Humou
the Couch

Exploring Humour in Psychotherapy and Everyday Life

ALESSANDRA LEMMA

Consultant Clinical Psychologist, South Kensington and
Chelsea Mental Health Centre
and
Honorary Senior Lecturer, Sub-Department of Clinical Health
Psychology, University College London

W

WHURR PUBLISHERS

LONDON AND PHILADELPHIA

© 2000 Whurr Publishers
First published 2000 by
Whurr Publishers Ltd
19b Compton Terrace, London N1 2UN, England and
325 Chestnut Street, Philadelphia PA 19106, USA

Reprinted 2000 (twice)

British Library Cataloguing in Publication Data
A catalogue record for this book is available from the
British Library

ISBN: 1 86156 145 8

Printed and bound in the UK by Athenæum Press Ltd,
Gateshead, Tyne & Wear

To Jeremy

I hope you never cease to see the world as you do

Talent for comedy is measured by you being able to detect the ridicule of them you love, without loving them less, and more by being able to see yourself somewhat ridiculous in their eyes, accepting the correction their image of you proposes. (Meredith, 1956)

Humour alone, that magnificent discovery of those who are cut short in their calling to highest endeavour, those who falling short of tragedy are yet as rich in gifts as in affliction. Humour alone (perhaps the most inborn and brilliant achievement of the human spirit) attains to the impossible and brings every aspect of human existence within the rays of its prism. To live in the world as though it were not the world, to respect the law and yet stand above it, to renounce as though it were no renunciation, all the favourite, commonly formulated propositions of an exalted, worldly wisdom, only humour has the power to make these paradoxes obvious...it is a third kingdom wherein the spirit becomes tough and elastic, a way of reconcilement, of extolling the saint and the profligate in one breath, and making the two poles meet. You should not take things too seriously... the immortals will tell you that...seriousness is an accident of time, it puts too high a value on time. Eternity is a mere moment, just long enough for a joke. (Hesse, 1929)

Contents

Acknowledgments

Jerry Lewis recounts the occasion when Jack Lemmon went to visit his dying friend, Edmund Gwenn. As he lay in his bed in a London hospital, he said to him: 'Edmund, it's a terrible thing to die'. Edmund looked up and replied ' It's not as tough as doing comedy' (Lewis, quoted in Grace, 1991: 6). Just as it is notoriously arduous to make it professionally as a comedian and to be a comedian, my attempts to find a publisher for this book alerted me to the difficult task that lay ahead in bringing together psychoanalysis and humour. One psychoanalytic publisher turned it down, as he wrote to me in his letter, on account that 'Humour does not do well professionally'! I fear that he may well be right since in Britain there are exceptionally few publications on psychoanalysis and humour. Out of all the available academic literature worldwide, comparatively little originates from Britain. This is curious indeed and one can only speculate that British academic writers and clinicians either lack the inclination to take humour seriously or they need to write books that will remunerate them. I am therefore grateful to Whurr Publishers for taking on this project.

The greatest reward in writing a book lies in the exchange of ideas that it promotes with family, friends and colleagues. I am indebted to several people who have listened to my views, shared their own and enthusiastically supported this project. I would like to thank, first and foremost, my husband Jeremy for his love, his gentle humour and infectious laughter, especially at those times when my own sense of humour failed me along with my computer. I would like to thank my family who, notwithstanding the challenges that life has thrown their way, have shown a remarkable aptitude for seeing the funny side of life. I am truly indebted to them for helping me to develop a sense of humour. I would especially like to thank my grandfather, Vittorio Lemma, for regularly taking me to see Italian comedy films when I used to spend time with him as a little girl. Those early shared laughs are still very much alive within me today even if he is no longer here to share them with me.

Mrs Baljeet Mehra taught me many valuable things but I am especially grateful to her for showing me how much can be achieved in psychoanalytic work through the use of humorous stories. I would like to thank Dr Arthur Couch for his support during my training and for wisely advising me, before my meeting with my first training patient some years ago, not to do anything 'spooky' to them such as not say hello or even smile! I am indebted to Dr Susan Howard for taking the time to read some of the chapters and for her very helpful comments. I am grateful to Dr Mary Target and Dr Heather Wood for supporting my enthusiasm for the subject of humour and for the helpful discussions we have had. I would also like to thank Madeleine Browning whose perspective on life, humour and psychoanalysis is, reassuringly, as surreal as my own. Without the help of Linda Farley I would never have managed to trace the numerous references she patiently searched for on my behalf – her help has been invaluable. Gill Crusey was, as ever, helpful in typing the manuscript.

Throughout this project my colleagues in the Psychology and Psychotherapy Department at the South Kensington and Chelsea Mental Health Centre kept my sanity afloat with their good humour and their accommodation of my idiosyncracies. In particular, I would like to thank Dr Nick Rhodes who, perhaps more than others, has had to endure my tendency to digress frequently into playful banter and laughter during our work together. I would also like to thank Adele Kosviner for taking seriously my thoughts about laughter therapy in the NHS - not many Heads of Department would!

Over the years I have had the good fortune to be taught and to be supervised by many psychoanalytic clinicians who have inspired me in different ways. Sometimes, of course, they inspired me to take positions somewhat different from the ones they themselves adopted. I do believe, however, that we can only learn through refining what others present us with. Disagreement and debate, though not necessarily easy to manage, are constructive. Each discussion refines, hones a point of view, and the latter, though a personal outcome at one level, can only be understood to be the product of a particular exchange. There would be too many people to mention who have helped me to articulate my ideas but I would like to acknowledge the learning opportunities they have offered me.

I would like to thank Sabine Catsiapis and the two British clown doctors, Doctor Mattie and Doctor Kiku, working for the Theodora Trust in London at Great Ormond Street Hospital and Guy's. I am grateful to them for their time and thoughts about the function of the clown in paediatric settings.

As will be clear in reading this book, I am a great fan of comedy – especially stand-up comedy – and I am deeply grateful to the comic artists who have given me so much pleasure over the years. I can but agree with Larry Brezner when he says, 'When you have laughed at comedians who are one of a kind, then the experience is more than simply the stand-up comedy experience. It's seeing Picasso painting live' (quoted in Grace, 1991: 10).

Last, but by no means least, I would like to thank my patients for their willingness to let me enter their world and to share their humorous slant on life.

Foreword

There is a story of a rabbi's wife who overheard her husband trying to settle an argument between two members of his congregation. One offered his opinion and the rabbi agreed with him, while the other offered the diametrically opposite case and again the rabbi agreed with him, at which point his wife felt compelled to intervene. 'They can't both be right', she pointed out. Her husband nodded his head wisely; 'You're also right' he said.

As the rabbi in question so deftly showed, there are always many ways of looking at one issue. In the same way, there are also myriad interpreters of the human psyche who have delved into all the complex aspects of humour. Of the most famous one of all, the great comedy clown, Ken Dodd, once remarked that the trouble with Freud was that he never played the Glasgow Empire (the theatre notorious for being the graveyard of so many comedians).

Now it is perhaps self-evident that it is much easier to theorise about humour than to actually create it on stage or indeed, in any other medium. Nevertheless, Alessandra Lemma (interestingly enough herself a self-confessed stand-up comedienne manqué and a life-long devotee of the art form) makes an important contribution to the whole subject in *Humour on the Couch*. Here she eloquently argues that the use of humour in both healing and understanding the perplexities of the mind has never received the attention it deserves, particularly in the UK. For many practitioners, psychoanalysis is too serious an area to be approached with any form of levity. There are a minority, however, who believe, as the author states, that 'psychoanalysis can only thrive if it can revisit some of its cherished assumptions'. To their credit, the Freud Museum did much to boldly further this process on the 5th November, 1994 by organising a one day conference entitled "Humour and Psychoanalysis" in the highly appropriate surroundings of the mecca of UK Stand-up comedy, London's 'Comedy Store'. The participants were Christopher Bollas, Jennifer Johns, Jerry Palmer and Valerie Sinason and representing the comedy side, John Cleese and myself. It is perhaps

worth observing that dialogue of this nature between practitioners and
theorists, while rare in the UK, tends to occur more frequently in the less
tradition-bound USA.

It is apparent that the roles of the therapist and the 'stand-up' have
much in common. By their very different disciplines, both can facilitate
personal insights and in doing so, help us to understand our problems
that much better. In *Humour on the Couch*, Alessandra Lemma highlights
stand-up comedy's special ability to also imbue audiences with a feeling
of communality, a reassurance that they are not alone in feeling as they
do. Paradoxically, this catharsis is often brought about by the wit of the
'existential outsider', the comedian. In this way, long-held taboos can at
last be confronted by saying the unsayable.

With their history of suffering, the Jews represent perhaps the
paradigm of the 'outsider', which explains their formidable contribution
to comedy (and, of course, psychiatry, psychotherapy and psychoanalysis). Incidentally, it has been said that Jews are exactly the same as
other people, only more so, which might explain the following anecdote
told by the American satirist, Mort Sahl, a contemporary of Lenny Bruce,
the seminal pioneer of subversive comedy who compelled society to
look at its inner soul. During the Depression, academics and intellec-
tuals like everyone else were forced to take any job they could get. The
story Sahl tells is of a bank robber who walks up to the counter and
shoves a note under the grille; 'I have a gun. Hand over the money. Act
normal'. The teller, a Doctor of Philosophy, reacts by handing back the
bank robber a note with the words, 'Define your terms'. (In offering this
as one of my favourite jokes, I am well aware this will inevitably place me
in the role of analysand for many readers).

'Normality' has always been hard to define, and the onus of the stand-
up comedian, in particular, to make a large number of strangers laugh
certainly does not appear to fit readily into this category. Nevertheless,
when the act does fall beautifully into place, there is no experience more
pleasurable and euphoric for a performer. Here, we are in Comedy
Heaven. The stories, the nuances, the facial expression, the pauses, are
all greeted with the laughter of unqualified delight. Happy to bask in the
sheer ecstasy of it all, the comedian can confidently assume - yes, they do
love me, and that perhaps is the covert intention of all joke-telling in
public. Conversely, everyone can closely identify with that feeling of
personal rejection when a joke one tells falls flat. Personally, my view is
that like may others, I suppose I went into comedy to get the attention I
never received as an adult. There is a child-like disinhibition in much
comedy and the author is surely right in advocating some application of
this playfulness as a potential psychoanalytical tool in certain cases.

Nowadays there is also a growing interest in the link between
laughter and health, (in this context, in 1997 Dr. Brian Kaplan, fellow
comedian Neil Mullarkey and myself presented a stage show at London's

New End theatre, entitled "Are You Feeling Funny?"). This is discernible when we consider the increasing volume of research that has been carried out evaluating the therapeutic benefits of laughter and, an exciting development, the introduction of Clown Doctors into paediatric wards in some British Hospitals. This is also an indication that as we approach the Millennium, at least in some quarters there is a more open attitude to the curative aspects of humour and its stress and depression diminishing effects.

Humour, too, can be a significant factor in releasing the powers of creativity. Arthur Koestler, in particular, advocated its special potency, observing that the humorist 'provides mental jolts triggered by the collision of incompatible matrices'. Perhaps a tangible illustration of this at work is the story of the elderly Jewish matriarch who calls downstairs to her husband, 'Harry, come upstairs and make love'. After a meaningful pause, the sorrowful riposte is made: 'Sarah, I can't do both'. As Woody Allen has so hilariously shown us, sometimes 'gallows humour' of this nature is the only weapon we have at our disposal to cope with the frailties of the human condition.

The author's message is simple yet powerful. If humour can do so much to enrich our lives, why is it so often underused and undervalued? Inventively and exhaustibly researched, Alessandra Lemma's *Humour on the Couch* is an imaginative and passionate plea for a liberating leap into the unknown by psychotherapists and patients alike. This is an authoritative and engrossing work that deserves a wider public forum beyond the professional and academic confines.

Arnold Brown
London 1999

Introduction
A funny thing happened to me on the way to therapy . . .

> The biggest joke in town for the longest time has probably been the psychoanalytic situation. Never before was there a human process with the potential for so many ironies, contradictions and opportunities for the emotional discharge of humour, laughter, criticism and a host of assorted feelings . . . if Freud had accomplished nothing else he created for the world a new type of theatre and literature, a new type of dynamic process and comedy. (Birner, 1994:88)

I am a psychologist and a psychotherapist. But, I must confess that this was not my first choice of career. I really wanted to be a comedienne. I wanted to make people laugh. Reality, however, presented me with an incontrovertible fact: at school, the stories I wrote and recounted to my peers were well received on account of their ability to make them cry rather than to make them laugh. As my talents appeared to lie more on the side of pathos than comedy I relinquished my secret wish and became a psychotherapist instead. The more I studied psychoanalysis, however, the more my original interest in humour was rekindled and brought to life in a different incarnation. Maybe this is not all that surprising, since there is an intimate connection between the two: psychoanalysis deals with personal tragedy and, as is well recognized, the flipside of tragedy is comedy.

The therapist[1] and the comedian may perform their tasks on different stages but otherwise they share a lot of common ground. They both aim to relieve others of their psychic pain (Birner, 1994). They give rise to similar expectations in other people regarding one's capacities to soothe and to comfort. As professions, both are emotionally taxing. We are just as disappointed when we meet a comedian in real life and he is not

---

[1.] Throughout the book I shall use the term 'therapist' as shorthand for both psychoanalytic psychotherapist and psychoanalyst, and the term 'psychotherapy' to refer to both psychoanalytic psychotherapy and psychoanalysis unless otherwise specified or unless differentiated by the authors I quote.

funny as when we meet a therapist outside of her consulting room and she is not understanding and sensitive.[2] The comedian and the therapist, both charged with the responsibility to relieve psychic burdens, arouse in us infantile expectations of being on call twenty-four hours a day to tender to our needs: 'make me laugh', 'understand me' – both are tall orders. The comedian and the therapist work with similar material: the unruly instincts which show us up in a rather unflattering light; the banana skins we slip on as we grapple with the task of being human; and the accidents of fate, or those we create as a result of our own self-deception. In other words, they both find their inspiration in the vicissitudes of life.

'Good' comedy and 'good' therapy also rely on timing: a good interpretation will fall flat if it is presented at the wrong time just as the punchline in a comic routine relies for its effect on timely delivery. Like comedy, psychoanalysis is a live performance of sorts. We can't rehearse a session. What the therapist has to offer the patient is created in the room and shaped by the patient's own contribution. Much like the stand-up comedian who delivers a good joke but at the wrong time or who misjudges his audience, the therapist cannot retract an interpretation and say to the patient, 'Sorry, got it wrong. Can I try again please?'. The therapist can of course attempt to understand, for example, why she may not have been attuned to the patient's need at that point or why she reacted in a particular manner, but she can never have a re-run; it is for real. And so it is with stand-up comedy too.

Even though the therapist's aim, unlike the comedian's, is not to entertain so as to amuse, one of her tasks is to enliven and to encourage curiosity in her patients about previously unacknowledged, unrecognized or repudiated aspects of their experience and of themselves. The therapist contributes to this by sharing her perspective, which she develops through careful attention to that which is spoken about as well as to that which is omitted or enacted in myriad ways. In so doing she presents the patient with a window on to his internal psychic landscape. This process involves questioning accepted truths and memories, those polished jewels that we sometimes hold up as hard-won trophies of our suffering. The therapist encourages her patients to examine more critically the narratives they have constructed to navigate through life so as to help them develop perspective or, in more analytic terminology, a 'self-observing ego'. Those of us who have been patients ourselves know only too well how difficult and painstaking this process can be. This is a process that the comedian also facilitates through the skilled use of

---

2. Since the majority of therapists are female I shall use the feminine pronoun throughout; since most comedians are male I shall use the male pronoun throughout. When referring to patients I have chosen, for the sake of clarity, to use the male pronoun throughout unless I am referring specifically to a female patient.

humorous stories, sketches and jokes which aim to get us to laugh but also to stop us in our tracks and think. He presents us with the incongruities we confront on a daily basis. Through his caricatures and observations the comedian enacts our struggles, the banality of our lives, the pitfalls of desire, our limitations and at times absurd or irrational behaviour. He says 'Take a look, that's you, that's me – it's serious but it's also funny'.

Comedy deals with the secrets of the psyche as well as of the body and it sometimes ruthlessly exposes both. In this respect comedy shares with psychoanalysis an attempt to bring the body into relief and to help reconcile us with what is basest in us (Jacobson, 1997). The comedian Robin Williams observes that:

> [comedy] makes people realise that you do trip, we fall, we fart, we touch ourselves. We have foibles. And that's all the strange things that make man man, and make it wonderful but also funny . . . we are incredible. Yeah, but you still smell. (quoted in Grace, 1991:168)

In reflecting back to us the crudeness of our physicality and the excesses of our instinctual nature, the comedian invites us to take a different perspective and herein lies the transforming power of humour. Humour, like metaphor, allows us to revisit and conceptualize 'familiar things in unfamiliar ways and unfamiliar things in familiar ways' (Borbely, 1998). The comedian's skill, as Pollio and Edgerly observe, lies precisely in his ability:

> to produce in us experiences involving the most fundamental and significant of human passions in a way that is restorative and cathartic rather than destructive and regressive . . . the comedian . . . as well as the naturally occurring witty person, provide a situation which allows each of us a bit of transcendence designed to make sport of those situations, events and taboos that lie hardest upon us if seen only from an earnest and serious perspective. (1976:240).

The psychoanalytic situation itself is a comic structure. Bollas incisively illustrates this point when he observes that 'A patient in analysis is straight man to his unconscious and it is a long time, if ever, before he comes to enjoy the comedy' (1995:224). This irony is often lost on us: it is a comedy routine we create at our own expense. When we can step out of the sketch and become the audience to our own unconscious we are assured an entertaining and frequently funny show. I recall one such instance when I was finishing my first analysis. I felt highly ambivalent about this as a large part of me did not want to finish. My analyst and I did, of course, talk about this within the analysis. Yet my desire not to end the analysis was most concretely expressed when I arrived for one session and, 'without thinking', I took my own keys out of my pocket and attempted to open the door to the house from which he practised. It was only when I found that the key did not work that I realized the comic enactment of my wish. This time the joke was not lost on me and it alerted me in a very immediate manner to my strong desire to have unlimited access to my analyst, and probably more!

Although my own personal experience of psychoanalysis was by no means devoid of humour and laughter, after years of sitting in clinical seminars and reading clinical papers I am struck by the conspicuous absence of reports of humorous exchanges between patient and therapist. So many therapists appear to leave their sense of humour outside the consulting room. What lies behind this? Is it the therapist who lacks humour or does she just reserve its use for her own life but not with a patient? Is it perhaps the case that therapists use humour far more than their accounts of their work would lead us to believe? Or is it the patient who simply has not yet become audience to his own unconscious and so cannot appreciate their unique comic narrative, as Bollas (1995) suggests? I think there is truth in all of these propositions. It does take time to be able to laugh at oneself benevolently – the punchlines in psychoanalysis are sometimes long overdue! (Bradshaw, 1999, personal communication). But even if the patient does laugh, to laugh alone in the presence of another who does not join him is rather inhibiting. Some therapists are undoubtedly rather sombre and grave in their manner and will not respond with laughter even if they consider to be funny something the patient has said. Others do use humour but either view it as inconsequential to the therapeutic process or they are reluctant to report their use of it. Given that psychoanalytic practitioners and theorists appear to pronounce themselves on virtually all aspects of human nature it is of note that so little has been written on the subject of one of the most ubiquitous means of communication in our repertoire. This reticence needs to be considered in the context of the analytic rules that are internalized by many psychoanalytic practitioners.

I started my own work as a clinician concerned that any change in the consulting room or any lapses from my (so-called) neutral therapeutic stance might threaten the sacred parameters of the therapeutic frame. I strictly monitored my inclinations to smile or laugh with my patients or to congratulate them or explicitly display my own pleasure at their achievements, anxious to avoid being inappropriately self-revealing or colluding with their need for narcissistic gratification. Over the years I have been fortunate, however, to have worked with clinicians who have pointed out to me that 'rules' are only a guide. Every patient we meet takes us into the uncharted territory of their unconscious. We need to be open to the novel experiences such journeys expose us to, not overly bound by rules which foreclose the imagination that is such an essential asset in our work. Ultimately, what matters most is the understanding we strive to arrive at on behalf of each of our patients which will indicate what they need and how we can best provide it within professional boundaries. Some of the patients we see may find a therapist's humour too threatening or too gratifying, whereas others will flourish on it.

Perhaps the use of humour in psychotherapy is generally thought best avoided due to a confusion between doing serious work and being serious. Serious work can be achieved without having to measure its seriousness through how many tears the patient has shed or how much anger or envy he has been able to express. Some of the most helpful moments in my own analysis were framed with humour. It is these moments I remember most vividly and fondly and for which I am grateful to my second analyst in particular. Although the transference coloured my perception of her and my relationship with her, at another 'real' level, she remained always a deeply human person whom I experienced as enthusiastic, playful and passionate about life. This enabled me to internalize an enlivening object with a sense of humour. I can therefore but agree with Grotjahn when he says: 'Therapy is no laughing matter but neither is it a Wailing Wall' (1971:238).

About the book

There is only one thing I can say with any certainty about this book: it isn't funny. I can only share your possible disappointment with this. Whenever I have read a book on humour I have felt invariably dissatisfied as a part of me always hopes for a joke or two, at the very least, only to be met with some rather dry, academic exposé on the subject. This is largely because, as Ferenczi correctly observed:

> Almost every joke can be robbed of its exhilarating qualities; in other words there is no joke so excellent that it cannot be spoilt by sufficiently thorough professional knowledge! (1911:333).

Writing on humour tends often to follow a similar fate. As you begin to analyse humour you invariably end up with something which is anything but funny. At its core humorous communication consists of the condensation of two messages, ideas or feelings into a single image which contains both funny and serious elements. Peel away the layers and you soon stop laughing.[3]

[3.] It is only when we begin to unravel the creative work of condensation (the process by which two or more images are fused to join one image, whose meaning is derived from both) along the lines described by Freud (1905a), that the underlying, serious message, is exposed. It was one of Freud's many insights into humour generally that the 'jokework' (essentially primary process thinking and censorship) is crucial for comical effect, as evidenced when a joke falls flat or misfires if the jokework is undone. This is highlighted when we have to explain a joke to another person who has not understood it. Often, by the time we have explained why it is funny, it is no longer funny.

I therefore embarked on this book with a degree of trepidation. I was reminded of Dixon's sobering remark when he notes that 'Just as sex research tends to shrivel romance, so pontifications about humour are death to amusement' (1980:287). There is truth in this. It is, to a large extent, unavoidable. I had even feared that in writing this book I would forgo some of the pleasure that humour has afforded me in my life. I am pleased to say that it has not and I hope that reading this book will not have that effect on you. The greater problem has been how to convey convincingly that, in my experience, humour is a very powerful and effective intervention in the context of psychotherapy. To illustrate this I have included some examples of humorous exchanges with my own patients. It is, however, notoriously difficult to recapture the quality of such exchanges on paper. As I reported them I was often inclined to put in brackets 'Well . . . You needed to be there really'. Humorous exchanges are the property of a particular relationship, at a particular point in time. And, importantly, the history of this relationship contextu-alizes the use of humour at a given juncture. The humour may be conveyed through a tone of voice, a subtle inflexion, rather than through the actual content of what is spoken. The moment you write it down, something is lost. Moreover, it may lead to misunderstandings both of the intentions lying behind the humorous remark and of its reception by the patient. I can only acknowledge this inevitable limitation and hope that you will bear it in mind when you come across these examples.

The aim of this book is primarily to highlight humour's 'communica-tive, relational and innovative value' (Morreall, 1987) in everyday life and in the privileged space, carved out of everyday life, that is psychotherapy. Chapter 1 traces philosophical, social and psychological perspectives on humour. In Chapters 2 and 3 humour is presented as a form of playing which origin-ates in the earliest exchanges between mother and baby and which confers significant advantages to our adaptation. In Chapter 4 the relationship between physical and mental health and humour is examined in light of the available research literature from both the fields of psychology and medicine. Although I have drawn on various sources in writing this book, Chapter 5 restricts itself to a review and discussion of psychoanalytic views on humour in psychotherapy. This represents a personal choice since psychoanalytic psychotherapy is the approach I practice and the one I find most stimulating. There is nevertheless litera-ture available about the use of humour within other forms of psychotherapy where it is often viewed less controversially. Indeed, in discussing humour in psychoanalysis a degree of controversy is unavoid-able. If humour is to be regarded a helpful intervention it then begs the question of whether such interventions are in keeping with the therap-ist's neutrality and anonymity and whether transference interpretations are the only, or at least primary, mutative agents in psychotherapy. Chapter 5 therefore addresses these questions before examining the actual use of humour in psychotherapy. Finally, Chapter 6 reviews evolutionary perspectives on humour.

Throughout the book, in so far as it has been possible, I have attempted to back up my arguments with research evidence; this has been limited by the comparatively meagre research available, especially about the use of humour in psychotherapy. Hence some of the arguments I present in this book are at times no more than an attempt to articulate my perspective, which I hope will nevertheless stimulate you to take humour seriously and perhaps even research this further.

As I reflect on why I have written this book, two reasons come to mind. Firstly, it represents for me an opportunity to share my enthusiasm for a subject I have long been interested in and which I feel has been comparatively neglected within psychoanalysis. Secondly, it is an attempt to explore aspects of the therapeutic process which interest me. Reading the final draft of this book I am struck by the fact that I started writing it contemporaneously with the ending of my own analytic training. This reminded me of the time when I passed my driving test. I recall the relief, excitement and anxiety that I experienced when I no longer felt that I had to do assiduously all those things I had shown my instructor I could do so as to pass. No doubt a similar dynamic is at work in processing the ending of my analytic training and articulating a more personal therapeutic stance. I do not wish, in any way, to denigrate what I have learnt, since it has been very stimulating and no one can develop a position without the benefit of its counter-example. Nor do I wish to 'break out' of an analytic mould since I value this approach and I have personally, as well as professionally, benefited greatly from it. However, I do think that psychoanalysis can thrive only if it can revisit some of its cherished assumptions. Even if in the end we realise that our original ideas were the most fruitful ones, criticism, like humour, regenerates us by turning things on their head and broadening our perspective.

Writing this book has been a pleasure as it has taken me on some unexpected excursions into many fields: psychology, sociology, anthropology, philosophy, socio-biology, medicine, zoology and education. This is a measure of how central humour is to an understanding of human nature. I have also come across some less interesting, albeit occasionally amusing, material. I have in mind here the literature exhorting us to laugh as the answer to life's problems. You need only search the Internet under the headings of 'laughter', 'humour' and 'therapy' and you will be invited to visit the 'Journal of Nursing Jocularity' or given tips for 'How to get more smileage out of your life'. More specific advice from the 'International Centre for Humour and Health' will encourage you to try out some of the following stress-reduction exercises: 'Dance naked in front of your pets' or 'Thumb through National Geographic and draw underwear on the natives'. And, if that has not lowered your stress levels, you could always try 'Reading the dictionary backwards and looking for subliminal messages'.

In America the perceived relationship between humour and health has created a market for so-called laughter therapy and in Britain we are now beginning to see an interest in this too. Although I would far rather be prescribed twice daily doses of *Fawlty Towers*, Arnold Brown, Bill Hicks and Eddie Izzard rather than medication or psychotherapy for my ills, I do not think life is that simple. I am not therefore proposing that being humorous is something we can simply will, or that the answer lies with 'laughter therapy'. The latter refers more to a mixed bag of ideas, strategies and attitudes rather than constituting a formal therapeutic approach. Overall, I am, however, sympathetic to the spirit and underlying philosophy of laughter therapy. I applaud its attempt to humanize the practice of psychology and medicine and remind us that pleasure and fun are as integral to healing as 'working through' pain and sorrow. To underscore the value of humour and laughter in our relationships is important. It is even more important to remind health practitioners that they do not have to reserve their sense of humour for 'after hours' but, rather, that they will be enriched by, and personally rewarded for, using it judiciously with their patients. Just as humour is an effective means of communication that we all use in our everyday lives, there is no reason to suppose that it is any less effective in our professional encounters. I subscribe to the view that humour is about far more than pleasurable distraction or a way of relieving tension. Indeed, I hope this book will highlight its mutative potential in the context of psychotherapy and the fundamental psychological and social functions I believe that it serves in our everyday life.

Chapter 1
On Humour's Tightrope

Tragedy requires less knowledge of the human heart than comedy.
(Mme de Stael)

Our hunger for comic amusement cannot be ignored. Humour pervades life. We can trace its significance as far back as the ancient Romans and Greeks, into the Middle Ages and up into the pressing Millennium. Depending on the particular society or historical period that is studied, the attitude, expression, form and content of humour will differ to a greater or lesser extent (Driessen, 1997), but its presence is undisputed. Laughter, as the most common response to humour, has also attracted a lot of interest. In ecclesiastical circles, from early Christianity onwards and up to the end of the Middle Ages, people were preoccupied with the question of whether Jesus had ever laughed during his earthly life (Le Goff, 1997), reflecting a concern with whether laughter was on the side of the devil or of God. Laughter has been both condemned and hailed as the quintessential human quality. In Umberto Eco's novel *The Name of the Rose* (1983) the question of the probity of comedy and laughter is examined through the attempt to resolve a series of murders for which the apparent motive is the theft of the sole surviving copy of Aristotle's Poetics which discusses comedy. In Eco's novel the monk, Jorge, views laughter as subversive and as a means of freeing man from fear of the devil. He believes that Aristotle's book will legitimize laughter and the 'low' comedy genre (Roberts, 1993).

The subversive nature of laughter and humour underpinned the rise of the more modern, Western trend towards so-called 'alternative comedy'. What we refer to as 'alternative cabaret' was at first a minority activity. The 1980s, both in Britain and in America, was the decade when the best of the hitherto 'fringe' or alternative comedy threatened to become, and then did become, mainstream. The last twenty years in Britain and in America have witnessed a proliferation of comedy venues and comedy series for television (Deayton, 1999). Although there has undoubtedly been an upsurge in our consumption of comedy, one of the constants in life, cutting across historical periods, has been the function of the 'comic spirit' (Boskin, 1987) as a way of managing the inescapable difficulty of being. In his own way, Charlie Chaplin recognized this essential function. Humour, he said, 'is a kind of gentle and benevolent custodian of the mind which prevents us from being overwhelmed by the apparent seriousness of life' (quoted in Boskin, 1987:154).

In this chapter we shall examine some of the functions of humour from three perspectives, namely philosophical, social and psychological.[4] The aim is to begin to understand why humour is so central in human interaction and to emotional and cognitive processing.

Humour and laughter

Humour has been variously defined as an action or statement that is comical or amusing; as whatever the individual thinks is funny; and as that which produces laughter (Dean, 1997). To possess a sense of humour involves not only the appreciation but also the production of humour, that is, finding humour in a situation that may not be immediately funny, as in irony. In this book the term humour will be used to refer to any verbal utterance or non-verbal behaviour that is experienced subjectively as amusing even if it does not necessarily produce the response of laughter or a smile. A sense of humour will be broadly used to denote humour production and appreciation; a sense of playfulness or whimsy; a personal recognition of humour; the capacity to laugh at oneself and problems; and the capacity to master difficult situations through the use of humour (Thorson et al., 1997).

Human laughter is said to originate from the open-mouth play face of primates that has been distinguished by ethologists from the silent bared-teeth display thought to be the precursor of human smiling (Van Hooff, 1972). There is some evidence that laughter and smiling signal different positive emotions. Keltner and Bonanno (1997) found laughter to be more strongly correlated than smiling with self-reports of reduced anger, whereas smiling was more strongly correlated with self-reports of reduced distress or fear. Humour and its frequent response of laughter or smiling undoubtedly spring from different emotional states and are therefore over-determined by varied and complex conscious and unconscious factors.

It is important to draw a clear distinction between what is perceived to be funny and what makes us laugh. The literature is replete with confusions between humour and laughter. Even though laughter and smiling converge functionally as non-verbal expressions of humour

---

4. Haig (1986) notes that there are well over a hundred theories of humour. The review here is of necessity restricted to those theories that have received the most attention.

appreciation, as responses they are multiply determined and not necessarily always responses to something perceived to be funny.[5] They can result equally from relief following fear or out of anxiety, for example. Although the function of laughter appears to be a discharge of energy, its trigger varies and so does its emotional meaning. Byrne (1958) cited the work of Kline (1977) who observed that survivors of the San Francisco earthquake appeared to laugh at the slightest provocation. Likewise, Hayworth (1928) reported that just prior to engaging in combat, soldiers would laugh at almost any cue. We need only turn to our own experience to note the tendency to laugh when we are anxious. The triggers for laughter are not only highly idiosyncratic and context-dependent but they are also reflective of cultural concerns or themes. Even though we laugh the world over and the physical manifestations are the same, we don't all laugh at the same things. Conceptions of humour across cultures are quite diverse, as are the norms concerning its occurrence and use (Apte, 1985). It is the wider socio-cultural context in which humour occurs that moderates the outcome of our perception of funniness.

Anthropological studies emphasize the influence of social and cultural factors. The extraordinary performances by the clowns in Zuni culture attest to this. Charles (1945) reports that these clowns, for example, drink urine to the amusement of the spectators. Such behaviour would most probably invite a very different response if it occurred as part of a Western comedy routine or indeed if a psychotic patient behaved in this manner. The context in which a joke is recounted will influence, for example, whether it will be deemed funny or not and whether it will be acceptable to reveal one's reaction in either direction. For example, you might not consider it appropriate to laugh at a funeral even though you felt like it, but equally you might not find a friend's joke funny but you feel you should laugh at it anyway.

The following joke, related by an Indian author (Mehta, 1998) would not be considered funny unless one was familiar with the particulars of life in Kerala, South India. In Kerala a vast number of people become government clerks because it has the highest literacy rate in the country. It is also a politically conscious state, with strong communist allegiances. So, someone asks the person from Kerala, 'Are you a capitalist or a Marxist?' 'I'm a typist', he replies. What is funny or humorous is determined then by subjective, intra-spsychic factors, as well as the interpersonal and socio-cultural context where the humorous exchange takes place. To understand its success or failure, it will be important to take

---

5. Thurber rightly observes that the belly laugh:' . . . dismays the writers of comedy because it is the laugh that often dies in the lobby. The appreciative smile, the chuckle, the soundless mirth, so important to the success of comedy, cannot be understood unless one sits amongst the audience and feels the warmth created by the quality of laughter that the audience take home' (quoted in Rosten, 1994:271).

into account the implicit rules which underline where, when and with whom it is possible to joke (Chiaro, 1992).

The first laugh

As many parents will remember, the baby's first smile and laugh are awaited and cherished moments, on to which many projections are made (e.g. this means the baby loves me/recognizes me/is happy/is having fun). The baby's smile appears to follow quite a clear developmental sequence and serves varied purposes. At first, smiles occur in response to internal stimuli. We can, for example, observe babies smiling in their sleep. To begin with, smiling is therefore reflexive. Between six weeks and eight months, smiles can be elicited by human or other environmental stimuli. Some research suggests that early smiling may reflect the operation of the 'pleasure in mastery mechanism' originally described by Piaget (1951). This proposes that after a period of accommodation to a stimulus the infant reveals his success at assimilating it by the experience of pleasurable emotions such as smiling (Kagan, 1971; Zelazo and Komer, 1971; Zelazo, 1972). Essentially, this posits a view of smiling and laughter in infancy as arising out of pleasure in cognitive mastery, that is, when some optimal, moderate amount of discrepancy is processed by the baby (Schultz, 1976). Indeed Minden defines the humorous attitude itself as 'a state of mind in which the individual reasserts his mastery over the environment and refuses to submit to threat or fear' (1994:126).

Kagan (1971) further proposes that infant smiling 'signifies a cognitive success following some doubt over that success . . . a feeling of uncertainty followed by resolution' (1971:157). This view is consistent with a biphasic sequence of arousal and arousal reduction which has been proposed as the underlying structure of humour as resolved incongruity, as we shall see later in this chapter.

Although smiling and laughter may be responses reflecting the pleasure derived from a subjective sense of cognitive mastery, it is important to appreciate their function in an interpersonal context. Simons et al. (1986) argue that humour – in its broadest sense – has 'survival value' for babies because it represents an avenue for communication with the caregiver. Smiles and laughter can exert profound effects on the caregiver, soliciting positive responses from them. At around four months the baby begins to appreciate the trade value in smiles: if I smile I can get something. By this stage then smiles acquire interpersonal significance and are produced to elicit positive responses from others, who are usually more than willing to oblige. If we observe babies from about six months onwards, it becomes apparent that they expect laughter from us and they gladly display their 'bag of tricks' to elicit this.

Unlike the smile though, the laughing response is not present at birth. When it first emerges, some time between two and eight months, it appears to be entirely in response to external stimuli, especially in interaction with others. Parents frequently initiate reciprocation by tickling the child thereby inviting smiles and laughter. By one year of age mother and baby can build up to a laugh by dialectically alternating their tone of voice, facial expressions and actions (Fogel et al., 1997). The reciprocity evident in shared laughter is developmentally significant. Most importantly, out of tickling and laughter, play develops which itself provides fertile ground for emotional and developmental advances, as we shall see in Chapter 3.

There is now a wealth of observational data tracing the baby's first smiles and laughs and their different triggers (e.g. Stern, 1977; Brazelton and Cramer, 1991). Studies which address the baby's development of affect or emotion are nevertheless beset with methodological difficulties since the emotion can be inferred only from the baby's overt behaviour on which the pre-verbal baby simply cannot comment. Yet such research is illuminating and suggests, at the very least, some interesting hypotheses. Developmental researchers have disagreed with Freud's original contention that all stimulation triggers excitement (i.e. internal tension) which is invariably experienced as unpleasurable. It was Freud's belief that pleasure resulted from the discharge of the tension that had built up. Nowadays this strikes us as problematic since we know that babies are active seekers of stimulation, especially of a social nature, and that they work very hard at regulating the amount of stimulation they take in (Brazelton and Kramer, 1991). In fact, both the baby and the mother, as a duet, regulate the baby's attention, curiosity and cognitive engagement with the world, to ensure that the baby is neither bored nor overwhelmed by the incoming stimuli. A build-up of excitement can clearly be pleasurable and hence sought after. Even though this runs counter to Freud's original theory, the notion that affect is related to the build-up and fall-off of stimulation and tension remains valid as this is a pattern that emerges clearly from observational studies (Stern, 1977).

Sroufe and Waters (1976) in a series of experiments on laughter in infants focused on the nature of the stimulus that elicited laughter. They found that the laughter-provoking sound needed to give rise to what they termed 'tension fluctuation'. The most effective stimulus was one that accelerated in intensity to an abrupt cut-off: a steep gradient of tension followed by a rapid recovery was most successful at eliciting laughter in the infants. This is a very interesting finding as it draws our attention to the very structure of what elicits laughter in early life and the possible parallels with the structure of comedy which elicits laughter in children and adults. Koestler (1964) observed that in a joke, the punchline 'derails a trainload of emotion' that has been set in motion by the first part of the joke. In other words, the punchline marks the abrupt cut-off following the increase in tension and emotion. The digressions characteristic of some comedians' routine are an effective way of keeping us hanging on from the beginning of the comic sequence so as to increase tension while the comedian 'teases us', as it were, and then releases us with the punchline or the final comic denouement. Likewise, some of the playful exchanges between mother and baby, such as peek-a-boo, consist of the mother gently teasing the baby until she reveals her face to him again.

Humour and intimacy

Since laughter can occur within an individual, Berlyne (1972) stated that it was unlikely that its prime function was an interpersonal one. This is something of a non sequitur. The observation that we can laugh or be amused on our own does not imply that laughter and humour evolved primarily for purposes other than social ones. Several authors have in fact emphasized humour's positive contribution to both social and intimate relationships. Fine points out that 'most humour and laughter imply a social relationship, a connection between self and other' (1983:159). Chapman observes that even though, most of the time, laughter arises infrequently when we are alone, we do sometimes laugh when reading a funny book or when we recall to ourselves an amusing incident. On these occasions,

> When we laugh it is as though we were actually present. Therein lies an explanation as to why laughter, an essentially social response, can find expression when we are on our own: *we may be alone physically but we are not alone psychologically* (Chapman, 1983:148, my italics).

Laughter of this nature is a by-product of interpersonal experiences, of the internalization of enlivening relationships. Nevertheless, it is true that laughter does most commonly occur with others, in their actual presence, and eases social interaction. Morreall (1991) has indeed described humour as a 'social lubricant'. So, let us begin by looking at the function of humour in social relationships before we examine its contribution to intimate relationships.

The role of humour in shaping particular societies and its boundaries has been well documented, for example, in a study of the use of humour in Trinidad. Jones and Liverpool (1976) suggest that humour in Trinidad is 'a way of life' which is best appreciated in the tradition of Calypso originally used to ridicule and so air grievances at those in power: 'Humour is no joke in Trinidad, because if you cannot appreciate it, you do not belong' (Jones and Liverpool, 1976:259).

Joking and humorous banter have been identified by anthropologists as defining particular types of relationships in certain cultures. In the literature there are various accounts of what are termed 'joking relationships'. Radcliffe-Brown (1952) observed joking relationships in his studies of tribal social structures. He described the presence of a set of institutionalized relationships that provide a framework for humour. In these relationships, he notes, 'one is by custom permitted, and in some instances required, to tease or make fun of the other, who in turn is required to take no offence' (Radcliffe-Brown, 1952:90).

In ethnographic studies it is clear that joking relationships occur quite widely in social life especially at points of transition such as at birth, during illness and at funerals. The relationship and the content of joking are highly structured. Rules abound and delineate what kinds of behaviour are allowed and those that are not permitted. Its very institutionalized nature keeps it under social control. Most of the relationships are based on kinship or friendship, but there are exceptions to this. For example, the Luvale in East Africa allow a joking relationship between people born on the same day.

The joking relationship espouses friendliness and antagonism. The particular exchanges that it sanctions between joking partners are such that in any other situation they would be interpreted as expressions of hostility and the recipient would therefore be quite likely to take offence. In other words 'the relation is one of permitted disrespect' (Radcliffe-Brown, 1952). The joking behaviour itself can be quite extreme: pantomime, the slapstick flinging of excrement and insults, attempts to copulate with one's grandmother, heavy sexual trading, gluttony and drunkenness, to name but a few. The main function of joking relationships is to maintain a viable relationship between people. Its aim appears to be to establish social harmony and stability. These relationships highlight the function of joking and teasing in the group context as adaptive strategies for managing relationships that involve attachment and detachment, social conjunction and disjunction. Apte (1985), however, draws attention to the difficulty in proving conclusively that it is joking per se that serves the function attributed to joking relationships. The effectiveness of joking compared to the other exchanges that these relationships allow for has not, in fact, been measured.

We can observe joking relationships in Western countries too, but they differ in important respects from the ones reported in the non-industrialized world. The joking relationship in industrial societies is voluntary, informal and less inclined towards the extremes of the behaviour sanctioned between traditional joking partners. It is, generally speaking, bound to the work setting in the sense that it does not necessarily give licence to joke in other situations. It is primarily used to establish group identity, whereas this aspect is less relevant in cultures where social relations are defined by kinship. When a new person joins a group, as when arriving in a new job, approbation of their joking is often an indication that the person has been accepted as part of the new social group. In this respect, we might say that joking acts as a 'screening procedure for membership' of a group (Apte, 1985).

Humour eases the social interaction and contracts forced upon us by the requirements of the work setting. Through its characteristically ambiguous nature, humour facilitates self-disclosure and social probing in an indirect, non-committed manner. This allows for 'face saving' since a potentially embarrassing situation can be dismissed by putting it down to 'just joking' (Kane et al., 1977). The advantages this confers in novel situations where there may be few cues as to how to behave, are considerable. Sharing jokes also enhances in-group solidarity (Martineau, 1972; Alexander, 1986) through mutual enjoyment and the achievement of consensus. Humour has indeed been found to increase self-reported cohesion in group members (Banning and Nelson 1987; Vinton 1989).

Just like play and other forms of pleasurable activity, humour binds groups together. It is a form of communication that encourages closer participation than many other forms of group behaviour. An invitation to join in laughter at a funny event highlights and indeed forges group consensus, the laughter itself signalling a degree of complicity. Humour and shared laughter are great levellers that can cut across differences imposed by age, gender, class or culture. Social barriers recede in significance because to laugh *with* others presupposes a degree of shared goal or consensus in a particular context where many other features of people's identity may be otherwise quite disparate. Vinton (1989), for example, suggests that colleagues at work use humour to include new colleagues and relax hierarchical differences within the work setting.

The power of humour to foster varying degrees of intimacy between people can of course also be appreciated when we consider its flipside, namely its potential to reject and exclude those who, for whatever reason, are unable to appreciate the humour. Bergson gives a flavour of the social boundary imposed by humour:

> It may perchance have happened to you when seated in a railway carriage
> . . . to hear travellers relating to one another stories which must have
> been comic for them, for they laughed heartily. Had you been one of
> their company you would have laughed like them but as you were not
> you have no desire whatsoever to do so . . . However spontaneous it
> seems laughter always implies a kind of secret freemasonry or even
> complicity, with the other laughers, real or imaginary (1956:64).

Humorous exchanges may be inaccessible to all but those who share information about one another's knowledge, beliefs, intentions and attitudes. Those who 'get the joke' become part of the group; those who cannot, are excluded. Some jokes require so much background knowledge and effort to be appreciated that they may exclude people; the obscurity of the joke may, at times, reflect an attempt to alienate another. Humour can therefore be used to create social distance, to reject and to maintain hierarchical relationships.

Humorous communication is so rich in social subtleties and nuances that it inevitably leaves itself open to varied interpretations. When we use humour we are therefore often taking a risk. In the context of a discussion on the use of humour in psychotherapy, Mindess correctly observes that:

> You can never be sure your humour won't be interpreted as derision or callous indifference, if not as calculated cruelty. In fact, you can be sure that it will unless, and this is the crux of the matter, the person you are trying to help unequivocally perceives you as his true ally (1971:10).

Mindess is making an important point since he reminds us that the quality of the relationship in which humour is used will determine, in large part, whether humour is experienced subjectively as an attack, a rejection or as a gentle, affectionate prod. It may indeed be appropriate, as Kahn (1989) suggests, to speak of a 'sliding scale' of humour whereby it can be used either to establish a social boundary that excludes others or to bridge social boundaries.

Although humour is most certainly used as an outlet for aggressive impulses (see next section), its constructive effects are best observed in its function as a means of reconciliation; affirmation of common values; asking and giving support; bridging differences and reassurance. A study by Coser (1960) looked at the contribution of humour to group cohesion and maintenance of a specific social structure. The study recorded the frequency and content of humorous comments/exchanges amongst staff working in a psychiatric hospital. Coser suggests that humorous exchanges serve the function of reducing social distance between colleagues occupying different hierarchical positions within the hospital setting by permitting them to share their pleasures and collectively withdraw their focal attention from the concerns of working with demanding patients. Kuhlman (1993) notes the importance of humour between staff in an inpatient ward for severely disturbed patients. He argues that humour increases cohesiveness, bringing together the staff as they struggle to reconcile themselves to the stressful exchanges with patients. In particular, he discusses gallows humour as a prime example of humour facilitating stress management in treatment settings that confront staff with ongoing, chronic stressors (see Chapter 4). Several theorists have proposed that humour is an effective strategy for reducing or diffusing tensions and conflicts (Chapman, 1983; Martin, 1989). Congruent with this notion is the research which suggests that increased humour is related to greater social assertiveness (Bell et al., 1986), greater mastery of interpersonal skills required to maintain and initiate social interaction (Turner, 1980) and higher levels of social competence in children (Pellegrini et al., 1987).

Coser's study provides several examples of humour's capacity to deflect more overt expressions of aggression whilst still allowing an outlet for such feelings. By converting hostile feelings into humour we can achieve a measure of control over them. Humour allows hostility sublimated expression and in so doing maintains a viable interaction between people. Bradney (1957) reinforced this point in an earlier study. She looked at the function of joking between colleagues in a department store. Her observations led her to conclude that through a tradition of 'joking behaviour' the staff were able to avoid considerable tension and disagreement that would have otherwise been likely to occur because of the formal structure of the store. By relaxing the rigidity of the prevailing social structure, humour brings people closer together, just as Radcliffe-Brown hypothesized to be the function of joking relationships, namely to reconcile tendencies of association and dissociation.

Although humour is a social lubricant it is also far more than this. At its best it is an expression of love. 'Humour' wrote Thackeray (1995), in an essay on English humorists in the eighteenth century, 'is wit and love'. In many respects this quote encapsulates the essence of this book as it conveys the connecting power of humour: it can make people feel closer, loved and ultimately fosters intimacy. Hampes (1994) notes a positive correlation between individuals scoring higher in 'intimacy' versus 'isolation' and a sense of humour when compared to those individuals scoring lower on intimacy. The importance of humour in our intimate relationships cannot be overstated. When couples are asked what is important in their relationships, a shared sense of humour frequently features in their replies. Scanning 'lonely hearts' sections confirms this; a good sense of humour (such a common requirement that it is invariably abbreviated to GSOH) appears to be a sought-after quality associated with attractiveness and esteemed above being likeable, helpful or influential (Goodchilds, 1972).[6]

Palmer (1987) documents how, in Luguru society, the participants in a joking relationship are actively encouraged to marry each other, since the Luguru think that the possibility of joking together provides an outlet for the normal tensions of married life. The Luguru also espouse the very sophisticated belief that it is through joking that potential married partners can get a feeling for each other. À propos of marriage, Greg Proops, an American comedian based in London, remarks:

> You can see the importance of the laughter molecule in a happy relationship . . . a prenuptial laughter agreement makes sense. I hereby promise to stop doing the squirrel noise after two years and you swear to come up with some new jokes . . . . Think of all the relationships that could be saved if couples could *surprise* each other with fresh stories' (1997, p.160, my italics).

---

6. There is also some evidence to support the notion that people react more positively to a speaker who uses humour (Gruner, 1976).

Humour can keep a relationship alive or even inject life into a stale relationship as it introduces the vital element of surprise. Humorous exchanges are a means through which people can jointly engage in a creative act. It can feel very exciting and certainly pleasurable to exchange a dialogue that is funny and, importantly, it can also help us to overcome impasses in relationships. Every relationship has to weather the inevitable ebb and flow of both love and aggression. Humour can help to tease and iron out tensions that may have not been clearly articulated and thereby clear the path for more creative solutions to interpersonal problems. Following a dispute or disagreement laughter can convey that there still exists a bond or working alliance that has survived the expression of hostility. Humour can of course be critical but loving other people is not just about supporting them. It is also about being able to challenge those we love so as to help them to change (Skynner and Cleese, 1993). Humour provides us with a very effective vehicle for affectionately criticizing others (Meredith, 1956).

Ziv and Gadish (1989) assessed the impact of humour on marital satisfaction in 50 married couples. The husbands' marital satisfaction was found to be related to their perceptions of their wives' sense of humour. Interestingly, however, the results for the wives' perception of their husbands was not conclusive. Blumenfield and Alpern (1986) also report results linking marital satisfaction with humour. They argue that: '. . . a sense of humour can help you be more accepting of your own imperfections as well as those of your spouse' (1986:153).

Keltner and Monarch (1996, quoted in Keltner and Bonanno, 1997) found that couples who laughed while discussing a mutual conflict experienced less distress during the discussion and reported increased relationship satisfaction. Baxter (1992) also found that the self-reported tendency to be playful (including humour) is associated with increased relationship satisfaction in romantic couples. It is also true, however, that the overuse of humour or compulsive bantering in relationships may serve the function of avoiding communication since it is primarily an indirect form of communication.

Not only is a good sense of humour potential cement for a relationship; its role in sexual seduction is subtle, yet powerful. A measure of the intimacy created by humour is conveyed in Alan Bennett's (1994) perceptive observation that it is far easier to share a bed than to share a joke. Anzieu (1980) believes that a man who can make a woman laugh has already lured her two thirds of the way to his bed. This may be on account of the fact that, as Strean (1993) suggests, the very act of telling and listening to jokes can be likened to making love. Similarly, the laughter that results from sharing a funny story has been likened to an orgasm. Like sex, 'comedy is irrepressible, laughter libidinous' (Stone, 1997). Grammer and Eibl-Eibesfeldt (quoted in Weisfeld, 1993) have proposed that humour communicates sexual interest. They recorded the spontan-eous conversations of German young adults who were initially strangers to each other. The more intense the woman's laughter, the greater her self-reported interest in meeting the man again. These researchers suggest that a woman's laughter can function to communicate interest in a man. Men's own laughter did not indicate interest in the woman, however. Rather, men's interest was indicated by the intensity of the woman's laughter. They attributed this sex differ-ence to the submission aspect of 'nervous' laughter; that is, the woman signals her submission to the man. Grammer and Eibl-Eibesfeldt also found that the more the couple laughed together in synchrony, the greater their interest in each other. They regard this as a social bonding behaviour that serves to cement the relationship once mutual interest has been established.

Elaborating the intimate connection between laughter and sex, Jacobson (1997) speaks of laughter as a 'foretaste and re-enactment of sexual abandon'. He draws attention to the physiological changes that take place during laughter (for example, the head thrust backwards, the chest heaving, quick breathing) which parallel so closely some of the changes that we can observe during sexual excitement. He describes a joke quite aptly as a kind of 'striptease'. It is indeed true that we reveal so much of ourselves through what we find funny as much as through what we fail to find funny. Humour exposes us quite crudely and so makes us vulnerable (Sinason, 1996). Because Jacobson (1997) identifies such a close link between sex and laughter, he argues that silence as a reaction to a humorous communication can feel so hurtful since it is experi-enced, at another level, as a sexual rejection. Although this may be one of the reasons why a silent response to a joke is wounding, this results far more frequently because it is experienced as a refusal to reciprocate in an exchange or to become intimate but not exclusively or primarily in a sexual sense.

A joke or a humorous exchange extends implicitly an invitation to be intimate, even if temporarily. The goal – not necessarily conscious – is the achievement of a kind of intimacy. Drawing a parallel between the function of metaphors and of jokes, Cohen (1978) describes the process by which the joker and the listener are drawn closer to one another. This process involves negotiations that are implicit. To begin with, the joker issues a concealed invitation to share a joke and to laugh to which the listener then responds. At the point of exchange this transaction consti-tutes the acknowledgement of a relationship. We may well ask then what is the interpersonal pay-off of such a humorous exchange. Cohen proposes that in order to appreciate a joke or humorous utterance, the listener has to engage, to penetrate, the speaker's utterance so as to explore and understand them, in order to grasp the import, for the latter does not reside in the joke itself. The joker knows that the listener is doing this, that is, that the listener is making an effort to understand and therefore to engage. In the 'co-operative act of comprehension' (Cohen, 1978) – which is far more than a routine act of understanding – we have, at that particular intersection, the creation of an intimate couple. Along similar lines Fine (1979) suggests that humour, allows the joker to engage the listener in a kind of collusion to bypass the superego thereby making it 'an exercise in communication'.

The desire to communicate is inherent in humour. The recipient of the joke or the funny story is as important as the joker (Palmer, 1994). Palmer emphasizes the implicit process of negotiation in humorous exchanges: 'humour is something negotiated rather than an imminent property of utterances' (1987:21). This concurs with the common observation that a response to the same joke may vary over time as well as between and within cultures and relationships. Not only do we then need to pay attention to the quality of the relationship within which humour is negotiated, but the intended humour in the remark has to be indicated by paralinguistic markers (e.g. intonation) and has to be sanctioned within implicit or explicit cultural roles. Participants willingly engaging in an exchange in which 'anything goes' (Palmer, 1994) (i.e. that would be out of the question in reality), as is often the case in humorous exchange, appear to be following tacit rules negotiated between the so-called joker and the recipient. A shared 'humorous space' (see Chapter 3) is thus co-created and entered.

Humour: weapon and shield?

Ambivalence is the emotional hallmark of humorous communication: it's funny but it's also serious, deadly serious sometimes. 'The ambivalence of comedy', writes Sypher, 'reappears in its dual meanings for comedy is both . . . rebellion and defence; attack and escape . . . . It is revolutionary . . . socially it is both sympathy and persecution' (1956:242).

The juxtaposition of comedy and tragedy can be traced throughout the literature on humour. The connection between pain and humour was embedded in Freud's thinking about the subject. In fact Freud predicated his own formulations on humour on the German meaning of the word defined as 'a series of painful emotions transformed in a manner that produces pleasure' (Bergler, 1956:39). In the English usage of the word the association with pain is not as explicit, but we are all too aware of humour's flipside. Expanding on this point Pollio and Edgerly observe:

Humour is a fragile phenomenon and the comedian as the custodian of the phenomenon is, and must be, ever mindful of the fine, delicate balance existing between kidding and hurting, between social commentary and prejudice, between controlled fantasy and madness, as well as between all those aversive states that comedy depends upon and their controlled comic counterparts' (1976:240).

In a purely physical sense there does appear to be an intimate association between pain and laughter since the grimace of mirth resembles so closely the grimace of suffering. Do we not also often hear people say: 'I laughed so much I almost cried', 'this is painfully funny'; 'this is so funny it is killing me', or 'this is side-splittingly funny'. Such expressions intimate that our laughter trades on pain and they invite us to be curious about what lies behind apparent amusement and the intent of humorous communication. Although humour can ease both social and intimate relationships it can also tantalize, deride, triumph over, ridicule and attack. In his classic study *The Nature of Laughter*, Gregory traces historically the aggressive element in humour and laughter:

> As laughter emerges with man from the mists of antiquity it seems to hold a dagger in its hand. There is enough brutal triumph, enough contempt, enough striking down from superiority in the records of antiquity and its estimates of laughter to presume that the original laughter may have been wholly animosity' (1924).

In thirteen out of the twenty-nine instances of the word 'laughter' in the Bible, it is associated with violence (Ziv, quoted in White, 1998). The close relationship between humour and aggression can also be traced in certain popular terminologies: people are 'mocked, ridiculed, parodied, wisecracked, ribbed, roasted, kidded, made fun of, poked fun at, cut up and laughed at', to name but a few. Because of its aggressive potential humour is an effective weapon. The Greenland Eskimos resolve their quarrels through 'duels of laughter' whereby the person who elicits the most laughs from the spectators wins; the so-called loser is humiliated and 'often goes into exile' (Robinson, 1977). Lorenz (1966) conceived of the 'humour-response' as a primal expression and motivation for aggressive behaviour. Freud (1905a) was explicit about the latent hostility in jokes. He believed that through verbal invective our perceived enemy was rendered comic. Likewise, Jones (1929) and Grotjahn (1957) thought that the use of humour evidenced the presence of repressed hostility, aggression and sadism.

The practical joke barely disguises its inherent aggression. Part of the pleasure derived from the practical joke lies in seeing another person caught out, metaphorically or literally 'tripped up'. The hostility, hatred and fear implicit in so many racist or sexist jokes requires no elaboration. In a review of self-report studies examining the specific situations in which laughter is evoked, Pollio and Edgerly (1976) conclude that situations involving clever remarks made by one person at the expense of another account for over half the responses. This supports the contention that aggression and hostility are significant factors that underlie what is often perceived to be funny and which frequently gives rise to laughter. Koestler argues that even though the more 'sophisticated' forms of humour belie more complex and mixed emotional determinants,

> . . . whatever the mixture, it must contain an ingredient whose presence is indispensable, an impulse, however faint, of aggression or apprehension . . . .It may be manifested in the guise of malice, derision, the verbal cruelty of condescension, or merely an absence of sympathy with the victim of the joke (1964:52).

If humour provides an outlet for aggression we might well suppose that listening to an aggressive joke might offer some relief if it resonates with an internal, hostile state. Quanty (1976, quoted in Buckman, 1994) indeed found that angry subjects appreciated aggressive humour more than their non-angry counterparts.

Of course, aggression in humour is seldom explicit. If it is explicit, the joke or comic routine run the risk of no longer being funny since the anxiety attached to the hostile impulses has not been sufficiently transformed through humour. In some instances the latent aggression is only revealed through an exploration of the humorist's state of mind and the internal phantasy and object relation that is being re-enacted in the humorous interaction, as became apparent in my work with Pete.

Pete was a 42-year-old man who sought psychological help because of stress. He worked in the City and was experiencing difficulties coping with his heavy workload. He had also been drinking quite heavily. He came to see me feeling uncertain as to whether therapy could be of any help, but his doctor had encouraged him to come. In our first meeting he 'cracked a few jokes', as he himself noted, while commenting on my failure to respond to them. He felt hurt by my silence. He said that it was important to look on the bright side of life. 'Maybe', he remarked, 'if more people looked on the bright side you would be out of a job'. I noted the significance of this in light not only of his anger towards me but also of his precarious hold on his own job – an anxiety he was desperately trying to deny through his apparent commitment to looking on the bright side. Life was too short, he advised me, to get too upset about things. Such statements were invariably followed by laughter.

Pete proudly told me that he was popular in the office because he always 'took the piss out of everyone and everything'. I asked him if he had always felt himself to be a funny person. Pete replied that he had. He recalled being the class clown and frequently getting into trouble for playing practical jokes on his classmates. I invited him to give me some examples of this. Aggression in humorous exchanges can take varied forms. It may, for example, be bound with affection as we can observe in friendly teasing. However, the incidents Pete recounted indicated the pleasure, accompanied by laughter, derived from seeing another person vulnerable, confused and lost while he and his friends looked on in delight, feeling superior. With the reduction of anxiety and under the auspices of this 'only being a joke', humour allows for a pleasurable release of destructive impulses. The very motive for sharing a joke is often an attempt to seek approval from others for the underlying guilt about the offensive and aggressive impulses concealed within it (Fenichel, 1946). The audience, as jury, absolves the joker through their laughter. Pete indeed emphasized how funny his friends had perceived these incidents to be.

I asked Pete whether anyone else in the family was funny. He replied: 'Well, my mother. She was born with a permanent smile – with her it's not so much a question of what could make her laugh but of what would *not* [his emphasis] make her laugh! If I came home with bruises from being involved in a fight she would always laugh it off.' As he spoke these words he also laughed off the pain of his experience of neglect. The more Pete spoke the more desolate I felt. It seemed as though he was trying to get me to laugh at his anxiety and pain too, thereby recreating his relationship with his mother who had been experienced by him as a permanent, uniform, 'smiley' face which never mirrored back his varied internal states. All emotional life had been flattened out into a superficially, 'happy-go-lucky', funny, exterior which had to be compulsively adhered to otherwise real feelings might seep through. I gained the impression that laughter was an effective emotional disinfectant in the family that foreclosed emotional experience.

Pete's greatest problem was that he had never developed any capacity to deal with the complexity of his emotional life. His descriptions of his mother in particular suggested that she had conveyed to him that to feel anything was dangerous. Consequently feelings were denied through being 'laughed off', mocked or belittled. Pete had internalized a similar way of coping with psychic pain. He re-enacted with others the internalized relationship with his mother. He could take no one seriously and 'everything and everyone' was dismissed through his compulsive bantering and ridiculing, and this permeated our relationship. This served the function of distancing others as well as myself, while making Pete feel that he was far superior and thereby supporting his belief that he was also self-sufficient.

Pete's brand of humour always required a victim. This feature is apparent in observations of some children's play which bear witness to the latent aggression in many of their so-called playful or humorous interactions. The sight of another child's looking foolish or simply different because of their colour, gender, physical appearance or disability may evoke laughter. Laughing *at* others is common – it is the extent and rigidity of this attitude that are the important variables. The earliest theories of laughter centred around the notion that laughter was closely associated with the degradation of another. These are variously referred to as the 'theory of degradation' or the 'superiority theory'. As far back as Plato we can find references to our mixed responses to other's misfortunes: 'When we laugh at the ridiculous qualities of our friends, we mix pleasure with pain' (Plato, 1925). According to Plato, our amusement is a kind of malice towards people who are perceived to be powerless.

Aristotle also draws attention to the feeling of superiority and the attendant wish to mock and deride, found in humour: 'Comedy is a representation of inferior people, not indeed in the full sense of the mere bad, . . . but the laughable is a species of the basic or ugly' (1927:18). Some humour is undeniably aimed at attacking another. American street gangs often indulge in competitive banter that aims to put down the perceived opponent (Jacobson, 1997) and enhances the status of the gang member who is most effective at this. Baudelaire (1855) articulated the philosopher's value position on this undeniable aspect of human nature as he held that laughter was indeed an expression of man's 'satanic spirit'. Laughter at misfortune is, however, clearly dependent on our affective disposition towards the recipient of the misfortune that befalls them; we are less likely to laugh if a loved one is afflicted (Wolff et al., 1974; Zillman and Cantor, 1976). The greater the misfortune of the 'butt of the joke' usually the less funny the joke is deemed to be (Zillman and Bryant, 1974). Moreover, there is some evidence that humour is far more likely when retaliatory acts compensate equitably for some perceived provocation than merely establishing the superiority of one party.

Generally speaking then, our affective ties to people determine whether or not we laugh at them and their misfortunes. When there are no such ties our laughter may express disdain caused, for example, by seeing someone's adversity or disfigurement. Nowadays the pressures of 'political correctness' inhibit many such responses, as we fear being publicly denounced as racist, sexist or just plain bigoted. There appears to be a strong relationship between such social sanctioning and our seeking of comedy as a release valve. Jacobson incisively observes that it is:

> exactly in proportion as we proliferate social boundaries beyond which we dare not step, careful of class, conscious of race, fearful of sex, each one of us a nurse to the other's crippled spirit, so does our hunger for the contrary consolation of comedy grow (1997:195).

For every tragedy on either a personal or larger scale, the jokes are not long to follow. McDougall (1920) noted that one of the functions of humour was to afford us some protection from the 'depressive influence' of other people's shortcomings or ill fate. Humour thus acts as a protective shield against fear arising from an awareness that those very attributes or circumstances that we jest about could befall us. The response of laughter appears to be based on the sudden and surprising relief from anxiety that it is not so – as if we had woken from a nightmare: 'it's only a dream; it's only a joke'. Indeed, this is one of the widely acknowledged mechanisms exploited to comic effect: increase tension and laughter will mark its release.

It is no mere coincidence that so much of what provokes laughter, forming the 'bread and butter' of a number of comedians' routines, are jokes that centre on difference (e.g. sexual, cultural, religious, etc.). The more talented the comedian the more sophisticated the construction of the joke and in some cases, the more benign its underlying intent, but their content varies little. In such humour the 'other' looms large as a menace which has to be defended against. Even in the routines of some of the so-called 'alternative', politically correct, comedians we can trace the vestiges of the threat posed by the 'other'. The main difference is that the latter use humour to give expression to this threat while exposing their own vulnerability rather than covering it up, and so shielding themselves from it, by using humour to ridicule the other. Racial stereotypes abound in jokes, bearing witness to our use of humour as an outlet for the less acceptable impulses and feelings that drive us. I have in mind here the aggression, hatred and envy that are also a part of our relationships with each other. It is as if we desperately need somehow to quench the anxiety generated by the perception of difference, for if something can be different then that which 'is' may not always remain so. Gilman (1988) argues that at the root of all bipolar images of difference, which underpin our construction of stereotypes, lies the phantasy of wholeness. We find it very hard to entertain the possibility of our own collapse, disability or loss of control. We find it easier to project it outwards into the world in order to localize it in the 'other', thereby creating a temporary illusion of control and safety. In many instances the fearful is made harmless through being rendered comic[7].

The theory of degradation is best exemplified in Hobbes' *Leviathan*:

Sudden glory is the passion which makes those grimaces called laughter; and is caused . . . by the apprehension of some deformed thing in another (Morreall, 1987:19).

---

7.   Not all jokes predicated on racial stereotypes are, however, racist. Rather, it is a question of how the stereotype itself is used and who tells the joke – a joke predicated on a stereotype of a Jewish person will not create much, if any, offence if it is told by a Jewish person. In this respect, Jacobson notes that some jokes play with the expectations implicit in the stereotype itself 'shaking them up as a kaleidoscope, making a glittering farce of all racial assumptions' (Jacobson, 1999:13). Moreover he argues that: '. . . fear of the stereotype is fear of comedy itself . . . far from nurturing racism, it [comedy] is the best ally reason has ever had in its long-running battle with intolerance . . . we look to it to aerate those antagonisms that fester in every heart' (1999:13).

Hobbes' position is largely in keeping with the views of Plato and Aristotle, but his theory introduces an important nuance (Zillman and Cantor, 1976). Whereas the Greek philosophers suggested that the powerful laugh at those who are less so, Hobbes argues that it is 'imperfect' people who laugh at those even less fortunate. Implicit in this position, therefore, is the notion of humour as somehow protective and restitutive of a precarious narcissistic equilibrium through the degradation of another who acts as the container of our projections. Glimpses of our own inadequacy and imperfection incite an attempt to ridicule another who thus acts as insurance against our own shortcomings. According to Bollas, a sense of humour takes pleasure in inadequacy because it originates within the early, inevitably unbalanced, power relationship between adult and infant:

> The mother–infant relationship, then, is something of a farce: one person
> – much the superior in power, treating the other as equal, though in fact
> the superior one takes pleasure in the inferior one's frailties, which then
> become endearing (1995:240).

Interestingly, Grotjahn (1957) frames his developmental analysis of humour in childhood within the context of a Freudian structural model wherein the quest for superiority is central. He argues that in the oral stage a smile will frequently elicit a favourable response from the other thereby imparting a sense of control over the object. Contemporaneous with the child's entry into the anal stage and the acquisition of control over bodily functions, is the child's awareness of laughter. As language is mastered between the ages of four and eight, jokes and riddles produce amusement. The child's mastery of his bodily functions affords him a sense of superiority which is itself a source of gratification. Grotjahn points out that it is when the child 'begins to feel superior [that] he has discovered the comic situation' (1957:75). Indeed, for every 'wit' there is invariably the 'butt' of the joke. Grotjahn argues that laughter takes us back to the pleasure we once all experienced as children as it gives voice to our aggression against all representatives of authority and order. As the child's ability to appreciate humour develops he discovers humour as a strategy for mastering aggressive and conflictual drives and so we witness, as it were, a symbolic turning of the tables on the powerful adult (Bergler, 1956). We might say then that children use humour progressively in the service of their growing mastery of reality (Wolfenstein, 1951).[8] It is adults who use it regressively.

---

8. Wolfenstein points out that jokes which evoke images of danger are amongst the play situations in which the child tries himself out facing and overcoming fears.

The existence of humour attests to our attempts to come to terms with our fragile narcissism either adaptively by developing a capacity to take ourselves less seriously, or maladaptively through our attempts to mock another so as to bolster our own narcissism. The narcissistic injury incurred so early on by all of us, confronted by our relative insignificance and powerlessness, leaves an indelible mark on our psyche. The good-enough mother, as we shall see in Chapter 2, steels her baby for future potential narcissistic wounds by imparting the skill of a sense of humour which can transform pain into pleasure. In this sense we might say that humour acts as a sophisticated, 'mature' defence mechanism – a point to which we shall return in Chapter 4.

Humour as corrective

The theory of degradation places humour firmly within an interpersonal context. Humour emerges as a vehicle which safely transforms but nonetheless gives expression, though by no means exclusively, to our destructive impulses. Bergson (1956) is another philosopher whose discussions on laughter and humour are firmly rooted in a social context. For Bergson the function of laughter is undeniably a social one. He argues that laughter pursues the utilitarian aim of general improvement by keeping us alert, pointing out our limitations. A comic impasse occurs whenever a human being ceases to behave like one, that is, when he resembles a 'thing'. The ridiculous is described by Bergson (1956) as 'something mechanical encrusted on the living'. In turn, laughter acts as a 'corrective' to rigidity:

> The comic is that side of a person which reveals his likeness to a thing, that aspect of human events which through its peculiar inelasticity conveys the impression of pure mechanism, of automatism, of movement without life. Consequently it expresses an individual or collective imperfection which calls for an immediate corrective. This corrective is laughter, a social gesture that singles out and expresses a special kind of absent mindedness in men and events (Bergson, 1956:117)

Although Bergson's theory differs from the earlier theories of degradation, it is interesting to note that even within Bergson's framework, laughter is provoked by the perception of a difference that has negative evaluative connotations. The 'thing-like' quality of the other is an 'imperfection' which is responded to with laughter and this entails a degree of humiliation even if its goal, as Bergson suggests, is to rectify and not to attack as an end in itself.

It is easy to relate Bergson's theory to many of the situations or comic characters that make us laugh. One need only think of popular British comedy characters such as Basil Fawlty or Mr Bean, or Jack Nicholson's recent impersonation of an obsessive-compulsive man in the film *As Good as it Gets* (1997), to appreciate the theory's explanatory power. All of these characters are funny largely because of their inherently inflexible personality structure – their responses to the events that befall them are highly predictable and unidimensional. The comic narratives are simply slight variations on a theme as we witness, for example, Mr Bean's blunders and misunderstandings, oblivious to the trail of chaos he is bound to leave behind wherever he goes. His inflexibility determines him predictably. So much humour is in fact based on caricature or impersonation. This process of transformation, for comic effect, results in the creation of an inflexible character whose caricatured idiosyncrasies have a mechanical quality exploited by the humorist. This is partly why obsessional people can so often be the victims of cruel mimicry which gives rise to laughter. The obsessional personality is caricatured inflexibility par excellence. Essentially what we are laughing at here are exaggerated character defences which have created an 'armour plating of the personality' (Reich W., 1949) which entraps the person. Cleese (in Skynner and Cleese, 1993) observes that repeated inflexible behaviour would eventually cease to be funny. That which ensures sustained laughter is, according to Cleese, the 'oscillation' between flexible behaviour and inflexible behaviour. But such oscillation or contrast need not be located necessarily in what we perceive 'out there', but may arise from a contrast between an internal expectation or wish and what we are met with 'out there'. In other words, even if, for the sake of argument, Basil Fawlty remains stuck in his behaviour, we will continue to laugh because our internal expectation, at times born out of an identification with him and his predicament, along with a wish for change, will create the necessary contrast.

Bergson's theory offers an account of why we respond to repetitive behaviour with laughter but it cannot adequately explain all laughter. Koestler (1964) wryly points out that if it were the case that we laugh each time a person gives the impression of being a 'thing' and repetitive behaviour were a necessary and sufficient condition of the comic, then: 'there would be no more amusing spectacle than an epileptic fit . . . there would be nothing more funny than a corpse' (1964:47).

Notwithstanding this limitation, the essence of Bergson's ideas on humour can be traced in the theories which emphasize humour's function as a form of social control of deviance. In these accounts humour is thought to act as a sanction against more minor forms of deviance such as bad manners or somewhat eccentric behaviour that does not carry a risk of harm to another (Powell, 1983, quoted in Palmer 1994). There is some evidence that laughter corrects deviant behaviour (Bryant et al., 1983), and criticism applied with the balm of humour may be easier to receive (Haig, 1988). Such a position advocates that when someone ridicules, mimics or jokes about a particular type of behaviour the listener is not only possibly amused but is also indirectly given information about faux pas or social subtleties. In an identification with the butt of the joke, but in the hope that we are not going to be the next victim by being similarly ridiculed, we learn how to avoid similar faux pas, and unacceptable or deviant behaviour is thereby reduced. Many forms of humour, including irony, satire, parody, sarcasm, and caricature, possess this corrective potential.

The gift of humour

Playing with Voltaire's original view that heaven has given us hope and sleep to get through life, Kant (1892) added '*and laughter*'. Although humour, as we have seen, can be murderous in its intentions and may serve to bolster our own fragile narcissism by humiliating another, there is also a great deal to be said in its favour. Perhaps, as Horace speculated, what we deride teaches us more quickly than does what we approve or revere.[9] This implies a critical and thus potentially constructive aspect of humour that could help us to expand our own self-awareness and knowledge.

Freud (1905a, 1927) carried out one of the most interesting psychological studies of humour that emphasizes its importance in our psychic life, even if he devoted comparatively little time to it in the context of his many works. In 1927 he wrote, 'Not everyone is capable of the humorous attitude. It is a rare and precious gift, and many people are without the capacity to enjoy humorous pleasure that is presented to them' (1927:166). Freud himself had such a gift. An often-quoted witticism was on the occasion of Freud's forced emigration from Vienna to London in 1938. After the Nazis had forcibly entered his apartment they required Freud to sign a declaration testifying to the 'good' treatment he had received from them. Freud obliged and is said to have added 'I can heartily recommend the Gestapo to everyone'! (Jones, 1957:226).

Although Freud's own personal style has been reported to have been quite humorous, his paper on 'Jokes and their relation to the unconscious', was spurred, according to Jones (1957), by complaints from his colleague, Wilhelm Fliess, that Freud relayed so many bad jokes! Rising to the challenge, Freud proceeded to develop his ideas on humour

---

9. Research does not in fact support the contention that the addition of humour to a message will increase what the audience can learn from it by increasing attention (Gruner, 1976). However, such research has typically focused on experimental situations in which attention to the message was mandatory and it is quite probable that humour operates differently in securing and holding attention in the real world. There is evidence to suggest for example that patients given pre-operative information using patient-related, overtly funny cartoons vs routine teaching, demonstrate greater recall of information that a control group (Parfitt, 1990, quoted in Dean 1997).

alongside his evolving ideas on sexuality (Spruiell, 1985). This connection is not surprising as Freud highlights links between the subject matter of jokes and the struggle to integrate within our personalities the pressures emanating from our sexual and aggressive impulses. As Phillips put it, 'the joke is so important for Freud because it is the most ingeniously efficient way of rescuing our pleasure from the obstacles' (1993:90). Phillips is referring here to the obstacles that stand in our way of deriving gratification – obstacles that are self-imposed but which also speak of the inevitability of the demands of civilization which requires us to inhibit our impulses. In our life-long balancing act between the demands of reality and the clamour of our instincts, dreams and jokes manage to bypass the censor and so are effectively 'saboteurs of repression' (Phillips, 1993:91). This is one of the ways in which we might say that humour is subversive.

In his early writings on humour, Freud (1905a) framed his ideas in the context of his then dominant topographical model of the mind within which psychic events were considered either to expand or economize psychic energy. At that time Freud believed that humour afforded pleasure because it spared an expenditure of emotion. Laughter was believed to release built-up nervous energy, thereby conserving the energy that would otherwise have been used to repress forbidden feelings or wishes. Within this model laughter springs from the fact that the intellectual or emotional effort that we would normally have to exert becomes superfluous as a result of condensation. The nervous tension is thus economized and abreacted involuntarily as a motor innervation of the muscles of laughter and is finally discharged in laughter. Ferenczi summarized the Freudian position thus:

> The man of humour . . . rises above his own troubles, his anger, or his feelings, economises in so doing his affective expenditure and employs this energy in laughter while the ordinary person abandons himself in sad emotion' (1911:344).

Freud (1905a) elaborates this 'economic' perspective by specifying what he perceives to be the different underlying mechanisms in the various humorous presentations. He concludes that the pleasure in wit originates from an economy of expenditure in inhibition; that of the comic from an economy of expenditure in thought and that of humour[10] from an economy of expenditure in emotion. Thus, in joking, the energy saved is that which would otherwise be used in the service of repression of hostile or sexual impulses. In the comic we are spared some cognitive processing. In humour, we prepare ourselves for feeling some negative

---

[10]. Freud's use of the term 'humour' is narrow. In its more contemporary usage, it subsumes joking and the comic.

emotion (e.g. fear, pity) but then realize that we need not be concerned, so that the energy summoned is discharged in laughter.

The exhilarating effect of puns, for example, results from our being spared the serious effort of intellectual work; we can 'play'. Through our witticisms we can give free reign to our hostility and resentment against language which is a reminder of the demands of reality, of reason and logic and, inevitably, of a given social order which keeps our impulses in check. Wordplay enables us to 'decathect' the latent content before it emerges into consciousness. It can thus be seen as affording a plausible front to consciousness. Young children's understanding of humour illustrates this point in reverse, since this is a 'front' that does not divert children from the latent meaning in the same way because it would appear that they ignore the double meaning of puns. Consequently, the phantasy images that are evoked are too strongly cathected to be dissipated by words. Wolfenstein (1951) provides several interesting examples of such 'failures' of humour which display the child as incapable of exploiting the defences that the joke would otherwise afford. For example, she refers to an eight-year-old boy who asks the riddle 'If you were in a room with just a bed and a calendar do you know how you would live?' to which the child replies: 'eat the dates off the calendar, drink water from the bed springs *and sleep on the bed*' (my italics). Wolfenstein draws attention to the fact that 'sleeping on the bed' is the boy's addition and is not a joke. It reveals how he is in fact transposing himself into the situation and 'seriously' trying to work it out for himself. In this instance then, the humorous solution is not effective in transforming the child's anxiety.

Fundamental to Freud's thesis is the notion that through the varieties of what is broadly here termed humour, we spare ourselves the affects to which a particular internal or external situation would otherwise give rise. The affective response is overridden with a jest – aborting it, as it were. It was only some years later, in a very brief paper in 1927, that Freud revisited the question of humour. Here he adds to his original economic formulation a dynamic one emphasizing the unique role of the superego in the humorous attitude. The paper is of note since it not only refines Freud's earlier conceptualization but also, in so doing, it develops further the very notion of the superego. At first Freud hypothesized that the superego was a function of the ego, largely concerned with the limitations to gratification: it monitored the ego, criticized it and punished it. This view of the superego was consistent with Freud's beliefs about the evolution of civilization. The coercive and hostile elements of the parental function were kept in the foreground by Freud who viewed their internalization as the basis of man's successful and lasting socialization as they kept the demands of the pleasure principle in check (Schafer, 1960). In humour, however, Freud recognized that, through a displacement of cathexis from the ego to superego, the ego can rebelliously and pleasurably adopt a more light-hearted attitude towards the impingements of reality.

In his 1927 paper on humour, Freud attributes to the superego a loving and comforting function – humour exemplifies this function. Freud suggests that in humour it is the superego that comforts the ego in the face of the stresses reality imposes by fostering a temporary illusion. He describes it as if the superego were sympathetically appealing to the ego, 'Look here! Here is the world which seems so dangerous! It is nothing but a game for children – just worth making a jest about!' (1927:166). The superego assumes a parental function relating to the ego as if it were a child who needs comforting.[11,12]A sense of humour becomes the hallmark of an optimal distance from inner conflicts and is based on a steady and free availability of libido in the superego. The loving superego is said to represent the loved and admired pre-Oedipal and Oedipal parents who provide love, protection and comfort. This identification facilitates an internalization by the child of the capacity to love and comfort himself. Indeed, Kris (1952) observes that such a reconceptualization makes explicit the value of the 'humorist's achievement, for he banishes man's greatest fear, the eternal fear, acquired in childhood, of the loss of love (1952:216). Chasseguet-Smirgel (1988) takes this one step further by suggesting that the humorist functions as a 'good enough' mother to himself. Along related lines Grotjahn (1971) observed that laughter frees the individual from the shackles of bad, persecutory, internal objects.

Freud's (1927) later conceptualization reveals humour as attesting to the 'triumph of narcissism', that is, a reassertion of narcissism via an adaptive regression. Humour allows the individual to triumph over the forces of repression or the pain of reality. The example of jokes will help to clarify this latter point. Freud believed that the pleasure obtained from jokes depended both on their technique or 'jokework' (e.g. condensation, displacement, symbolization, breaking the rules of logic, establishment of unexpected connections between disparate ideas) as well as their 'tendencies'. According to Freud, tendentious jokes involve latent content that is taboo; that is, he refers to those jokes motivated, on the whole, by erotic and aggressive impulses. Such jokes allow access to ordinarily suppressed or repressed phantasies and combine them with pre-conscious phantasies on another level. The result is a discharge and a saving of energy, as we saw earlier, equivalent to the forces usually sustaining the repression. In a psychoanalytic sense, humour, like dreams, opens up for us another fruitful road to the unconscious.

[11.] Oberdorf (1932) draws attention to the American slang expression 'kidding' meaning to 'treat like a child'.

[12.] Freud presents this parental function as a paternal one – a point which is disputed by Chasseguet-Smirgel (1988) who views it as a maternal function.

Although the analogy between jokes and dreams is clear, Freud nevertheless differentiates them from dreams in so far as jokes are necessarily social. The joke's *raison d'être* is the other person (Kline, 1977).

At the core of a psychoanalytic perspective is the view of humour as an adaptive ego defence mechanism, a position which has been repeatedly reiterated by other theorists since Freud's original views on the subject (Jones, 1929; Dooley, 1934; Grotjahn, 1957; Bergler, 1956, Vaillant, 1971). Humour is so effective as a defence since it does not altogether smother the painful affect. Rather, it allows the affect to be discharged, once disguised through the jokework (Buckman, 1994).

This understanding of humour is echoed in those accounts which view it as an invaluable safety valve. For Sypher, 'Comedy is a release, a taking off of the mask we have put on to deal with others who have put on decent masks to deal with us' (1956:221). Fisher and Fisher's study of comedians emphasizes this point. They observe that 'in general comics play themselves' (1981:81). In an interview, the comedian Jerry Lewis describes how 'A comedian is literally allowing the underlying real thing to come out in front without any guise . . . In the dramatic, you have a mask . . . but in comedy you are naked' (Wilde, 1973:318). The comedian exposes himself to us and so leads the way, taking us with him to another place where everything is turned upside down, where our values, our cherished beliefs and our impotence and irrelevance are all ruthlessly exposed (Bollas 1995; Jacobson, 1997). The comedian 'defrocks' us as he is himself elevated to a 'priest, a mystic and release valve for clogged social tensions' (Lee, 1997:20). The comic routine performs the function of presenting anxiety-provoking material and simultaneously reassuring the audience that the dangerous content and its associated emotional response will be safely contained. Studies of comedians reveal that their success depends on their capacity to work successfully with topics that are emotionally threatening to the audience (Pollio and Edgerly, 1976).

We may abandon our masks through comedy and see ourselves a bit more crudely and realistically, but comedy itself exploits humour's tightrope to give expression to that which would otherwise be repressed. 'It's only a joke' . . . we see it and then we don't. This clever mechanism allows us to approach what is feared at a safe distance and in so doing tension is released. Yet, the changes that humour can facilitate are even more far reaching than this.

Critical and subversive humour

A psychoanalytic perspective highlights humour's psychically integrating function bringing together the contradictions and conflicts that are an unavoidable part of being human. The humorous vision facilitates a psychic elaboration and mastery of unpleasant and discongruent or conflictual situations or emotions (Sacerdoti, 1992). Integrating paradox is the province of the professional comedian who has been accurately described as ' . . . precariously immersed in contradictions. He becomes a master at integrating what seems not to fit together . . . The joke is so often the mastery of disparate pieces' (Fisher and Fisher, 1981: xiii).

Moreover, comedy, as Jacobson (1997) suggests, transforms what is base in us and allows us to enjoy it. Indeed, reading Freud, we can be left in no doubt as to the value he placed on humour as a significant developmental achievement. This has been emphasized by other authors too, especially by those focusing on humour as a positive social force. Such perspectives have highlighted the essentially critical nature of humour and hence its subversive potential. Freud singled out jokes by virtue of their capacity to subvert criticism itself as they can bypass our internal censor thanks to the jokework, a point echoed by Palmer:

> Only one feature of jokes and jests, of all forms of comic utterance, is universal in them and distinguishes them from mere comic utterances: the subversion of criticism (Palmer, 1987:218).

Humour, then, by subverting our own internal critic emerges as one of the most powerful critical tools we possess. It is, in a manner of speaking, 'the critic's critic'. Humour kicks us into thinking, re-evaluating implicit assumptions, seeing new possibilities for the first time:

> Whatever is funny is subversive . . . .a dirty joke is not of course a serious attack upon morality, but it is a sort of mental rebellion, *a momentary wish that things were otherwise* (Orwell, 1961:176) [my italics].

Orwell here highlights the close, and psychologically significant, association between humour and the imagination. Humour expands our imagination allowing us to entertain the possibility of something being other than it is, a point to which we shall return in more depth in Chapter 3. Writing on the subject of satire, Graves observes that its function is 'to destroy whatever is overblown, faded or dull and clear the soil for new spring' (Graves, quoted in Jacobson, 1997:117). This implies a kind of regeneration through humour, sweeping away the cobwebs of our rigidities. If this is indeed so then comedy's purpose is to upset established personal assumptions, beliefs or values, as well as external social order in the service of change and hopefully progress. Jacobson echoes this when he writes that, 'In the deranging, disarranging communal laughter occasioned by the contrary clown, we see what isn't possible, thereby make it possible' (1997:195).

Lorenz (1966) suggests that behind the comedian's or clown's masks we meet a moralist striving to rebalance that which is unbalanced or repressed in a given society. These views find some support when we consider the function of such social events as, for example, carnivals, and of the archetypal figures of the Fool and the clown. According to Sypher (1956), carnivals represent an outlet for our resentment as they upset the social order, by turning everything on its head. Tracing the function of carnivals and of clowns historically and cross-culturally, Jacobson draws attention to their inherently rebellious nature:

> . . . what is holy is profaned, what is elevated is lowered, where there has been respect and awe there is now travesty, where modestly, lewdness. Nothing stays still, nothing is as it was, every possible fantasy of social revolution and retroversion is realised . . . until the renunciation and restitution of Lent (Jacobson 1997:198).

The Japanese form of vaudeville known as *taishu engeki* is a case in point. In a culture organized around notions of reverence and obedience, *taishu engeki* theatres legitimize an orgy of insubordination, punctuated by breaches in the time-honoured Japanese rituals of propriety. Jenkins (1998a) argues that its main function is to fulfil the spectators' 'urgent need for release'. He describes *taishu engeki* as 'year round festivals of non-conformity' in which cultural taboos are inverted, genders are reversed, patterns of *kata* (Japanese formal speech and behavioural patterns) are distorted and barriers of social status are bypassed (Jenkins, 1998a).

Anthropologists have recorded ritualized clowning in many societies even if the content of their performances varies cross-culturally (White, 1998). In a survey of the anthropological literature Charles (1945) found that out of a total of 136 cultures, 56 contained information about the social role of the clown or the Fool, both of which emerge as important figures in the social life of the community.[13] Defying various demons, Balinese clowns offer laughter as an antidote to the threat of annihilation. In Balinese culture, clowns are central figures in the temple festivals which are held regularly. The clowns introduce contemporary anachronisms into ancient myths, thereby highlighting the conflict between tradition and modernity that dominates the Balinese. For example, evil spirits are dressed in Western-style galoshes and fifteenth century battles are staged and disrupted by clowns mimicking tourists trying to take photographs (Jenkins, 1998b).

The central role of the clown was not lost on Charlie Chaplin (1960) who shrewdly observed: 'I remain one thing and one thing only – and that is a clown. It places me on a far higher plane than any politician.' Approaching the subject from a Jungian perspective, Charles (1945) views the clown as an archetype which alerts us to primitive concerns which have been either neglected or totally excluded from a social

---

[13.] Among the Tubatolabol, for example, the office of clown is hereditary, passed on from father to son (Apte, 1985).

group. Levine (1961) in a study of American Indian ceremonials, views the ritualized clowning performance as affording a contained and controlled expression to repressed aspects of a given society. He presents humour as a form of social regulation that protects a society from acting out sexual and aggressive drives. In the shared laughter at the clown's antics the audience partake in the violation of taboos, bypassing guilt or fear of punishment or disruption of the community. Bakhtin (1968) regarded the clown as the embodiment of a comic attitude towards the world and carnival laughter as a manifestation of popular folk humour which subverted authority and so brought liberation. Laughter 'degrades us', according to Bakhtin , in the sense that it takes us down to earth, reconnects us with our origins, as he emphasizes the necessary digestive, sexual or scatological acts which are the human common denominators and which feature in so much humour. A renegade aspect of our experience which requires integration is thus allowed into both individual and collective consciousness. The exaggeration which is so characteristic of both clowning and comedy represents, according to Charles, an attempt to:

> . . . symbolise the exaggerated size and quantity . . . of an element which is causing unconscious conflict, and also the better to emphasise and to hold up for clear understanding . . . the clown performs an extraordinarily alive and immediate ritual of induction into the consciousness of his audience, of relatively neglected elements in the life of the individuals in the community (1945:33).

In an historical study of Fools and clowns from medieval times onwards, Welsford (1935) argues that the salience of the Fool can be seen to reflect its function as the 'creator of freedom'. It is the Fool's prerogative to act out forbidden wishes and so give our instincts free reign. It is also his privilege to voice truths that others may not be able to contemplate: 'The Fool is the primeval condition that churns and rumbles within us all as we seek to know and he represents the ground that assures us that we do not' (Janik, 1998:20).

Traditionally the Fool is a close confidante of the ruler's most intimate experiences, as dramatized in Shakespeare's *King Lear* (Rose, 1969). Knight (1931, quoted in Hager, 1998) viewed the Fool as the critic and psychologist unsuccessfully trying to make Lear laugh at himself. The Fool's and the clown's antics also reassure us, not simply because we vicariously give expression to repressed aspects of ourselves, but also because, for all their acting out, both the clown and the Fool survive and, significantly, survive in our sympathy. This is apparent when we consider the *schlemiel* (badly done) and *schlimazel* (bad luck) comic characters – originating in medieval ghetto folklore – that emerge in various incarnations in Jewish humour. They exemplify some of the ways in which the Middle-European Jews used humour and the Fool figure as a way of managing their predicament (Shatzky, 1998). Notwithstanding their mishaps these characters' intransigent optimism transcends their ineptness and misfortune. Indeed Pollio and Edgerly suggest that 'the clown is successful not because he gets slapped or degraded, but rather because he is none the worse for his slapping' (1976:216). Furthermore, through their mistakes and mishaps these characters highlights what is valued and important (Klapp, 1972).[14] We can trace here echoes of Bergson's theory of laughter as corrective as the Fool emerges as the symbol of the 'moralist in reverse . . . stressing what he violates by emphasising what is beyond him' (Pollio and Edgerly, 1976:216).

What can we conclude from all this? Carnivals, clowns and Fools appear to bear witness to our instincts unleashed, yet contained within a ritualized activity. They expose the intimate connection between the sacred and the profane (Douglas, 1966). The comedian, the clown, the humorist in each of us, manipulate something embarrassing or shocking:

> The clown holds the licentious thing in his hand psychologically speaking . . . he knows, his audience knows, and both he and his audience know that the other knows, that he is not that thing . . . He is playing with fire, but he is not fire. In the moment he identifies himself with the fire he is no longer funny; that fine delightful sense of balance and mastery is lost and the clown becomes pathetic, ineffective, disgusting (Charles, 1945:32).

The clown, the Fool and the comedian all reflect back to us the hungry infant wanting more, expressing his 'polymorphous perversity' (Freud, 1905b), his greed and envy: the internal revolution of our instinctual life enacted under the guise of a public, 'funny' celebration. In humour, though regression takes place, it is not tantamount to a total relinquishment of ego control (Levine, 1961). Indeed, A. Reich observes:

> The grotesque-comic play cannot be understood as a more or less disguised breaking through of instincts . . . [it] has the meaning of confession, self-humiliation and self-punishment. Thus the requirements of the superego are fulfilled simultaneously. So many psychic needs are satisfied by this achievement. So many instincts find discharge, not flooding the ego but subjugated to its mastery. These instincts are deliberately evoked by the ego that makes use of them for the purpose of gaining pleasure. Thus the anxiety, which under ordinary conditions is always the consequence of such a return of the unconscious, is controlled (1949:165-166).

[14.] The clown exploits none other than the mechanism of 'negation' that, paradoxically, reveals through its denial.

Through humour we can get away with it and so re-invent our beginnings but maybe we seek to return to a place we have never in fact inhabited. Perhaps, as Levy-Strauss observes, 'Festivals turn social life topsy-turvy, not because it was like this but because it has never been and can never be any different'(1949:98). Ultimately, however, these figures are important not primarily by virtue of the relief they afford us but, largely, because they remind us of what has been ignored and are thus instrumental in prodding us to take act of our awareness. They can thus instigate social and intrapsychic change.

Humour and incongruity

The varied perspectives that have been reviewed so far appear to suggest that where there is life there is humour. Indeed, Kierkegaard (1841) viewed the 'comical' as intrinsic to life, arguing that wherever there is life we find contradiction and wherever there is contradiction the comical emerges. The notion of contradiction or incongruity can be traced in the work of other philosophers such as Kant (1892) and Schopenhauer (1819). Darwin's (1872) original 'theory of incongruity' stated that nothing produces laughter more than the meeting of two incongruous ideas that result in two contradictory responses related to two conflicting emotions. Incongruity is usually defined as a conflict between an expectation and what actually happens. It invariably reflects a relationship between two objects or events whereby the first sets up an expectation that is not met by the second. For something to be incongruous it must be both different from what we anticipate and it must violate our conceptual patterns. Schopenhauer (1819) thought that laughter resulted from the perception of incongruity between our ideals and the actuality before us.

So much humour in fact consists of bringing together that which 'rationally' would appear antithetical, or highly unlikely. Incongruity accounts well for the underlying structure found in most jokes that culminate in a punchline which is then experienced as a surprise. There is some evidence to suggest that an increase in the experience of incongruity is accompanied by an increase in the proportion of people laughing in a situation (Nerhardt, 1970). Incongruity underlines irony, a figure of speech in which the intended meaning is the opposite of that expressed by the actual words used. It plays on a contrast between appearance and reality and condenses contradictory emotions into one ironic expression. The funniest jokes or situations are those that run counter to expectations. It is of course the case that this holds only for those expectations towards which we feel either indifferent or we are keen, or emotionally ready, to be liberated from (du Pre, 1998).

Incongruity poses a challenge to our wish for an orderly world, both external and internal. The human challenge we might say is to find ways of

managing conflict or contradiction constructively. Paradoxically, our enjoyment of humour testifies to our enjoyment of incongruity. We appear to
seek out that which disturbs us at some level but which, through humour,
is transformed in such a way that anxiety is lessened and we can experience pleasure. Although incongruity is important, that alone provides an
insufficient account of humour. Perception of an unexpected event may
lead to fear, curiosity or problem solving and not necessarily amusement
and/or laughter. Rothbart (1976) proposes that the emotional outcome
of a confrontation with incongruity will depend on a number of factors:

*   the perceived danger of the stimulus
*   the perceived challenge of the stimulus to the person's knowledge
*   whether the incongruity is resolvable.

Such criteria are no doubt related to the final outcome of a humorous
communication. Schultz (1976) argues that it is a more subtle aspect of
jokes that renders incongruity meaningful by somehow resolving it.
Such a perspective proposes a biphasic sequence whereby incongruity is
first perceived and is then followed by its resolution (Schultz, 1976).[15] It
is the resolution phase that distinguishes, for example, humour from
nonsense. Even this account is incomplete since not all incongruity
needs to be resolved for it to produce a humorous effect. Some people
appreciate humour that makes them feel uncomfortable precisely
because it is less disguised, more raw or crude, and does not offer a
resolution to the incongruity it confronts the audience with. The
humour of comedians such as the late Bill Hicks is a case in point. The
readiness to engage with this type of humour may reflect a capacity to
play with ideas and possibilities more imaginatively without being
enslaved to a need to resolve the dilemmas or paradoxes that are
presented.

Koestler (1964) developed his notion of 'bisociation' around a
consideration of the nature of humour and its link with incongruity: 'the
sudden bisociation of an idea or event with two habitually incompatible
matrices will produce a comic effect provided that the narrative . . .
carries the right emotional tension' (1964:51). 'Bisociation', for Koestler,

---

15. This sequence appears to engage us at quite a fundamental level. Sloboda (1998)
    has in fact proposed a similar theory to account for the widespread appeal of
    certain musical patterns. When we listen to music, he explains, our brain is trying
    to guess what comes next – music, like humour we might say, can surprise our
    expectations. Sloboda argues that when the music we hear does not fulfil the
    normal pattern of our expectations, our brain registers surprise that it interprets
    as an emotion. In music this device is called an 'appogiatura' and occurs when
    the first note is discordant – it produces emotional tension and a bittersweet
    tone. The second note then falls inside the chord and produces the resolution or
    relaxation, just as the punchline does in a joke.

demarcates an important distinction between the 'routine skills of thinking on a single 'plane' and the creative act which operates on more than one plane' (1964:36). Koestler refers to the latter as 'double mindedness'. This represents a coming together of lines of thought from different levels of the mind, from the unconscious to the pre-conscious and the conscious. It could be argued that 'single-mindedness', in Koestler's sense, is reassuring. Such a perspective simplifies our experience by doing away with the nuances, the options and hence the decisions we have to make and so the responsibility we have to assume for them. Conversely, 'doublemindedness' involves a state of 'unstable equilibrium where the balance of both emotion and thought is disturbed' (1964:36). If we can tolerate the tension generated by the disequilibrium that incongruity brings about, the bisociative act can facilitate the connection of previously unconnected 'matrices of experience'. Koestler argues that this paves the way to a creative path.

Other philosophers and theorists underline the sudden shift in cognitive perspective that marks the humorous moment. O'Connell observed that the humorist is 'skilled in rapid perceptual-cognitive switches in frames of reference (1976:237). Morreall (1987) suggests that laughter results from a 'pleasant psychological shift' brought about by incongruity. He argues that in order for us to appreciate incongruity we need a system of 'mental representations', that is, we need to manipulate concepts in a non-practical, even 'playful' manner, so that the violation of our expected conceptual patterns will not give rise to negative emotions. Morreall focuses on why we enjoy incongruity by exploring the varied emotional responses to it. Amplifying Rothbart's list (1976) Morreall suggests that incongruity can give rise to the following responses:

- fear or anger
- practical concern for how the incongruity can be resolved
- cognitive dissonance which we aim to reduce, or
- humorous amusement.

The last, according to Morreall, requires a degree of emotional disengagement. This is what Bergson (1956) aptly referred to as a 'momentary anaesthesia of the heart'. Such emotional disengagement, rather than being viewed as pathological, may in fact be highly adaptive (it is of course a matter of degree) for it allows for some emotional distance that may facilitate both cognitive and emotional processing of a given event. In an emotional state we are engaged in a highly charged and personal manner with a situation. Our attention is focused primarily on how a given situation is related to us rather than how it may relate to other people or other situations in a broader sense. In this state we are somehow restricted in our range of experience and consequently in the scope for potential responses, some of which may turn out to be more adaptive than others. Such ideas can be traced to Kant's writing, where we find humour defined as:

> The talent of being able to voluntarily put oneself into a certain mental disposition in which everything is judged quite differently from the ordinary method . . . , and put in accordance with certain rational principles (1892:50).

To be able to confront incongruities in our own experience with amusement rather than anger or sadness, enables us to adopt a more objective and rational perspective. 'Emotions', writes Morreall,

> can be valuable in providing automatic, practical responses in concrete situations, but they do not promote the cognitive orientation to the world we call rationality. In amusement, by contrast, our cognitive processes operate not in a practical but in a playful mode, where there is room for theoretical understanding, imagination and creativity (1987:223).

Morreall's original thesis is that we strive to seek variety in our cognitive input through incongruity. Although variety and novelty make us anxious about our environment as they confront us with the unknown, humour allows us to enjoy novel experiences in a controlled fashion. In this sense humour is a manifestation of our cognitive adaptation that may have survival value (see Chapter 6).

To laugh or to cry

An examination of humour, as I hope this book will testify, can illuminate the varied ways we manage the task of being human. It is unlikely that any one theory can wholly encapsulate the nature and function of humour and why we laugh. As Darwin observed, 'many curious discussions have been written on the causes of laughter with grown up persons. The subject is extremely complex' (1872:200). Nevertheless, cutting across the differences in the varied conceptualizations of humour reviewed in this chapter is the positive value of humour. It operates both as an individual or group psychological defence mechanism that acts as a release valve and thus contributes ultimately to the healthy functioning of society, as well as a critical tool that aids learning and may contribute to individual and social change. If it is so central to our cognitive, emotional and social adaptation, that we cannot then ignore the 'critical' part it plays in our lives. Consequently, its role and potential also need to be considered in the context of the therapeutic relationship, as we shall examine later, in Chapter 5.

When we consider the nature of humour it quickly becomes apparent that it produces laughter not so much by capitalizing on what we perceive to be pleasurable but from the metamorphosis of pain into a psychically more manageable form (Jacobson, 1997). Baudelaire (1855) was clear that the wise man 'laughed only with fear and trembling'. For Baudelaire, at least, laughter was inextricably bound up with the tragic. He argued that man laughs because he has lost his state of completeness that exists in Paradise: 'Neither laughter nor tears can show themselves in the paradise of bliss. They are both equally the children of sorrow' (1855:143).

Our response to suffering is typically more consonant with the Western tragic-heroic tradition. To an extent we mystify suffering and elevate its experience to a higher moral plane. This is implicit in so much writing on the therapeutic endeavour itself. A painful psychotherapy session is one worth paying for. If we laugh we harbour, both as patient and as therapist, the secret concern that no 'work' has been achieved. Bound by the belief that the road to greater insight is earned through cathartic expression of our emotional pain, humour is all too often dismissed as of little therapeutic import. Life is, of course, in so many ways tragic but our reaction to that which life throws our way can evoke both tragic and humorous responses which reflect different narratives. Although the humorous narrative sometimes represents an attempt at denial, this is not always the case. Moreover, sometimes, a temporary degree of denial is adaptive. The tragic response too can be said to involve a denial of our impotence since it can confer an illusory sense of self-importance by viewing our defeat as somehow lending meaning to the conflict, thereby reconciling ourselves to it (Schlesinger, 1979). In the tragic narrative the defeat or the victim role can become the trophy. The humorous response may well deny impotence, to an extent, but it does so by conceptually resolving the incongruity in its capacity to tolerate the pain 'without extolling it and retain the sense of selfhood in a world of pain and ambiguity' (Schlesinger, 1979:322). At its core 'comedy is truth and pain' (Vorhaus, 1994). Almost every joke attests to this. Take as an example jokes about sex; sex at some level or at some point in our experience has been anxiety-provoking for most of us. The joke reflects the pain and the truth of this common experience. As Sypher wrote:

> There is a comic road to wisdom as well as a tragic road. There is a comic as well as a tragic control of life. And the comic control may be more usable, more relevant to the human condition (1956:254).

Chapter 2
The First Clown[16]

You laugh sometime after your fortieth day and then you become human.
Aristotle

Laughter for all?

Laughter has been singled out as an essentially human characteristic (Bergson, 1956). The Navajo Indians in fact elevate the child's first laugh to the status of a rite of passage marked by a sumptuous celebration to which all the family are invited (Jacobson, 1997). Laughter is part of a universal human vocabulary whose structure is highly consistent across cultures, unrestricted by either linguistic or cultural codes (Apte, 1985). The physical expression of laughter is the same in all humans, and was described anatomically by Darwin (1872). In other words, we all speak 'Ha, Ha!' from very early on even if we may not understand anything else the other person is saying, and even prior to the development of language itself (Provine, 1998). In this sense we might say that laughter is both instinctive and primitive. If by humour we mean the process that mediates the responses of smiling and laughter, then clearly we could view such behavioural responses as evidence of humour.

Just as the anthropologist searches for universals amongst human beings some authors, perhaps carried away on anthropomorphic flights of fancy, argue that animals also laugh and have a sense of humour. Masson singles out teasing and playfulness in dogs and concludes that ' . . . many dogs have a good sense of humour' (1998:106). Lorenz (1994) also describes dogs who laugh when playing with their human companions. Human laughter is thought to be phylogenetically descended from the relaxed, open-mouth display, or play face expression, of non-human

---

[16.] I am indebted to Dr C. Bollas (1995) for his original description of the mother as clown to the baby.

primates (van Hooff, 1972). Darwin (1872) compared the sound of human laughter to the vocalizations of apes being tickled and there is some evidence that primates laugh in much the same way as people do, closely resembling the laughter of children at play (Yerkes, 1943; Monro, 1951; van Hooff, 1972). Kohler (1927) identified teasing behaviour in primates and Goodall (1968) reported laughing accompanying wrestling and tickling in chimpanzees (see also Berntson et al., 1989; Aldis, 1975). More recently, studies of recorded vocalizations of rats interacting with each other in what is assumed to be playful behaviour have revealed a striking patter mirroring human laughter (Fridlund, 1998).

These comparative observations suggest that laughter itself may have some equivalent in other primate species, and that it is therefore likely to have an evolved basis in humans (Weisfeld, 1993). To say that other animals make vocalizations that closely resemble human laughter is by no means equivalent to saying that animals possess a sense of humour. There is, however, some anecdotal evidence of humour appreciation – not just laughter accompanying play or tickling – in captive apes. For example, McGhee (1979) reports the cases of chimpanzees and gorillas who have learnt sign language giving a series of incorrect linguistic signs, often accompanied by laughter. Chimpanzees have also been observed to throw debris at or to urinate on people, and then to sign 'funny'; this sign has also been used to accompany tickling or chasing games. Apes also sometimes use the sign for 'funny' to refer to human behaviour that is silly, unusual, or out of context. Such research and anecdotal observations would suggest that what we may be observing in animals are instances of the evolutionary forerunners of human laughter and indeed of a sense of humour itself. Contemporary researchers studying both animals and humans argue that laughter is an ancient response which represents mid-brain activity. A sense of humour is understood to be the more recently evolved activity which rests on more 'modern', advanced areas of the brain which allow for sophisticated linguistic and cognitive processes.

In this chapter we turn our attention to the newborn infant in order to trace the developmental processes which, it will be argued, lead to the acquisition of a sense of humour. This will involve visiting such areas as the mother-baby relationship,[17] the development of emotion and cognition and the capacity to symbolize. We cannot begin to understand an adult sense of humour and its value in everyday life without paying attention to some of the earliest emotional experiences and the developmental advances on which a sense of humour rests. To begin with, we

[17] Although it is acknowledged that the child's main caregiver is not invariably the mother, for the sake of clarity I shall use the term 'mother' as this is the case for the majority of babies, and I shall refer to the baby as 'he'.

consider how the prevailing assumptions about development that
dominate contemporary psychoanalytic thinking create a very particular
context for an examination of humour and its value throughout development.

Learning the hard way

Writing about pleasure, fun and humour within a psychoanalytic framework is not easy. This is not because their role in our psychic development has not been formulated. It is, rather, that discussions about such
matters are invariably framed in the context of notions of conflict. If we
can speak of pleasure or fun it is always therefore in a rather ambiguous
sense, where pleasure results from a prior renunciation. It is, in other
words, a dampened notion of pleasure, a compromise reached which
may leave us yearning for more but realizing that it is an achievement to
be able to settle for less. The prize at the end of our struggle between
our instincts and reality is, in Kleinian terms, for example, the successful
negotiation of the depressive position. The very notion of a *depressive*
position as goal affords a glimpse of what fun and how much laughter
awaits us. Relinquishment and acceptance are common currency within
psychoanalysis. As a movement, psychoanalysis may be besieged by
theoretical splits but everyone agrees on one thing: conflict is inevitable
and this is no laughing matter. Psychoanalysis, writes Phillips, '. . . is
about what stops good things coming easily; about how we have to
acknowledge, but also how we seem to need to create, accurate obstacles to satisfaction' (1998:7). The psychoanalytic literature is replete
with formulations about the experiences of loss, conflict and pain as
spurs to development, in particular the development of our capacity to
symbolize and hence to think. This emphasis is significant and one could
be forgiven for agreeing with Phillips when he bluntly remarks that,
'psychoanalytic theory has become obsessed by, indeed obsessional
about, loss' (1998:19). 'Fun' appears to be of secondary importance in
the grander scheme of things. So what is so significant about loss and
renunciation? What do such experiences teach us?

Psychoanalytic theory has always posited that disillusionment and
frustration are intrinsic to development. Within Freudian theory, renunciation is a necessary evil if society is to survive. The hard lessons begin
at birth. As reality impinges on the unity of the mother-baby dyad and its
imperfections and limitations dawn on the baby, the experiences of
frustration, disappointment, loss and longing make their entry into the
chronicles of existence. These very experiences, however painful, are
those which have been singled out by psychoanalysis as privileged in our
development towards adaptation to the so-called real world. Even if it
were possible to create a situation in which the baby's every need was
satisfied, this would not be desirable since it would not equip the baby
with the resilience born of the endurance and survival of moments of

frustration and distress. Our capacity to delay gratification, to withstand absence and loss, are hard-won lessons which remind us that we are not omnipotent but that, nevertheless, we can face reality without being overwhelmed by the enormousness of the task. Winnicott (1965) emphasized the role of the mother as facilitating 'de-adaptation' – a graduated failure in attunement – according to the needs of the baby. Along with others, Winnicott underlined that we simply cannot have it all our own way.

Psychoanalysis reminds us that the dictates of the pleasure principle need to be subordinated to the demands of reality so as to aid adaptation to the external world. Phantasy[18] is the solace of the unhappy, the unsatisfied – and here psychoanalysis does not discriminate; it is our common fate since, for Freud, hysterical misery, once cured, is only replaced by the fact of our 'common unhappiness'. Phantasy, for Freud, is essentially escapist; a turning away from reality rather than a preliminary to altering reality in the desired direction:[19]

> We may lay it down that a happy person never phantasises, only an unsatisfied one. The motive force of phantasies are unsatisfied wishes, in every single phantasy is the fulfilment of a wish, a correction of an unsatisfying reality' (Freud, 1924:146).

Acceptance of our limitations and of the ultimate limit, death, is the goal and it is one which creates inevitable conflict between that which we want and that which we can't have or feel we should not have, or between who we are and who we wish we could be. One way in which we manage to integrate our instinctual urges with the demands of reality is through sublimation. Sublimation allows us to give expression to our sexual and/or aggressive feelings but in a way that is more acceptable. Humour of course provides a good vehicle for this, which is why so much humour is fuelled by sexual and aggressive feelings struggling to find an acceptable outlet.

Jones (1916) hypothesized that when a desire has been renounced because it would otherwise give rise to conflict, it is then repressed and may express itself in a symbolic way. The object of desire which has to be forsaken is replaced by a symbol. Kleinian theorists speak of the necessary integration between the good and the bad: the acknowledgement and management of ambivalence is the goal. More than the Freudians, Kleinians have written extensively on the nature of symbolization which is viewed as key to the healthy development of the ego. According to Klein (1930) children's play is the prototypical example of the sublimated activity which represents the symbolic expression of anxieties and

---

[18.] This spelling of 'phantasy' denotes its psychoanalytic usage to refer both to the conscious and unconscious phantasy. Where I am referring to its more everyday usage I shall retain the spelling 'fantasy'.

[19.] See Chapter 3 for a discussion of the value of the imagination.

wishes (see Chapter 3). If symbolization does not occur, Klein thought the whole development of the ego was arrested. Children who display a paralysis of phantasy life, and hence a failure in symbolic formation, cannot play. Symbolism is thus understood to be the basis for all talents.

The capacity to symbolize is viewed as a significant developmental achievement, indicative of whole object relationships. These more integrated relationships rest on an awareness of separateness and differentiation between the self and the object, paving the way for the development of a stable sense of reality. This is considered to be an essential component of Klein's depressive position. With the dawning realization that the good and the bad object are one, that the loved mother is also the hated mother, the child becomes increasingly preoccupied with protecting her from his aggression. It is this predicament which acts as stimulus for the creation of symbols: 'the symbol is needed to displace aggression from the original object . . . and in that way to lessen the guilt and fear of loss' (Segal, 1957:394). The symbol, according to Segal (1957) is used not to deny but to overcome loss and it is therefore a critical tool in our adaptation. Disturbances in the ego's relationships to objects are thus reflected in disturbances in symbol formation. The capacity for humour appreciation and generation can emerge only when the child has developed the capacity to assimilate experiences, feelings and thoughts in a phantasy or make-believe world and so is able to play with ideas (McGhee, 1974). It is therefore also dependent on the capacity to symbolize. This capacity reflects developments in cognitive processing but also in emotional development, as it rests more fundamentally on the ability to distinguish reality from phantasy.

Much effort has been invested within psychoanalysis in an examination of how our sense of reality develops. Typically, the conclusions reached point to the central importance of loss and absence. Klein developed further the ideas expressed in Freud's (1917) paper 'Mourning and melancholia' by establishing a clear connection between the process of relinquishing something with that of mourning. For Klein, this process involved anticipation and disappointment through the realization of absence. In keeping with formulations of loss as central to development, O'Shaughnessy (1964), in a classic paper, outlines her views on the intimate connection between thought and absence. She argues that to begin with we need to develop a capacity to 'think of' before we can 'think about'. In her opinion, the development of the former capacity is stimulated by absence – the absent breast representing the first such experience (i.e. the baby has to think of the breast in its absence):

> The history of the absent object is this: first it is the bad breast present; second it is thought of as a bad aspect of the breast; and third it is a good breast missing (O'Shaughnessy, 1964:120).

In a similar vein, Britton (1989) singles out loss and renunciation as he views the resolution of the Oedipus complex as critical to the child's emotional and cognitive development. The reality of the parents' exclusive relationship presents the child with a prototype of a relationship in which he is an observer but not a participant. This, Britton argues, is at the root of the capacity for empathy since it involves seeing ourselves in interaction with others and so entertaining another's point of view while retaining our own. Another renunciation, another developmental trophy for the child who manages to accept the loss of an exclusive relationship with the mother and the reality of her relationship with the father. Symbols then are needed to bridge that inevitable and developmentally necessary separateness between self and object. Dispossessed of the person who nurtures and loves him as if one, the child endures frustration and disillusionment. How and when such separation occurs is critical for how the child manages this painful aspect of reality. If through pressure of unsatisfied need the child has to become aware of his separate identity too soon or too continually, then the illusion of union is shattered and this may lead to premature ego development (Milner, 1985).

The leitmotif in psychoanalysis, as I hope will be clear by now, is conflict, pain, renunciation and loss. This whirlwind overview of the literature suggesting a link between these experiences and development provides some support for the contention that psychoanalysis is, as Phillips put it,

> committed to the idea of life as somehow organised around, in relationship to, absence. We are the animals for whom something is missing and for whom what is missing is always privileged (1998:20).

Perhaps what is missing is privileged precisely because this is the only way we can rationalize the loss. We transform the overcoming of our adversity into the triumph of acceptance. So what about pleasure? Are pain and frustration the most significant stimuli that contribute to our development? Is there a place for fun and humour in our development?

The enlivening object

Of course, as was noted earlier, it is not the case that psychoanalysis ignores altogether the value of fun or humour. In fact Freud was the first to point out the value of play in the child's attempts at mastery, as we shall see in the next chapter. It is not therefore a matter of either/or, but rather of emphasis. Absence and loss do trigger an internal conflict which pushes us on to the tortuous path of separation and individuation. But so can an enlivening presence and the playful, fun and pleasurable experiences that can ensue, including the sharing of laughter and a humorous perspective on life. As Alvarez observes,

Pleasure should not be thought of as inferior to pain in its capacity to
disturb, alert and enliven . . . arrivals and returns can be just as stimulating and thought provoking as departures (1992:64-7).

Alvarez posits the important maternal function of 'claiming' whereby the
mother provides interest and surprise by drawing the baby's attention,
not simply in response to the baby's withdrawal. She is an active
stimulus, inviting the baby to join her in exploring the world. She
conveys the excitement that lies ahead and which itself then acts as a
spur towards separation. There is little incentive to learn how to crawl or
to walk, for instance, if the baby is not encouraged to take those critical
first steps, and the mother cannot enjoy this significant achievement
because she needs the baby to remain dependent on her or because she
fails to convey that life can be enjoyed. Under normal circumstances, the
mother communicates the advantages of independence to the baby
primarily by making learning fun, through play and humour, and so facilitates the baby's freedom to become a person in his own right. Failures
and disappointments cannot be avoided but their blow can be lessened
if they can be successfully integrated. Humour provides a route for
integration.

The origins of a sense of humour need to be traced back to the early
exchanges between mother and baby. Tucherman (1998, personal
communication) refers to 'smiling encounters' to denote the early
exchanges between mother and baby where maternal warmth is permeated with smiles. A distinction commonly drawn in the literature is
between Duchenne and non-Duchenne smiling and laughter. In the
former, both the lip corners and the cheeks are raised pulling the skin
from the cheeks and forehead towards the eyeball, while in the latter,
zygomatic muscle action only pulls the lip corners up obliquely. Only
Duchenne smiles are associated with pleasant stimuli and with self-
reported pleasure in adults (Keltner and Bonanno, 1997). Under six
months of age infant Duchenne smiling has been found to be related to
frames of visual mutuality, of eye contact and/or mutual smiling (Fogel et
al., 1997). Fogel and colleagues suggest that Duchenne smiling is a
'salient constituent of an experience of positive connectedness between
the infant and the mother' (1997:13). Observations of mother–baby
dyads attest to the rhythmic, coherent configuration of verbal and non-
verbal reciprocations, to which both mother and baby introduce
immutable elements of communication such as smiles, vocalizations and
tactile signals. Stop-frame analyses reveal that the interactions between
mother and baby follow a cyclical pattern of looking–not looking, of
engagement–withdrawal. This latter rhythm is critical to the baby's need
to regulate his comparatively immature psychophysiological system and
in so doing he learns a great deal about basic self-regulation (Brazelton
and Cramer, 1991). Condon and Sander (1974) coined the term
'entrainment' to describe how in such early interactions each partici-

pant's contribution seems to be submerged in a momentum which allows them to control the level of exchange. Stern (1977) suggests that early games such as peek-a-boo are built on such entrainment. This popular game highlights, Stern (1985) argues, the mutual interaction which gives rise to the baby's,

> self experience of very high excitation, full of joy and suspense . . . this feeling state, with cycles of crescendos several times over, could never be achieved by the infant alone at this stage, neither in its cyclicity, in its intensity, nor in its unique qualities. Objectively, it is a mutual creation, a 'we' or a self-other phenomenon (1985, p102, my italics).

A sense of fun or amusement – the earliest manifestation of a sense of humour – is, I would like to suggest, a 'we' phenomenon, created by the mother and baby as the mother uses humour to help her baby regulate affective states. Parents play a very significant part in regulating the baby's emotional experiences. Despite neurological maturation, the baby's innate potential requires an interactive, intersubjective environment to be optimally actualized. In this unique environment, co-created by both participants, most of the baby's and parents' time is devoted to active mutual regulation of their own or the other's state. State is used here to refer to the 'semi-stable organization of the organism as a whole at a given moment' (Stern et al., 1998). Regulation of states within the mother–baby dyad is jointly choreographed through the flowing exchanges of information from perceptual systems and affective displays. Some of the states that are regulated in the early months are hunger, sleep, activity, arousal, to name but a few. So much of what the baby will feel is possible only in the presence of, and through the interaction with, another person who acts as mediator and consequently whose own emotional states will colour the baby's experience. Brazelton and Cramer (1991) underline this point:

> As infants achieve an inner balance and then go on to experience expectation and excitement within a safe, predictable relationship, they begin to discover the capacity for emotion and cognition with which they are endowed (Brazelton and Cramer, 1991:128).

The level of activation and intensity of an interaction will determine whether the experience will be emotionally digestible and can be thought about, as much as whether its actual content is positive or negative (Alvarez, 1992). Timing, therefore, is critical. A mother who is insensitive to her baby's need to tune out and overexposes him to too much excitement, may lead him to withdraw.

The mother of early childhood is one of the greatest sources of stimulation for the baby. It is in this context that Bollas (1995) suggests that she may well represent the child's first encounter with the 'clown'. He describes how a mother's face exaggerates human expression 'so as to stimulate the baby into smiling and even laughing'. Sinason (1996) also locates the origins of a sense of humour in the early games between mother and baby, such as peek-a-boo. Underscoring the importance of the sensitive attunement and therefore 'timing' between mother and baby in these playful exchanges, Sinason observes that, as adults,

> perhaps the reason we find a failed joke or an unsuccessful comedian so unbearable is because it takes us back to the feeling of betrayal when mother mistimed an interaction (1996:24).

'Missteps in the dance' – to coin a very apt description by Stern (1977) – between mother and baby can and do occur. No attunement can ever be so perfect and, even if it were, as we saw earlier, this would not aid development to take its healthy course. Accepting these imperfections is one of the important developmental tasks facing the baby. When confronted with his own limitations and those inevitable existential 'givens' and human fallibilities, the mother can nevertheless help the baby to develop a sense of amusement about his own predicament and so also about the human condition. This relies on the mother's own capacity to manage her relationship to reality in this emotionally adaptive manner. The emotional state of others is fundamentally important to the baby's own emotional state. This is not on account of passive processes such as mirroring. Rather, it results from the baby's active use of the mother's emotional expression in forming his appreciation of an event and using it to guide behaviour. Through the mother's capacity to adopt a humorous and playful attitude she can transform, as Bollas suggests:

> potential trauma . . . by turning it into pleasure . . .. In thus developing her infant's sense of humour, a mother brings under temporary human control something that is in fact beyond human influence. Beyond the infant/mother couple, outside the comedy club, is a world of the real that is deeply thoughtless. By clowning, the mother represents this world and allows vestiges of trauma to show in the human face, turning plight into pleasure (1995:243).

The function performed by the mother is that of transforming the baby's experience into something emotionally digestible. Within psycho-analysis, the mother's function has been likened to that of a container for the painful states of being, which the baby experiences but has not yet developed the capacity to process (Bion, 1962). The earliest forms of communication take place without any mediation by verbal or non-verbal symbols. The baby often conveys his feelings to the mother in a very raw manner and in so doing causes the receptive mother to experience as her own, feelings that the baby is not yet able to articulate or, indeed, emotionally process within himself. The mother who is not overly preoccupied with her own difficulties is able to respond to the infant's behaviour – his cries, but also his gurgles, smiles and laughter – conveying her belief that such behaviour is a meaningful communication which requires understanding and response. By the very act of responding, the mother provides the baby with an essential experience which enables him gradually to build up a sense that his own behaviour is meaningful and communicative (Fonagy et al., 1991). Amusement and laughter, provided their underlying intent is benign, may be understood as further examples of the mother's processing of her baby's experience, which encourages the baby's development of a playful attitude towards his own predicament. The intent underlying the mother's laughter is of vital significance. If the mother laughs in a mocking tone she will undermine the baby rather than helping him to develop a more flexible and benign attitude towards his predicament. In turn, the child later on may well use humour as a way of disparaging others and distancing himself from his own internal experience of humiliation, in an identification with a mocking internal mother. Our sense of humour is one of the many windows on to our internal world of object relationships. People reveal their unconscious both by what they find funny and the jokes they tell (Friedman, 1994). In a humorous exchange we invariably repeat or defend against a particular object relationship. Humour may thus be used to communicate gently and affectionately with someone we love, but it may also be used to triumph sadistically over another.

Humour we might say, transforms our conflicts and preoccupations into something pleasurably digestible, and in so doing contributes to an emotional processing of our experience. Tronick (1989) argues that positive development may be associated with the experience of co-ordinated interactions between mother and baby and the transformation of negative affect into positive affect:

> The experience of interactive reparation and the transformation of negative into positive affect allow the infant to elaborate his or her other-directed affective, communicative and self-regulatory capacities and to use them more effectively, that is, to be able to maintain engagement with the external environment in the face of stress (1989:116).

From such an experience the baby accumulates evidence of relationships as reparable and of his effectiveness in bringing about such a positive resolution. Healthy development is thus not necessarily the product of an absence of, or limited, negative experiences. Rather, resilience is built upon the successful transformation of negative into positive. It depends on the accumulation of interactive and affective experiences with different people in different contexts, which lend shape to the baby's regulatory processes and self and other representations over time. The function of humour and shared laughter following a disagreement in a relationship may well be to signal that 'everything is all right' and hence that the rupture is reparable. Perhaps one of the most important features of humour in relationships is that it provides routes to reparation. It can be used as a gentle, affectionate way of alerting the other to their limitations or how they may have hurt us. A well-timed joke or humorous observation or tone can communicate understanding as well as forgiveness. Humour at its best is essentially an expression of love.

Back to the beginning

There have been ample speculations as to what it is that humour, in adults, seeks to recreate. Some have argued that we are seeking to return to the regressive happiness of childhood, to unburden ourselves of the demands of logical thought and so 'revel in a long forgotten freedom' (Kris, 1938). Both Kris (1938) and Chasseguet-Smirgel (1988) believe that one of the more notable accomplishments of a sense of humour is that it can keep at bay the fear of loss of love. Such conceptualizations suggest that when we seek to be amused, we are essentially seeking for a reassurance that it is really 'all right'. One of the hallmarks of humour is that it conveys a sense that 'all is well' (Leech, 1968). Our actual enjoyment of the comic involves a feeling of complete security from danger. In his study of military behaviour, Dixon (1980) emphasizes a similar function of humour as used by military leaders:

> A colleague's or leader's humorous aside, under dangerous or threatening conditions, seems to carry the message 'If he or she can joke, then he or she is evidently not afraid, therefore there is nothing to fear.' (1980:282).

Humour therefore acts as a contextual clue that there is nothing to fear. Hence, our capacity to generate humour under conditions of internal or external threat may serve the function of self-reassurance. The seeking of reassurance suggests that in humour we may be observing, as Freud (1927) himself pointed out, the superego comforting an intimidated ego by repudiating reality and serving up an illusion. Freud's hypothesis, as we saw in Chapter 1, led him to a reformulation of the nature of the superego which, up until that point, had been characterized as the critical, punishing agency of the personality. Such a novel perspective on the nature and function of the superego highlights the way in which humour metabolizes our experience and represents it to us in a more manageable form, which is experienced as reassuring. Perhaps this partly accounts for the popularity of observational comedy. This genre is born out of everyday observations of human behaviour with which most of us can identify, as it draws heavily on our commonalties rather than on our differences. In such humour we recognize its essentially human inspiration. The comedian holds up a mirror to our fear, anxiety, naivety, stupidity and arrogance, and we feel known and understood in a comforting rather than critical manner. Such narcissistic wounds are made bearable because the humorous structure creates a space or a 'pliable medium' (Milner, 1985) through which we can become our own observers from a safe enough distance. Through the guise that 'it's only a joke', we can acknowledge something of our own conflicted nature. In this respect, humour transforms the inherent anxiety that is triggered when we are faced with life and who we have become, into something more bearable. It is important that anxiety be made more bearable because if we are overwhelmed by it we cannot confront the reasons for it (Pasquali, 1986).

We feel safe, comforted and reassured through humorous interaction because, I would like to suggest, it rekindles the early experience of the 'we' (Stern, 1985). The self–other fusion is the background state to which the very young baby returns whilst separateness can gradually develop. Separateness is not, however, a once-and-for-all state from which we never digress. On the contrary, throughout development, many situations in life invite regressions into more childlike states which can be experienced as pleasurable and reassuring. Bollas (1987) describes how early on the mother is not yet identified as fully other but rather as 'a process of transformation' which alters the self. He considers certain forms of object-seeking in adult life as reflecting the wish to find an object – a 'transformational object' – (e.g. place, event, person) that promises similarly to transform the self. The promise, as it were, is only mere projection on our part that this object will deliver what we seek. Through humour and in humorous interaction we seek such a transformation and in so doing hope to recreate the form of the earliest object tie. The sharing of humour and laughter allows us to regress back to a comforting feeling of oneness. Whether we seek to be amused by actually attending comedy shows or in our own intimate relationships, the person cast in the comedian's role is charged with soothing our troubles away through laughter.

Chasseguet-Smirgel (1988), in a most insightful analysis of one of humour's psychological functions, suggests that the humorist acts as a 'good-enough mother' to himself.[20] She proposes that at the moment at which the humorist produces humour he is protecting himself against the ultimate narcissistic injury, namely the loss of love:

---

[20] The American comedian, Jerry Lewis, made an interesting observation in this respect: 'Everyone that walks out on that stage is a child. They're out there for one reason, to get parental love and affection and understanding. Applause is 'I love you, baby' (quoted in Grace, 1991:94).

I believe that the adult part of the ego in humour represents, in their totality, all of the mother's efforts of care and attention, efforts liable to cloth the naked infant with the narcissism she has forfeited in its favour (1988:205).

Chasseguet-Smirgel believes that the relationship often noted – especially amongst comedians – between humour and depression can be understood as reflecting a precocious lack of maternal affection. The humorist acts, according to her, as his own 'loving mother' reassuring himself that everything will be fine. Although I am in agreement with Chasseguet-Smirgel's suggestion that humour is an attempt at self-soothing and self-care, I am less convinced that this invariably results from a failure in the pre-Oedipal relationship with the mother. Indeed, the few available studies of comedians report contradictory findings in this respect. In one psychological study of comedians they revealed, on the whole, far more positive relationships with their mothers, who were more likely to be portrayed as affectionate, supportive figures whereas the fathers were more typically described as either absent, uninterested or disapproving (Janus, 1975). Another study reported, on the other hand, that mothers were typically experienced as punitive and critical and were ascribed more 'non-maternal attitudes', whereas the fathers were depicted on the whole as figures they admired (Fisher and Fisher, 1981). Given such mixed findings it may be more appropriate to say that humour is an attempt to comfort oneself but that the direction and quality of the underlying parental identifications will vary between individuals depending on their own unique developmental histories.

To seek a transformational object is, as Bollas put it, to recollect an early experience 'to remember not cognitively but existentially' (Bollas, 1987:17). If humorous interaction (whether within ourselves or between people) triggers such an early emotional memory, this may offer an account of the pleasure afforded to us by humour's complicitous nature. Shared jokes create an impenetrable boundary. When couples first meet, one of the common early, joint elaborations are the funny stories, incidents or jokes that reveal to others that there is something shared, something special between two people. It signals intimacy. This is why when we don't get the joke we can feel very excluded.

Shared laughter signals understanding which bypasses language. Writing from an anthropological perspective Barley observes:

After a day eliciting recondite and unconvincing explanations from local people at an Indonesian funeral, building a rickety bridge to human understanding, nothing conveys a greater certainty of real mutual comprehension than catching a villager's eye as the beautifully dressed high priest trips and sprawls full length in the mud and you explode in laughter. Then, for the first time all day, you *know* you have understood each other (1995:15)[original italics].

The shared laughter rekindles the pre-verbal memory of similar exchanges in infancy, when the mother's smile and face lit up and conveyed that there was nothing to fear, that we were understood and loved. To appreciate a joke or a funny incident implies that the spectators recognize something similar and so laughter binds them together, even if only momentarily. If we take the above speculations to reflect the reality of what happens in humour, then this enables us to account for the universal appeal of comedy, even though its content will differ cross-culturally.

The parental double-act

We have so far focused on the role played by the mother in the development of a sense of humour. However, she is not the only source, or contributor, to this development. Equally important is the internalization of benign and playful aspects of the parental couple which together contribute not only to a more tolerant and guiding superego but also provide the prototype for the complementarity of opposites. Healthy humour, as we shall see in the next two chapters, rests on the capacity to tolerate antithetical ideas, to manage opposites. This capacity is won at a cost. We all have to tread the arduous route of identification and dis-identification from our parents. This rests on a relinquishment of an exclusive relationship with both parents along with the acknowledgement that they have an exclusive relationship with each other. If the child negotiates the Oedipal stage in a relatively healthy way he acquires an internal model of an intercourse (between the parents) which is, on the whole, a creative activity (Feldman, 1989). In a discussion on play and creativity, Caper elaborates this point:

> . . . the degree to which one has been able to accept an internal parental couple whose sexuality is pleasurable, creative and non-destructive plays an important role in one's ability to establish [the kind of] playful, experimental relationship to reality (1999:90).

The 'acceptance' Caper refers to relies on the child's capacity to relinquish omnipotence, to accept the difference between wishes and reality. In relation to his parents the child has to accept that they have a relationship from which he is excluded.

The pain of this exclusion was described by Tony – a young man in his late twenties who started therapy with me because he felt 'bored with life'. Tony had been the second child born to parents who had only started a family in their mid-forties. He depicted them as 'artistic types' whom he had experienced predominantly as very involved with each other and their respective pursuits. He felt that children had been an 'afterthought'. One of his most striking memories was of lying in his bed as a young boy hearing his parents laughing together. He described standing at the top of the stairs, feeling very upset, as he wanted to be with them.

As an adult, Tony was highly sensitive to situations in which others were laughing together since he invariably felt on the margins. He had difficulty joining in and was so self-conscious in his attempts to make others laugh that he was not really funny. His sense of humour was contrived and hostile, often at the expense of another. Yet, he entertained a view of himself as witty and clever and though he was bright I often found myself feeling quite bored listening to him. The boredom arose from his self-absorption, so much so that I often felt like 'surplus' in the sessions. The absence of a real emotional connection, which would have destabilized his tenuous hold on the belief in his self-sufficiency, contributed to the boredom.

Laughter had become erotisized for Tony as it symbolized the coming together of his parents in a union from which he had felt bitterly excluded. In his relationship with me he complained that I was 'far too serious' but imagined that I probably laughed with other patients. He said he found me and psychoanalysis 'boring', thereby casting me in the role of the humiliated, inconsequential one who could not stimulate him and so be a worthy partner in our relationship. This reflected the battle staged in his internal world where Tony repeatedly came up against his humiliating rejection when he felt himself to be cast aside amidst the parents' exciting laughter.

For Tony, the phantasy was that he had been excluded from an exciting and pleasurable experience. For some people, however, the phantasy is that any connection or intercourse is between a destructive couple. The anxiety about a couple coming together destructively may generalise to thinking itself whereby links between different experiences and between thoughts themselves cannot be allowed. In turn, this may lead to inhibitions in thinking and learning that are manifest in an absence of a sense of humour. Humour relies on a loosening of thought associations so that they may be brought together in an unusual, surprising manner.

Simon, with whom I worked for six months in weekly psychotherapy, provides an example of how the phantasy of any kind of intercourse as destructive precluded the development of a sense of humour.

Simon is a forty-six year old accountant. He suffered a severe psychotic depressive breakdown and was still very depressed when we first met. He was an only child. He described a desolate childhood dominated by the exacting demands of his parents to achieve academically. If he failed in any school activity he was punished and belittled by his father, whose mocking tone he vividly mimicked. His father had been in the Army and had received commendations for his achievements. Simon recalled frequently being reminded of these. In particular, he remembered one thing that his father always used to say to him: 'count yourself lucky'. His father had become disabled when Simon was twelve years old and he felt that since then his father had become very intolerant and 'picky'. He told me that his father had always seen himself as somehow superior to other people. His disability appeared to have dealt a very severe blow to his inflated, yet very fragile, self-image which he had seemingly managed by turning the disability into a virtue to be admired, by Simon in particular. His mother was a very religious woman who had always insisted that Simon should put the Church before any more frivolous activities.

Simon did not recall his parents ever doing things together or going out as a family. He had few memories of playing and he felt that fun, generally speaking, had been taboo. He could never bring his friends home and the one memory he had of a friend visiting him had been stained in his mind since his father had smacked him in front of his friend. Simon harboured a deep sense of humiliation about this particular event around which his many grievances towards his parents were now crystallized.

Although Simon had few recollections of arguments between his parents, those that he did remember were very violent and had led him to feel that it was better to be alone than risk being with others. In his adult life he avoided relationships since he invariably felt himself to be at odds with what other people enjoyed and valued. In a very fundamental sense Simon had no hope that people could understand and support each other. His internal world was populated by mocking and contemptuous objects to which Simon felt tied.

Simon was very reserved and almost obsessionally polite. His rage was evident in the lengths to which he went in order to deny it. He channelled his energy into his work but beyond this he had no friends. His breakdown followed the end of a brief, but significantly his first, relationship with a woman several years his senior who also had mental health problems. When I first met Simon he lived a rather monastic existence deriving apparent masochistic gratification from his suffering. He harboured very critical thoughts about other people and spoke derogatorily about people having fun. I sensed that he felt he was the only person carrying such a heavy burden and that he was also the only one who seriously cared about what happened in the world. Thus, his masochism also gave way to his sadism as he triumphantly raised himself above the mere mortals whom he thought were ultimately worthless as human beings.

In our sessions Simon was always demure and correct. I never detected a smile. His seriousness was impenetrable. I asked him early on if he recalled ever laughing with his family. He replied quite simply that there had never been anything to laugh about. Simon inhabited a humourless internal world in which nothing good, pleasurable or reassuring could survive. There was no sense in which Simon was able to stand outside of his predicament so as to take perspective. His descriptions of events lacked vitality and colour and revealed the narrowness of his vision. If he were to relax his serious stance Simon feared the admonishment of his internal father and the abandonment by his internal mother whose piousness had been translated into an indignant self-righteousness.

In its origins, a sense of humour is essentially what Freud referred to as a sense of the comic. Here, two participants are necessary: one person who is comical, the other who perceives what is comical and enjoys it. Of course, as we develop, we are able to perceive what is comical in ourselves. This way the comical can become an internal experience, a dialogue within the self. It is the sense of the comic or the sense of amusement (Bollas, 1995) that the mother encourages in her baby through their playful interactions. The mother perceives what is comical in her baby's behaviour and through her own amusement conveys to the baby that there is a different perspective, another possible emotional response. Someone like Simon recalled no such experiences. Personal shortcomings were not to be benevolently acknowledged or laughed about; rather they had to be overcome at all costs. No thinking could take place as, for Simon, options simply did not exist.

Under ordinary circumstances the origins of the sense of the comic, we might say, are pre-Oedipal. As the well dosed frustrations are administered by the good enough mother, the baby comes to realize his own separateness and consequently that of his mother. If she is separate then she can also have wishes and loves of her own which exclude him. It is therefore not surprising to find that it is during the Oedipal phase, when the child begins to realize the existence and threat posed by rivals, that the appreciation of jokes develops. Jokes do require three people, as Freud suggested, namely the joker, the listener and the derided. The 'other' is reduced to the butt of the joke, thereby solidifying the relationship between joker and listener and excluding the third party. Brazelton (1992) suggests that a sense of humour emerges at about the age of three years but it may be more accurate to speak of the precursor to a sense of humour, and to restrict a sense of humour proper to the later developmental achievement contingent on the resolution of the Oedipal phase. A healthy, 'mature', sense of humour reflects a higher, more sophisticated, level of development which marks the successful resolution of the Oedipal stage. The latter rests on an internalization of the benign parental relationship. This contributes to the development of the benevolent aspects of the superego and is based on an identification with the loving and admired Oedipal and pre-Oedipal parents (Schafer, 1960; Offen and Burrough, 1987).

The mother, and later the parents as a couple, impart to the child a vital piece of 'psychological equipment' (Jacobson, 1997): a sense of humour. Bollas' description of the mother as clown is deeply evocative and singles out the reassuring, and I would like to suggest, psychically necessary, transformation of 'plight into pleasure' that humour allows for. Humour, as Thurber put it so beautifully, is after all 'emotional chaos remembered in tranquillity'. It provides us with a 'psychic reservation' (Freud, 1924) within which our experience is not denied but can be thought about in tranquillity.

Chapter 3
The Playroom of the Mind

Man alone suffers so excruciatingly in the world that he was compelled to invent laughter. Nietszche

It was a strange laugh – nothing funny had happened after all – and yet pleasant and infectious. It was a challenge to Tamina to forget her anxieties, it was a promise of something vague – joy perhaps, or peace. Milan Kundera

Freud is well known for recognizing the intimate connection between our ability to work and to love and mental health. Therapists of all persuasions are invariably interested in their patients' capacity to form and sustain meaningful relationships as well as in their ability to engage in purposeful activity. An absence or deficit in these areas of functioning is a reliable indicator of psychological difficulties. Winnicott's work with children sensitized him to another core area of functioning, namely, play. Expanding on Freud's original formulation, Winnicott recognized that mental health depended on our capacity to love, work *and* play.

There is still disagreement amongst theorists as to whether verbal play and humour are distinct, or whether humour is a subset of play, or whether play is a particular type of humour (du Pre, 1998). In this book humour is understood to be a form of playing and one that is very common in adults. In order to understand its adult form and functions, it is important to understand its origins in children's play. In this chapter we therefore begin by exploring the nature of play in children and its continuity into adulthood. We shall focus in particular on the emotional and cognitive processes facilitated by play, which are central to our adaptation to the external world.

Playing for real

As suggested in the last chapter, it is through the playful, humorous, interactions with the mother that the baby develops a sense of amusement. Winnicott observed that the development of play depended upon trust in the environment. In the early stages, the mother *is* the environment, though the father's equally important contribution should not be ignored. Winnicott therefore thought that the ability to play originates in the earliest exchanges between the baby and his environment which, under normal circumstances, conveys enough security.

Playing is fun but it is also through play that children can discover and approach what is serious or, as Freud put it, what is 'real'.[21] Indeed Freud (1920) did not merely regard playing as a pastime but as a developmental achievement. He viewed it as a striving towards mastery; an invaluable aid in the child's attempts to come to terms with emotional experience. The importance of play is, however, best articulated in the work of Winnicott (1954; 1971). He believed that we should take heart from a child's capacity for play even in the presence of symptoms since if a child is playing this is, in itself, an indication that 'there is no very serious trouble afoot'.

Child psychologists and psychotherapists have long considered inhibitions in play as significant, indicating inhibitions in phantasy life and consequently in both cognitive and emotional development. Without play we are truly impoverished. It is a basic urge shared across species and recent research supports the notion that play is essential to our adaptation. For example, studies looking at children's behaviour before and after play breaks at school suggest that the more children are allowed to play the less impulsive and overactive they are subsequently in class and the better they are able to concentrate on work tasks (Pellegrini, 1998). Play facilitates the development of a sense of mastery as skills and aptitudes are put to the test in the play situation. Consequently it also provides invaluable opportunities for developing skills (Boulton and Smith, 1992). Through play, the child is actively experimenting; trying things on for size, as it were. If we take the example of playful tickling it can be understood as a mock attack at vulnerable body parts (the soles, armpits, etc.) thereby providing children with a safe arena within which to practise defending themselves (Hayworth, 1928; Weisfeld, 1993). Play takes us to the perimeters of knowledge and, importantly, provides a pliable forum for learning about social subtleties (Panksepp, 1998).

Play is also central to emotional development because it bridges unconscious phantasy and external reality. The presence of playing reflects the child's capacity to distinguish reality from phantasy whilst encouraging a 'creative imagination which is neither delusional nor lateral' (Hopkins, 1996:26). Children may make use in play of real objects but they invest these objects with meanings which derive from the world of their unconscious. The symbolical area of play is best

---

[21.] For Freud the opposite of play is not what is serious but what is real.

thought of as a relatively safe area in an emotional sense. When it can be used, anxiety can be experienced in a modified way because the child does not have to face directly the anxiety or guilt which he might experience if he expressed and imposed upon his environment the full force of his conflicting instinctual urges. Equally, he does not have to face the responsibility and consequences of the limitations of his capacity to cope with dangers and difficulties in his external environment. Play is therefore especially important to the child as it provides possibilities for anxiety-provoking situations to be faced in a symbolical way. The child's anxiety may be thus reduced to a more manageable level but if the anxiety remains too great we shall see the child breaking off his play at the point of danger. We can recognize a parallel here in the experience of people losing their sense of humour. On such occasions it would appear that the anxiety is so intolerable that it cannot be modified in a displaced fashion through humorous communication. The similarities with humour are noteworthy since humour can also be said to provide a bridge between unconscious phantasy and reality to that afforded by play, by allowing us to express and modulate primitive drives, conflicts and anxieties. In other words, play and humour are adaptive inventions of the ego. In children, Kris writes, '. . . fun is over and over again favoured as the chosen means of mastering aggression or more correctly ambivalence' (1952:183). Our impulses are not mastered in a once-and-for-all fashion. Rather, they can exert pressure on us at different times so that we continuously bring into play strategies for managing them. A retreat into a humorous mode may thus signal the emergence of difficult impulses.

In both play and humour we witness an interaction between the inner and outer world which allows for the elaboration of imaginative, creative, solutions to internal conflicts. A good index of a child's imagination is their pretend play. From about the age of eighteen months, children start to endow physical objects with pretend properties and thereby bring to life a make-believe world. In Piagetian terms the developments of symbolic representation reflect the child's capacity to differentiate between the 'signifier' (i.e. the appropriate object and its pretend use) and the 'signified' (i.e. the schema as it would ordinarily be applied and its normal object). Although children may be deeply immersed during their play in their make-believe creation, they are nevertheless capable of distinguishing this from the real world. This distinction is critically important. Without it we enter the realm of psychotic elaborations or symbolic equations (Segal, 1957) where the 'as if' quality of the pretend experience cannot be appreciated. The ability to pretend is believed to be central to the child's engagement in an imaginative understanding of other people's mental states. In other words, it assists the child in his capacity to form and sustain relationships. For example, through their pretend play children can imagine believing or feeling something that they do not in fact believe or feel at the time. This is, of course, the basis of empathy, of being able to put ourselves in someone else's shoes. The ability for empathic resonance with another person's predicament reflects a flexibility in emotional and cognitive processing which is essential to reciprocity in relationships. It denotes the ability to view problems, situations or emotional experiences from different perspectives and thereby modulates the tendency, we can all at times succumb to, towards ego-centric positions, especially regarding emotional matters. Given that supportive relationships are crucial to our own well-being, such flexibility is therefore also essential to mental health. This 'psychological' flexibility frees us from the tyranny of rigid patterns of feeling, thinking and behaviour. It develops out of the playful exchanges in the early years where the young child can experiment within the confines of a safe space provided by the environment.

Fonagy and Target (1996) stress the importance of play in developing children's understanding of psychic reality. They emphasize its central function in the child's development of thinking as well as in the integration of emotional experience. According to Fonagy and Target (1996) the 2-3 year old child's sense of psychic reality is characterized by what they term the modes of 'psychic equivalence' (i.e. ideas are not felt to be representations but are replicas of reality and consequently are experienced as true) and the 'pretend mode' (i.e. ideas are representations but their correspondence with reality is not of concern to the child). It is around the ages of four and five that these two modes become integrated. In the pretend mode, ideas cannot threaten the child because they have lost their equivalence to what is real. This is one of the reasons why play can be such an effective way of working through certain anxieties, since eventually a child can always brush it away by saying 'it was only a game'; likewise, with humour. If we start to jest and gradually become anxious as we realize that in jesting we are expressing sexual or aggressive drives, we can also brush it off by saying 'I was only kidding'. We retreat into pretend mode as a way of disavowing our intentions.

In the pretend mode, ideas are representations and they can be played with. In humour, we can observe the activation of a pretend mode similar to that which we observe in young children's play. When we enter a humorous interaction, for example, by listening to a joke, we are essentially 'entering a world of make believe' (Jacobson, 1997). Humour creates a fictional space, a potential space which I would like to argue, as in play, is essential to our adaptation and survival. It is a pretend mode that utilizes the adult's play tools: words. Playing in adults, writes Winnicott, 'manifests itself in the choice of words, in the inflection of the voice and indeed in the sense of humour' (1971:46). Bergson is also most evocative and clear about the continuities between playing in childhood and humour in adult life: 'there can be no break in continuity between the child's delight in games and that of the grown up person. Now, comedy is a game that imitates life' (1956:105). Humour is evidence that the child in us has survived in the unconscious. As Ferenczi remarks:

> It takes . . . many artifices to get the adult human intellect which is addressed to the realities in life and inclined to seriousness to lay aside its inhibiting function and let us go back into the playful, crazy, laughing times of childhood (1911:338).

Play, as we have seen, facilitates the capacity for pretence which is the playground in which incongruity is first approached. Schultz (1976) proposes a view of pretend play as 'self-constructed incongruity', that is, there exists an incongruous relationship between the object and the schema applied to it. He argues that this explains the common observation that pretend play is often accompanied by smiling and laughter. Given this, Schultz suggests that pretend play may represent an essential foundation for the development of the ability to appreciate humour. The development of a sense of humour relies at a fundamental level on some awareness of the distinction between appearance and reality. What we may regard as some of the early manifestations of a playful and humorous attitude, such as teasing, offer us some good examples of the importance of this distinction. Reddy (1991) notes that little is written on infant playfulness as a phenomenon in itself, especially that revealed in what we might call teasing, joking or mucking about. Reddy clearly views playfulness as a cause of developmental advances. His interest is on teasing, as he considers it to be an important behaviour which has specific consequences in relationships. In particular, it is aimed at having an affective impact on others. He argues that an early understanding of other people's teasing relies on the ability to distinguish between what are serious and non-serious intentions. For example, in order for me to acknowledge that I am just 'mucking about' or 'just joking' I need to be able to distinguish the external reality from what I might be feeling inside. It is very likely that the ability to impute mental states to others underpins the capacity to joke about the foibles of others as well as our own. Stern (1985) argues that you can't tease other people unless you guess what is in their minds and 'make them suffer or laugh because of your knowing'.

Observations of infant–parent teasing and cheekiness reveal that such interactions set the ground for, and provide, the interpersonal context for pretending. To begin with, Reddy suggests, the baby's appreciation of such pretence need involve nothing more than an understanding of the playful quality of the parent's intentions which may be communicated non-verbally. In this respect we can see that Bollas' (1995) description of the mother's clowning function is an example of this playful quality which indicates a benign intention on the part of the mother, even though she may at times actually be, as it were, laughing *at* her baby. As with play, in humour, there has to be metacommunication which signals the frivolousness of the interaction.

Humorous space

Winnicott's original idea of the 'potential space' is helpful here in understanding the nature and function of humour. In his work, Winnicott hypothesized an intermediate area of experience that lay between phantasy and reality. He believed that this intermediate area originated in the physical and mental space between mother and baby. Playing, in Winnicott's theory, occurs in this potential space which is a 'hypothetical area' used by him to denote the special quality of phenomena which are given the collective name of playing. The latter subsumes creative activities and humour. In his inimitable way Winnicott strove to conceptualize how we might describe what we are doing, for example, when we listen to a piece of music or share a joke. He asks:

> . . . what is a child doing when sitting on the floor playing with toys under the aegis of the mother? It is not only what are we doing? The question also needs to be posed '*where are we?*' (1971:96, my italics)

According to Winnicott, we are in a kind of transitional, paradoxical, state which partakes both of the world of dream and phantasy and the world of shared reality. Although developmentally we have to acquire the capacity to distinguish reality from phantasy and establish our own sense of personal boundary, the potential space transcends such boundaries. In the course of development the individual becomes capable of generating their own potential space. Winnicott believed that symbols originate within potential space. The use of symbols denotes the capacity of being in touch with internal psychic reality and represents an aspect of what Winnicott calls 'creative apperception'. The early roots of such perception are to be found in the exchanges between mother and baby when the baby looks into the mother's eyes and discovers himself there and consequently is able to discover meaning in the world of seeing things: 'It is creative apperception more than anything else that makes the individual feel that life is worth living' writes Winnicott,

> contrasted with this is a relationship to external reality which is one of compliance, the world and its details being recognized but only something to be fitted in with or demanding adaptation . . .. In a tantalising way, many individuals have experienced just enough of creative living to recognize that for most of their time they are living uncreatively, as if caught up in the creativity of someone else, or of a machine (Winnicott, 1971:65).

It is important to appreciate the developmental advantages conferred by the capacity to enter Winnicott's potential space, as it is here that there can exist a rich interplay between reality and phantasy allowing creativity and spontaneity to flourish. Ogden also advocates an intimate relationship between potential space and creativity:

> . . . that space between symbol and symbolized, mediated by an interpreting self, is the space in which creativity becomes possible and is the space in which we can be alive as human beings, as opposed to being simply reflexively reactive beings (Ogden, 1985:133).

Play's central function is to help us to establish contact not only with internal, but also with external, reality. This point is emphasized by Caper who argues that

> . . . one establishes contact with external reality in part by linking it in a particular way to internal reality, [that] one establishes contact with internal reality in part by linking it in the same way to external reality, and that this link is basically playful (1999:85).

Ogden discusses the different possible outcomes contingent on the nature of the dialectic between reality and phantasy for any given individual. Of particular interest to this discussion are those cases when reality is used as a defence against phantasy, as we then observe a foreclosure of the imagination. Such difficulties arise, according to Ogden, from the premature disruption of the mother–baby unit, which leads to a failure to create or maintain the psychological dialectical processes between reality and phantasy. Where there have been such early disruptions we can also typically observe a failure of the development of a sense of humour. This was the case for Sean.

Sean is a rather desolate man in his mid-forties. He has a history of hospital admissions for depression and suicide. When I first met him he lived alone in supported accommodation. His relationships were very distant and superficial and were restricted to the other residents of the hostel where he lived. Sean felt very shy in the presence of women and he felt especially ashamed of the fact that he had never made love to a woman. In the sessions he could barely look at me. His anxiety was so heightened that, at first, I felt somewhat pessimistic about our chances of working together.

Sean's father had died when he was four years old and he had few memories of him. His older brother had died in a tragic accident when Sean was only five months old. He remembered his mother, who was now also dead, only very vaguely. She had been internalised by him as this rather amorphous, shadowy, figure with little presence. Sean was struck by the fact that he could never remember her face and that even if he looked at a picture of her now the image would soon be lost and he had no representation of her. It felt as though there were no memories to help Sean piece his experiences together. A sense of 'absence' permeated his life and the quality of his interactions. One can only speculate as to the quality of the relationship Sean must have had with a mother confronted with the birth of a young baby and the death of her other son in very close proximity to each other. My experience of being with Sean suggested to me, however, that she had been quite depressed and unable to interact with him in a spontaneous manner. It appeared as though she had never recovered from the loss and withdrew into her own private world of sorrow, shutting Sean out.

My questions about his feelings or fantasies were met, in our first encounter and for the first nine months of psychotherapy, with blankness as if we were speaking a different language. When I invited Sean to tell me about his day-to-day life, the sense of desolation was quite overwhelming. Even though he struggled to articulate his feelings, the barrenness of his internal emotional life was striking. He was very concrete in his descriptions of events and people. He described his alienation from social situations. He recalled school as one of the most 'painful' experiences since he felt he was 'too slow' and never kept up with others. Without any prompting on my part he told me how he could 'never get the jokes'. Although Sean had left formal education at the age of sixteen and had always worked in manual jobs, he was far from unintelligent. But his communications lacked spontaneity and imagination. When I asked him if he remembered playing he said he did not. He could not even remember if he had any toys beyond a few crayons and model cars.

I worked with Sean for twenty months on a weekly basis. At first the sessions were very monotonous and it proved difficult to engage him. Yet over time he began to make use of the space in more creative ways. My interventions were at first focused on mirroring his internal states to encourage him to develop an emotional language and some curiosity about his emotional life. Gradually, Sean himself would refer to things I had said and I was struck by the fact that he repeated my interventions with considerable accuracy. I sensed his hunger for these interventions and this gave me hope. The sessions acquired at times the feel of a frenzied feed as if tomorrow might never come. This poignantly reflected how Sean lived in the perpetual shadow of loss.

Although I sensed Sean's gradual engagement in our relationship, the first year of therapy was devoid of any playful exchanges between us. When we entered the second year Sean had begun to relax more in our sessions and to feel that there was some continuity. In one session he had been talking about his shyness and then, in a rather embarrassed manner, said that the previous night 'I had thoughts of a woman running through my mind'. I was struck by the use of the word 'running' and I replied, quite spontaneously, 'Women have to run through your mind, you would not dare let them walk'. For the first time in twelve months I heard Sean's laughter. At first, he hesitated and then laughed out loud. The following week he referred to this exchange and told me that he had thought about it when on the bus as he had looked across at a woman he had found attractive and had thought to himself: 'This one, she can drag her feet if she wants!'.

The humorous exchange between us had enabled Sean to allow himself a bit more freedom in his fantasy life and in the sessions with me. I was very touched listening to him relate this experience to me in a light-hearted manner, clearly excited at the discovery of his ability to be humorous and the freedom that comes from being able to play with thoughts and fantasies. It had a similar quality to a child coming home from school eager to share his achievement. I think that my more humorous intervention had given Sean permission to think about himself in a different manner. Sean had discovered the relief that can be found when we code events humorously. Indeed this exchange was referred to in subsequent sessions and became a landmark in our work together. This intervention would probably not have struck a chord earlier in the therapy and I think it unlikely that I would have responded in this manner sooner. The timing was right when this exchange took place. It was important that, by then, we had established quite a solid working alliance and that Sean was that little bit more receptive to playing.

According to Winnicott, play affords the child and the adult an opportunity to be creative and to deploy the whole personality. He believes that it is through being creative that we actually discover our own true self. As adults, we can recreate the freedom of the playroom of our childhood through our humorous exchanges with others which allow us to play with ideas, often incongruous ones, and so we carefully tread the tightrope between phantasy and reality. In so doing, we can often discover aspects of our personality that may not have been previously expressed. It can also help us to meet our anxieties in a way that feels safe since it does not involve a direct confrontation with them. One way of managing anxiety is by reducing our weaknesses, misfortunes or dilemmas to an object of fun and invite others to laugh with us. The latter strategy affords us an important psychological resource, especially in helping us to sustain the integrity of the ego and our narcissistic equilibrium. The capacity to be humorous and to enjoy humour reflects an ability to play with reality thereby creating a safe space within which possibilities can be entertained as rigidities of thought and feeling are relaxed. I shall call this safe space the *humorous space*.

If we look at comedy itself, the basic comic premiss – what makes a story or a joke funny – is the gap between comic reality and so-called real reality (Vorhaus, 1994). Take the pun as an example. The pun is a function of the gap between the real meaning of the word in normal usage and the comic reality of the way it ends up being used in a joke. Comedy exploits this gap or, if you like, it exists in the humorous space which is accessible to us all. Like play, the humorous space can allow for a new, creative, structuring of concerns and anxieties as it allows for a greater receptiveness to novelty by challenging rigidity in our emotional attitudes.

Comic perspective

The imagination can flourish within the safe confines of humorous space. The imagination is an essential component of humour because it affords us perspective. Perspective implies that we can assume the role of observer. In order to have perspective we need to have developed the capacity to stand outside of a situation, to gain sufficient distance from it so that we begin to think about it in a different way. The unity of the mother–baby couple has to be relinquished if perspective is to develop since, in the dyadic position, there is no possibility of knowing oneself because there is no third dimension to provide perspective (Mollon, 1993). Britton (1998) hypothesizes the developmental significance of that which he calls 'triadic triangular space'. He argues that it is within this space that the development of a 'third' position – from which the child can observe his own subjective beliefs about an object – can thrive. The third position can only mature if the child can accept that there exists a relationship (i.e. the parental one) from which he is excluded. This represents, as it were, the first emotional appreciation of the role of 'observer of' rather than 'participant in', a relationship. Comic perspective rests on a capacity to observe oneself. It requires the adoption of Britton's 'third position'. Although the origins of humour are to be found in the earliest exchanges between mother and baby, the capacity to laugh at oneself can only develop out of the successful negotiation of the Oedipal challenge. When we witness such humour it reflects the individual's capacity to stand alone and think about himself in a flexible manner. This is qualitatively very different from the humour which is at the expense of another, for example, or where the pressure on the listener is to join in an attempt to recreate the blissful dyadic unity of the pre-Oedipal couple where differences are minimized or altogether negated. The latter is characteristic of the earliest forms of humour, as I experienced in my work with Sarah.

Sarah is a successful thirty-seven year old woman who started therapy because of difficulties in sustaining intimate relationships. She reported a long history of brief sexual encounters which left her feeling unsatisfied. She also found it difficult to reach orgasm and this troubled her. From the outset Sarah impressed me as very articulate. She gave invariably detailed and graphic descriptions of her life which had the effect of drawing me towards her in a rather engrossing manner. She was adept at relating events in a humorous manner which could be quite entertaining. I felt frequently inclined at least to smile and at times actually laugh in response to her stories. Yet I did not always feel comfortable doing so. I soon became preoccupied with a sense that we were not really 'working', even though, at the surface at least, it appeared that she was discussing pertinent issues and she was very motivated to come. A rather insidious sense of complacency (Britton, 1998) pervaded the beginnings of this therapy.

Sarah described a very enmeshed attachment to her mother who had, by her own account, been depressed for part of her childhood. She maintained a very close relationship with her, especially since her father's death some ten years before she started therapy. As she spoke to me about her shopping trips with her mother, their similar taste in clothes and their 'gossipy' discussions about other people, I felt that this was an apt description of the relationship we had recreated in the consulting room. Rather than challenging her or interpreting what was happening in the room, it was as if we got together for 'gossipy' sessions which were injected with jocularity and were experienced by her as exciting. I came to understand the way she used humour in the sessions as an attempt to recreate a rather complicitous relationship between us. I began to feel that what kept Sarah in therapy was not the possibility of change but the illusion that change was taking place while, all along, the status quo remained unchallenged. Our joint laughter was reassurance that we were one against the world outside.

In one session Sarah related, in a light-hearted manner, an incident which had amused her involving a friend of hers in analysis. I shall not enter into all of the details of the story as they are not all salient. But it was significant that the story depicted a therapist whom Sarah perceived to be rather inept and who had very poor eyesight. The farcical element of the incident was a powerful metaphor for the farce that our work together had become. At one level Sarah perceived me, quite accurately I am afraid, as lacking perspective, as blind to what was happening between us. I had colluded with her wish to recreate the enmeshed relationship with her mother that was the obstacle to her having any other relationships as it could allow no third party to enter.

The hostility embedded in her descriptions of the inept therapist gave expression to her contempt for me. Yet, through using humour, Sarah could continue to deny her hostility towards me just as she denied it in relation to her mother by whom in fact she felt quite suffocated. The contempt had echoes in her relationship with her father. Her father had been a very intelligent and successful academic, whom she had nevertheless experienced as inaccessible and passive. The good memories she had of him were few. As she had been an only child she recalled him as encouraging her to go out and make friends while she preferred to stay at home with her mother. If he was around she remembered feeling very competitive for her mother's attention and she proudly stated once that she could make her mother laugh whereas her father was far too serious and always wanted to discuss politics. The sense of triumph as she reported this was striking.

Sarah's case highlights the importance of assessing the quality of the humorous exchanges that can take place between therapist and patient as these may signal the wish to recreate a narcissistically fused object relationship which thwarts progress. Although Sarah's use of humour was an attempt to foster an exclusive, pre-Oedipal relationship with me, the content of her humour had a very Oedipal flavour, characteristic of humour that is frequently at the expense of others and that contributes to a feeling of triumph over another. In other words, the content of humour is not always an indication of the type of relationship the patient may be re-enacting in the transference.

Sarah's use of humour denotes how it can recreate a relationship which impedes progress; however, at its best, humour reflects possibilities and openness. Moreover, it affords us an effective strategy for integrating the multiple meanings and experiences that may conflict with each other, thereby introducing complexity to our emotional life. Central to psychoanalytic thinking is the assumption that a major developmental task facing us all is the integration of opposites or, if you like, of incongruities. The development of the self may indeed be said to rest on the 'constructive reconciliation of such incongruities' (Schlesinger, 1979). For example, we need to learn to become independent although acknowledging our inevitable dependence on others; we need to learn to bind love and hate, good and bad, that is, to manage ambivalence. Even if we seek intimacy we may nonetheless fear being taken over by the other and we have to find a way of reconciling our wish to be close with our need to retain a sense of being separate. These developmental goals involve a degree of conflict and pain. The difficulties inherent in working through these dilemmas frequently act as spurs to seeking psychotherapy.

Like psychoanalysis, comedy deals with incongruity (see Chapter 1). Indeed, humour thrives on contradictions, paradoxes and ambiguities. It can be seen to be a process of incongruous creation and resolution where incongruity leads to disequilibrium and its resolution restores equilibrium (Palmer, 1987). It may indeed feel like an emotional roller-coaster, as we can sometimes experience at a comedy show, as the comedian turns our established reality on its head. He confronts us with a contradictory world, rubs our face in it and expects us to laugh. If we can rise to the occasion we have reached an important developmental watershed: we can integrate opposites, we can live with uncertainty, we can even bear to contemplate the greatest paradox of all, namely that that which gives our life meaning is what ultimately takes life from us. So much humour does in fact centre on our relative inconsequence and finiteness. Paradoxically, however, through humour, we can derive some narcissistic pleasure as we metaphorically turn the tables round and perceive the world in 'pygmy proportions' (Dooley, 1934). This is because it allows us to indulge in fantasy that clothes the harshness of reality, with comforting, gentle playfulness.

When we first experience incongruity we may not, however, respond humorously. On the contrary, we may feel anxious, fearful or enraged. If we manage to resolve the incongruity we are faced with, the outcome is frequently a feeling of relief and even joy. However, some of us try to simplify our emotional life because we fear being overwhelmed by a mass of confusing feelings that we are unable to integrate. By simplifying our emotional experiences, we do not do justice to their complexity and we restrict the range of our experience. We cannot really progress unless we can manage the differences, conflicts and paradoxes which threaten to overwhelm us. The adaptive solution is to develop enough ego strength to hold such conflicting experiences or feelings/thoughts in mind without resorting to projective mechanisms of defence which aim to get rid of unwanted feelings. When we overuse projection we simply perpetuate our problems since the feelings we seek to disown are subsequently no longer accessible to us but continue, nevertheless, to exert a hold over us. Since we find it so difficult to entertain two conflicting emotions, we all to readily fall into the blind alley of polarized thinking and feeling which reinforces a rigid perspective on life, which is marked, characteristically, by an absence of humour.

Ian is a forty-five year old man I assessed only over two sessions as he never took up the option of psychotherapy. He was married with no children and worked in administration. He was referred because of obsessional rituals around washing which had gradually begun to take over his life and were contributing to tensions in his marriage. He was highly ambivalent about therapy and had in fact cancelled the first two consultations. He had come in the end because his wife had threatened him with a separation. He described a very tense atmosphere both at home and at work. At work, his colleagues teased him about being 'anal'. He decried the lack of values amongst his colleagues and showed irritation with his colleagues whom he viewed as 'slapdash' in their approach. He thought they spent more time 'playing around' than working.

In his childhood, Ian described stern parents. He had felt his childhood had been dominated by the guilt they harboured as they were both first-generation Holocaust survivors. They had started a family quite late. His father had a serious heart problem that had restricted his ability to work. Consequently his mother had carried the burden of working as well as caring for the father. His sister had left home early at the age of eighteen as she had always argued with the father. Ian bemoaned her irresponsibility and had very irregular contact with her. His father was now dead but his mother was still alive, though very elderly and frail. Ian felt he 'had' to see her once a week and would go over to the home where she was being cared for and 'give her room a good clean'. He saw it as his duty to look after her in her old age. Ian harboured guilt at his own inability to keep her at home with him since she needed too much care. It was not possible to elicit more information about the quality of his relationship with his parents. Generally speaking, Ian found it very difficult to elaborate his answers to my questions. His communication was telegraphic, except when he engaged in a tirade against other people. Then, it was actually difficult to interrupt him.

Ian's life ran according to a strict routine. Just listening to it felt stifling. His murderous rage, though denied by him, was imbued in his virulent judgements of others and his harsh attitude towards himself. There was no shortage of what others did that was wrong. Although Ian was often in the role of the critical person who could do everything much better than anybody else, at times he found himself in the position of the victim, persecuted by his own and other people's judgements of him. Minor mistakes would compel him to tortuous self-reproach which echoed the parents' own self-reproach for having survived.

Ian was aware that he was much disliked at work. He had got into work one morning and he had found his drawer full of staplers and toilet paper. When I asked him what he made of this, he said he had been very irritated at work the day before because someone had removed the stapler from his desk and he had made it clear, several times before, that his stationary should not be removed. He related this incident angrily to me. His colleagues had seemingly retaliated by filling his drawer with staplers and toilet paper, a reference presumably to his anal tendencies though Ian himself could not understand the significance of the toilet paper. At some level this incident had deeply upset Ian but he could not openly acknowledge his humiliation and hurt. He simply persevered in his admonishment of his colleagues. The joke they played on him was most likely an expression of their hostility towards him and was intended to ridicule him. It was not funny but it was a communication about how they viewed him. But although he felt attacked Ian had been unable to decipher the symbolic meaning of the toilet paper – the joke was on him but it was totally lost on him. He simply could not see himself as others saw him and he was certainly a very long way off from laughing at himself. In the session I sensed that exploration was not possible as Ian's way of dealing with this incident was to dismiss the whole thing as further evidence that 'people are simply not worth the effort'. Comic perspective emerges only when we can take a double view of ourselves – a perspective by incongruity (Sypher, 1956). Sadly, Ian was incapable of this.

The humorous position requires a shift of focus from a self-centred, subjective, mode of functioning, to a more critical, objective, mode. It is a position of 'internal objectivity', to borrow Britton's (1998) phrase, where we assume the role of observer rather than active participant with respect to our own emotional life. An objective mode does not imply that we feel neutral about that which is laughed at. If we can speak of an emotional detachment this is only relative (Kris, 1938). More often than not, what is laughed at resonates deeply within us. To be distanced from an event does not necessarily entail that we are totally emotionally cut off from it. The emotional response is simply managed differently. Humour metabolizes our otherwise immediate emotional response and enables us to create a space for playing with it. It is an example of the interplay between a state of amusement – an emotional state – and cognitive processes generally.

Creative solutions

Many humour theorists have followed in Freud's footsteps and they have concentrated primarily on humour's role as a means of reducing tension. They took from Freud his most rudimentary understanding of humour as elaborated in his first paper rather than his later, far more sophisticated, formulation. Consequently, humour as a creative act, providing a vehicle for coping with life, has been comparatively under-played (Fry and Allen, 1975). Nevertheless, some theorists have concentrated on the latter. In his seminal discussion on humour, Koestler (1964) argued that the humorist[22] provides 'mental jolts' triggered by the collision of incompatible matrices. He posited the necessary experience of 'a jolt' or 'an associative shock' resulting in a new 'kind of fusion' that was itself creative. Humour may be said to be a creative act in as much as it encourages the exploration of associations between events that have been previously ignored or unprocessed. Within this conceptualization of humour there is an implicit acknowledgement of the importance of the imagination and creativity.

The subject of the imagination has been of interest to philosophers and writers but it is perhaps unsurprising that within psychology as a whole the subject has played a somewhat marginal role in relation to cognitive and emotional development. Freud himself, though he showed a strong interest in phantasy life, viewed phantasy as essentially escapist, a means for wish fulfilment or drive satisfaction. It represented a turning away from reality rather than a preliminary to altering it in a desired direction. Though he defined humour as the hallmark of maturity he simultaneously labelled it as an outstanding denial of reality, the measure of neurosis (O'Connell, 1976). In a parallel manner, the psychological literature on the development and acquisition of cognition bears witness to a bias away from a consideration of the value of the imagination towards more systematic and analytic cognitive efforts. In these accounts, the imagination appears to carry a contradictory set of associated meanings (Meadows, 1993).

[22.] I use the term *humorist* to refer the comedian in us all. I reserve the term *comedian* to refer to those who work professionally as comedians.

The etymological root of imagination is the Latin *imago* meaning image or representation. At its core, the imagination has the ability to conceive of what is not actually happening at a given point in time. The evolutionary function of the imagination may not appear immediately obvious since, it could be argued, what is the value of investing energy in developing a fiction which takes us away from our goal of adapting to our immediate external environment. The imagination does allow us to escape from our current reality, but I would like to argue that such an escape is functional and makes evolutionary sense and that humour provides one such escape route. The capacity to conceive of what is not actually present may encourage important elaborations as it propels us into a different emotional and cognitive space replete with possibilities. The imagination has to work with skills and knowledge and provides a playground for their exercise even if its ultimate goal is to transform them into the unreal or the impossible. To view the imagination as a means merely of distorting or denying aspects of reality is to ignore its potential as 'a fiction of prolific consequences' (Phillips, 1998:5). It also ignores its intricate connection with the exercise of our higher cognitive functions to aid our adaptation to the external world. The imagination, along with humour as one of its creations, allows us to entertain possible realities and, of particular importance, to entertain possible realities that other people might entertain, thereby encouraging us to expand our curiosity about the world and other people and so assists our adaptation.

Reasoning and imagination are not truly independent, though a survey of the literature may lead one to believe that the imagination has nothing to contribute to the development of our capacity to reason (Reddiford, 1980). John Dewey's definition of the imaginative as 'a warm and intimate taking in of the full scope of the situation' highlights the contribution of the imagination to the development of cognition. In a discussion of children's cognition, Meadows (1993) suggests that young children's mental lives are full of imagination because they are actively engaged in trying to make sense of the world. The exaggeration and freedom which are core components of the imagination and of fantasy (both conscious and unconscious) are an important means to this end. Both fantasy and imagination involve the elaboration of impossibilities and thus they both offer routes to creativity. The essence of creativity is the ability to take a fresh look at familiar objects and situations, enriched by past experience but not constrained by it:

> Creative people make new things but these are 'new' not because they are the only ones like that which have ever occurred, but because they reveal reality in a new way (Russell 1991:176).

Storr (1989), in his study on solitude, discusses the nature of creativity. He puts forward a strong argument that an 'inner imaginative world' is an integral part of man's biological endowment. Adopting an evolutionary perspective, he argues that man's success as a species has depended upon this particular endowment. Given this hypothesis, Storr argues that we should not strive to replace fantasy by reason, since it is the inevitable discrepancy between the inner world and the external world that propels man to become imaginative and hence inventive. According to Storr, the creative imagination can 'exercise a healing function'. This is a view echoed by Alvarez (1992) who argues that the imagination is a 'healing ground, an area of potential development for that which can and ought to be'. It is possible to respect this potential without necessarily having to collude with a denial of reality which might be present in some aspects of fantasy and imaginative thinking. Brazelton believes that 'The richest source of humour, empathy and compassion is the child's imagination and all the rich experiences that his fantasies provide him' (1992:209).

Alex was an adolescent boy I worked with some years ago. He was fourteen years old at the time I saw him. He was said to have mild learning difficulties and significant interpersonal problems. His appearance was quite downtrodden and he often looked unkempt and dirty. At school he was frequently picked on and made fun of by his peers who teased him because he wore unfashionable clothes. His background was very deprived. He had been born to a single woman diagnosed with schizophrenia and had been taken into care at the age of three, having been found unfed and unwashed by a visiting social worker. He had spent some years in institutional care following which he had been adopted by an older couple. At the age of twelve he had been sexually abused by an older man who visited the adoptive parents' house. Alex's relationship with his adoptive parents was very distant and he was generally withdrawn with others.

Alex had developed quite obsessional tendencies and displayed ritualistic behaviour. In the sessions he was difficult to engage. He would religiously bring his scrapbook in which he collected various pictures and he would sit in a corner of the room leafing through it and rarely speaking. One day, however, he came to the session carrying an Argos catalogue with him. I noticed this was different and I asked him if there was something he wanted to buy. Alex replied emphatically that he wanted 'everything' in the catalogue. At this point I could of course have made some interpretation about his omnipotence or his need to acquire material things so as to be able to compete with his peers who teased him because he did not possess all the latest accessories. Or I could have interpreted his need covering up as greed, which of course made sense given the extent of Alex's early deprivation. I could even have chosen to focus on the anger that had been present in his tone when he spoke, or I could have heard his statement as expressing his wish to have me all to himself, all of the time, since this session had followed a week's break.

Of course, I could also have chosen to say nothing. Instead, regarding it to be much more important to enter into an elaboration of his phantasy wish, I said 'Well, if you could have everything, where would you put it?'[23] Alex looked up and started giggling. I sensed he had appreciated what I had said and thought it funny. I smiled. He then returned to leafing through his catalogue and showed me a bicycle he wanted.

The following week Alex came to the session and announced, for the first time, that he wanted to do a collage. He retrieved from a plastic bag the Argos catalogue and a cut-out picture from a Levi's jeans advertisement, showing an attractive man, bare-torso, wearing jeans. Alex proceeded to stick the picture on to a piece of paper and then cut out from the catalogue numerous pictures: a bicycle, some toys, a new bed and so on. He stuck these things next to the picture of the man and gave it to me. The page was covered to the brim with pictures. I said that he was letting me know that perhaps it was important that I should see him as the handsome man who has lots and lots of nice, new, things. Alex laughed and then said : 'Just a few things because I can't find room for everything!'. I was very struck by his response, especially since he spoke confidently and in an articulate manner. We both laughed.

In subsequent sessions Alex started to tell me jokes and riddles. He had got a book out of the library which was full of jokes. I sensed he felt powerful when he made me laugh and I decided that, at that point it was important to laugh with him, to allow him to experience himself in this different light. Some months later he reported that he had shared one of the jokes in class and his peers had laughed. He was clearly so proud of this achievement and he eagerly told me about it. Even though he still continued to have numerous difficulties, Alex had begun very gradually, through humour, to experiment with a different way of being and of relating that had brought him some rewards. By laughing with him I was not denying his pain and anger which, as you read this account, will no doubt strike you. Alex had a very long way to go but it was important to acknowledge his attempts to entertain himself, at least in fantasy, and gradually in reality, not as a victim but as someone who could be admired and could make people laugh with him, not at him.

Humour, like the imagination, has a healing function. Being humorous is a creative act that strives to synthesize experiences and thoughts into a new unity by bringing together disparate ideas and feelings. In the context of a discussion on creative people, Storr (1988) makes observations that are equally applicable to the everyday use of humour: 'by creating a new unity, in a poem or other work of art, the artist is attempting to restore a lost unity or to find a new unity within the inner world' (1988:123). He considers that the imagination drives us

---

[23.] This is in fact an observation once made by the American comedian Steven Wright.

to seek new understandings and new connections in the external world but at the same time it also reveals our 'hunger for integration and unity within'. If we return to Chasseguet-Smirgel's (1988) view of the humorist as consoling himself as his mother would have done, we can find some parallels with the views expressed by Storr more generally about creative acts. For Storr goes on to say that,

> the creative act is one of overcoming the state of helplessness which . . . is so important a part of the depressive state. It is a coping mechanism: a way of exercising control, as well as a way of expressing emotion. In fact, the act of expressing emotion itself gives the sufferer some source of mastery, even if he or she is not particularly gifted (1988:129).

The ability to integrate the ambivalence of opposites, of conflict, is indispensable to the emergence of a sense of humour. Christie (1994) argues that our creative imagination depends on our capacity to tolerate antithetical ideas simultaneously and the attendant anxiety. 'Laughter', writes Sacerdoti,

> testifies both to the existence of incongruity and the capacity to resolve it at the level of inner reality, of a broadening of insight that understands, through laughing at it, external reality (1992:162)

To be able to face incongruity in our experience with amusement allows for a more objective and rational perspective on it. Humour is in fact critically important to the development of reason. This is because humour requires us to suspend our emotional involvement in that which ostensibly concerns us. Bergson (1956) spoke of humour demanding a 'momentary anaesthesia of the heart'. We will recognize this requirement from our own experience. When we are distressed and involved in an emotional exchange, for example, it may be very difficult to take some distance and laugh at our own predicament. A few hours or days later, when we are feeling less raw, we can often begin to see the funny side to an incident that, at the time, may have been quite harrowing for us. Humour then appears to emerge when we are capable of stepping out of a self-conscious frame of mind, and enter the humorous space where we are less concerned with our personal relationship to things (Morreall, 1987). From such a position we can broaden our perspective to consider the relationship between things, ideas, events and people. This is because the cognitive system underlying amusement orients us to the world in a different mode from the way our emotions orient us. Morreall (1987) draws attention to the incompatibility between the response of amusement and 'practical concern' with a given situation. In other words, when we find something funny we are emotionally distanced from it. This underlies our attempts to cheer someone up where they feel sad, for example.

It is well recognized that good moods generally have a positive impact on our ability to think flexibly and with more complexity, thereby allowing us to find solutions to problems. Goleman, in his discussion of the notion of 'emotional intelligence' suggests that:

> Laughing, like elation, seems to help people think more broadly and associate more freely, noticing relationships that might have eluded them otherwise – a mental skill important not just in creativity, but in recognising complex relationships and foreseeing the consequences of a given decision (1996:85).

There is some research evidence to support Goleman's contention. In one study, participants who had watched a video of 'television bloopers' performed better in a problem-solving task than a group who had watched a film on mathematics and another group who had simply been asked to exercise (Isen et al., 1991, quoted in Goleman, 1996). Ziv (1976; 1983) found that the laughter response to humorous stimuli increased creative thinking in adolescents as measured by scores on creativity tests that essentially measure divergent thinking. In his later study Ziv (1983) also found that it was not only direct exposure to humour which produced a shift towards more divergent thinking and hence creative responses. When participants were given instructions to use humour, rather then being exposed to humour, this was perceived as a cue to use more non-conventional modes of thinking. Such studies are not of course suggesting that 'a good laugh' can transform us into creative people but rather that the expression of a particular mode of thinking not bound by a concern with rigidity and conventional answers is facilitated through humour. This type of thinking is closely associated with creativity.

The view of humour as 'liberation' or 'freedom' (Penjon, 1893; Dugas, 1902; Mindess, 1971) can be traced in the literature and emphasizes the value of a humorous attitude in freeing us, amongst other things, from conformity, seriousness, reason and language. Humour enhances our ability to think broadly and flexibly, and most importantly with more complexity. This is so because, as we have seen, humour relies on a freeing or loosening of associations which, in turn, highlights relationships between things that may have eluded us previously. It allows us to play with new ideas by giving us temporary leave from the demands of logical thinking. There are important implications here for the role of humour in psychotherapy. Allowing ourselves entry into the humorous space can be likened to allowing ourselves to use the analytic space. If humour encourages a loosening of the shackles of logical thought, it is in keeping with the aim of psychoanalysis, which encourages a similar loosening of associations. Although we may give instructions to our patients to say what comes to mind, I am not advocating explicitly encouraging patients to be humorous. Nevertheless, if, as therapists, we feel at ease with the humorous mode, by using it ourselves, we are implicitly giving permission for humour to emerge within psychotherapy. The examples of Sean and Alex given earlier in the chapter illustrate this.

It is through our free associations that we can arrive at our unconscious concerns and mobilize our resources to deal with that which is troubling us. Although, it can be argued, that comedy provides us with an escape, we are essentially escaping through looking and laughing at the imperfections of the world about us and at our own imperfections. The comic artist releases us from the limitations of things as they are, and in so doing offers us an invaluable opportunity to stand back and to observe how different they could be (Sypher, 1956).

Mastery through humour

One of the most important functions of humour is that it represents, as I have repeatedly emphasized, an attempt at mastery and consequently has adaptive value to us as a species. In order to appreciate this more fully, we need first to return to Freud's original description of the function of play. In his paper 'Beyond the pleasure principle', Freud (1920) gives a detailed description of an eighteen month old child at play. In this excerpt, the child repeatedly throws his toys under the furniture and plays with a wooden reel attached to a piece of string which he then throws out of his cot and subsequently pulls back again. Freud notes the context in which this game occurs, namely, the child's relationship with his mother and his reaction to her absences and returns. To Freud's mind, the meaning and function of the game is clear. It represents:

> . . . the instinctual renunciation . . . which he had made in allowing his mother to go away without protesting. He compensated himself for this, as it were, by himself staging the disappearance and return of objects within his reach (1920:285).

In so doing, Freud argues, what we can observe is the child's attempt to turn a passive experience, that of being left alone, into an active one through the process of playing. Essentially, Freud is describing here the use of play as an attempt at mastering an emotionally difficult situation. Humour may be used to similar ends. For example, people may lightheartedly recount an embarrassing incident which, at the time, caused humiliation or triggered some anxiety. In retelling the incident, the desire to gain some mastery over an experience in which we most probably felt out of control, is gratified. Our capacity for humour wanes when we are overwhelmed by anxiety, persecutory or depressive feelings, or feelings of shame and guilt, so that we fail to laugh at ourselves at that point but may recover this ability subsequently through the humorous storytelling. In the humorous storytelling, we turn a passive experience into an active one. We can observe a similar mechanism at play in certain comic performances, which we also all stage in our daily lives, where the person who is laughed at in fact retains control of the situation by deliberately providing entertainment at their own expense (Reik, 1954).

Humour as an attempt at mastery and control is highlighted in the very poignant recollection by Brian Keenan when he was held hostage. In retelling of his interactions with John McCarthy, he writes:

> Our humour was not heroism. Quite the reverse. It was a way of putting the previous night at a distance from us, screened behind humour and affection, so we could take control of it before it took control of us (Keenan, 1992:120).

This is an example of 'gallows humour' or 'black humour' about which Freud (1927) originally wrote. It has since been documented in particularly harrowing situations such as among Czechoslovakians suffering under Nazi regimes (Obrolik, 1941) and Viktor Frankl's (1959) own accounts of his time in Auschwitz. It is the 'humour of survival' (Boskin,1987). Solzhenitsyn (1973) shares one of the many anecdotes among prisoners in the concentration camp where he was prisoner: 'What is your last word, accused?' 'I beg you to send me wherever you please, just as long as it is under the Soviet government and the sun is there!' (1973:269-70). Such humour appeared crucial as a means of survival and for the maintenance of human dignity in the face of a dehumanizing process. Discussions on the nature and function of Jewish humour have trodden a similar path. In a paper on Jewish identity Schlesinger (1979) argues that:

> Jewish humour as an oral tradition handed down over generations of joke telling is a form of secular communal ritual which both binds and characterises the community, and *acts adaptively for its survival* (1979:319, my italics).

More specifically, Schlesinger suggests that self-assertion in situations where our sense of being is under threat can be integrated through the use of humour which allows for a sublimated and constructive expression of hostility. Barchilon (1973) has emphasized the rebellious gratification afforded by the manipulation of language such as the use of nonsense, mockery and absurdity. Schlesinger's analysis of Jewish humour is very pertinent to this discussion since he views the origins and function of humour as arising out of a need for the integration and mastery of incongruity. For Jewish people, the need to find a way of coming to terms with the repeated experience of loss, without succumbing to despair, presented a poignant incongruity.

Humour thus facilitates a conceptual resolution that has important emotional consequences:

> Humour can be considered as play in which the ego constructs ambiguities and incongruities and then solves them. The humorous mode is applied to the incongruities of inner and outer experience in an attempt to resolve them (Schlesinger, 1979:318).

The individual's refusal to be 'distressed by the provocations of reality' (Freud, 1927) is actively translated into the imaginative and adaptive development of verbal, conceptual congruity out of absurdity or contradiction thereby leading to a sense of mastery. The following Jewish joke, reported by Schlesinger, illustrates how humour may be used to manage an unpalatable reality by altering one's attitude towards it:

> An Englishman, a Frenchman, an American and a Jew are engaged in a discussion about their hypothetical responses to their imminent death due to a flood from which they are unable to escape. The Englishman says: 'I would open my best bottle of port, sit and enjoy it, think about the life I have had and surrender to the water'. The Frenchman says: 'I would drink a great Bordeaux, prepare some good food, make love and let the waters take me'. The American says: 'I would eat, drink, make love, try to improvise a raft and swim as far as I could. I would fight to the bitter end and then die'. The Jew says: 'I would do all that you describe and when the water goes over my head I guess I would learn to live underwater'!

This joke juxtaposes, according to Schlesinger, the tragic-heroic and humorous positions. It is the Jew who through the humorous response articulates the creative solution of underwater life. This epitomizes the adaptive value of humour.

Kris (1938) describes the inherent feeling of anxiety over our own powers of mastery, which accompanies humour. He considers the question of when a child, for example, may find an experience funny. According to him, a child may laugh at an absurd movement in another person only when the child has himself mastered the same movement. Kris concludes that even though laughter, as Hobbes originally suggested, results from a realization of our own superiority, it also results from the realization that we can actually do something and not just do it better than another person. Kris argues that the reason that we might repeat a joke or continue to derive pleasure from some humorous exchange is because we derive a permanent delight at the harmlessness of what once felt out of our control, dangerous and in some way elicited our anxiety. Humour thus combines a sense of mastery with a feeling of pleasure. What today strikes us as funny is what yesterday might have been overwhelming. From this arises the well-recognized tightrope of humour since the laughter it produces can so easily reveal its flipside. As Sinason (1996) observes, this why comedians have to be so good at what they do.

Humour puts us in touch with repressed sexual and destructive impulses and subjects them to a transformation that renders them acceptable to consciousness. Spruiell links creative acts and jokes by pointing out that what they have in common is 'the sudden, shocking, joining by the viewer or listener, of previously buried sexual and aggressive fantasies with fantasies more closely related to everyday perception' (1985:482). The transformation which takes place through humour facilitates psychic integration and insight. If the individual is receptive to the meaning revealed through the humorous communication, it then facilitates an examination of the anxiety which has been stirred up by the humorous communication as a whole. Christie (1994) argues that it is precisely through its very structure that humorous communication raises and at the same time reduces the anxiety to a bearable level. The relief often arises from the psychic structuring of one's emotional experience facilitated by the humorous response. This is most evident, as we saw earlier, in extreme situations which give rise to 'gallows humour'. Here humour is, first and foremost, used both to assert and rebel against one's helpless condition. Just as through play children can discover and approach what is serious or real, through humour we also emotionally manage reality (Pasquali, 1986). This is a process that we can also observe in other creative acts. This creativity stands in sharp contrast to a more repetitive way of living life which forecloses more imaginative, creative, solutions.

Uses, misuses and abuses of humour

This book, like all books, is inevitably biased. I am a firm believer that the capacity to enjoy and to produce humour – in particular, to be able to laugh at oneself – reflects flexibility in emotional and cognitive processing and is therefore adaptive. Nevertheless, my own prejudices do not preclude an appreciation of how humour may also be open to misuse and abuse, that is, to ends which are not adaptive. We can all probably think of instances where humour has been used in order to deny, attack or humiliate, as well as contributing to a stalemate in communication. Before we consider some such uses of humour it is important to clarify a common assumption made about humour, namely its inherently aggressive nature. This is one of the reasons some therapists avoid using it as they recognize this feature and are therefore understandably concerned about its effects on the patient. All humour may be said to contain an element of aggression in the sense that aggressive instincts are a component of what drives behaviour. Our self-preservative instinct relies on a measure of aggression at its disposal to fulfil its aims. In other words, it is imperative that we do not lose sight of aggression's 'propelling function essential for the construction of life' (Perelberg, 1999:23). Some humour, even if affectionate in its intent, may nevertheless contain a challenge which is a manifestation of aggression. However, we would not consider such humour to be destructive. On the other hand, humour may be primarily aggressive and intended to discharge feelings indiscriminately or may actually be intended to hurt another.

Teasing, as we saw in the last chapter, begins very early on. It is an interesting behaviour since it is a good example of the tightrope we tread when in humorous interaction with another person. Teasing can be felt as an affectionate prod but it can also certainly feel like a stab. After all, teasing quite literally means to shred finely, to tear into pieces. The aggression inherent in that is explicit. As Brenman points out:

> Teasing seems to stand somewhere between aggression and love, but is modulated by various processes – on the highest level by the adaptive, creative, ego product, humour, as well as by single and complex defensive processes . . . when the behaviour loses this precariously poised middle position, it may proceed to pointed wit or become clearly hostile as in the derivative form of ridicule, mockery, derision or tantalising, or it may 'graduate' into the socially adaptive behaviour of humorous banter, relatively free of barbs (1952:265-266).

Teasing may be expressed in the context of humorous storytelling. In such situations, the person telling the humorous story may use this as a vehicle for teasing someone and so to express their retaliation by unmasking the other. Such behaviour may encourage the approbation of a group who laugh at the story and thereby marginalize the person who is the butt of the joke.

Although irony can be a great source of enjoyment, ironic comments may also be intended quite viciously. They hit the jugular, as it were. Irony can be used as revenge, as a sadistic attack or a means of preventing defeat (Alexander, 1969). More insidiously, it may also lead to a stalemate, an absence of action, even if the ironic message conveys the dissatisfaction with a state of affairs. In a discussion about the similarities between the English and the Irish, the actress Fiona Shaw observes, 'Both nations suffer from the disease of irony. And it is a disease, because of a refusal to deal with anything.' (1998:16). Shaw highlights how irony, and indeed any kind of humour, can create an impasse. We may laugh but it is not a creative laugh; on the contrary, it is an abdication of sorts. However, as Sacerdoti notes:

> Ironic play risks remaining play indefinitely, but it may also use ambiguity as a temporary means of arriving at an active and serious choice of greater strength (1992:14).

Humour may also be employed in the service of denial and it is in this sense that much of the psychotherapeutic literature has conceptualized the use of humour in that particular context. It is of course true that the use of humour is sometimes a manifestation of a defence precluding any exploration of what is ostensibly troubling the person, as was evident in my work with Alice .

Alice is a twenty-six year old scriptwriter who collapsed from 'nervous exhaustion' at work. She had been working very hard on a project and had felt unable to tell her boss that she was behind schedule. Consequently she had been pushing herself very hard and finally her body gave in. She came to the initial consultation with very mixed feelings. She spoke quite rapidly and punctuated her speech with laughter as she tried to relate incidents in her life. Everything she spoke about was turned into a joke and it was difficult to gain any sense of her or of the emotional significance of the events she related. It felt as though she fired jokes like a machine-gun to keep me at a distance. Her life was fast paced, like her speech, and though I could see why she was successful at writing I could also see why she had collapsed.

In our initial meeting Alice told me that sitting in my room reminded her of Tennessee Williams saying that he gave up seeing his psychoanalyst because he was meddling too much with his private life. Conscious that she was working hard to keep me at a distance, I found myself responding to this by saying: 'An opportunity would be a fine thing!' Alice laughed and replied that she had always had 'trouble with punctuation'. I encouraged her to pause and reflect on what she had been doing in the session – how she had prevented me, as well as herself, from really thinking about what had brought her to therapy. Although Alice did pause temporarily and was more thoughtful, the therapy was characterized for some time by her need to distance herself from her emotions. She undoubtedly used humour in this way and I was therefore very cautious with her with my use of humour since I felt we could both easily get caught up in a whirlwind of witticisms.

When humour is employed in this defensive manner and occurs in the context of the therapeutic situation, it is important to address the denial and the feelings that the humorous communication attempts to deflect. However, it is important to do so thoughtfully and not jump to conclusions too readily. It is incumbent on us to ask ourselves in such cases what is the difference between avoiding and facing up to reality? (Brandon, 1996). How do we in fact distinguish as Brandon (1996) points out, a manic state that represents a denial of depression and a manic state that in fact signals a recovery? This requires us to examine our own assumptions about the nature of defence and the role of the therapist in relation to the patient's defences. In her discussions on the function of play in children, Alvarez (1992) makes the very apt observation that even though play may be used defensively to avoid or to triumph over an unpalatable reality: 'In some cases play may help the child to explore the possibility of one day being strong even if their present reality may be quite the opposite' (1992:178). She goes on to observe that:

> A mask or a lie may involve an offering which contains, not necessarily a denial of a past reality or a current pain, but a tentative question about the possibility of *a new version of the present and even a new view of the future* (1992:81, my italics).

Alvarez is making a very important point, which, as clinicians, we all too often fail to consider in our eagerness to 'catch the defence' and to remind our patients of the arduous task of facing up to reality. It is not solely a question of the timing of our interpretations of defensive structures. Timing is important so as to ensure that the patient can actually hear the interpretation and so make use of it. It is also essential to consider the purpose of distortion or denial for a given individual. In some patients, the very act of creating an illusion, or a funny story, is in fact an indication of progress. Just like play, humour may contain an expressed hope that things could be otherwise, even if they are in fact not so at the time. The humorous perspective releases us from the limitations of things as they are, and in so doing opens up new possibilities: 'In the deranging, disarranging, communal laughter occasioned by the contrary clown, we see what is not possible and thereby make it possible' (Jacobson, 1997:195).

Likewise, the patient who tries to make humorous contact may be tentatively exploring another version of himself, one that may, in the longer term, prove more adaptive. When Sean returned to his sessions observing that the woman he had seen on the bus could be allowed to 'drag her feet', he had played in his fantasy with my original intervention and made it his own. It gave him a glimpse of how he *might* be able to see women and himself in relation to them. My response of laughter, indicating my appreciation and pleasure in this developmental shift, was important. Perhaps as clinicians we have become so adept at spotting the denial in wish fulfilment that we have, as Phillips suggests: 'denied what wishing affirms'. For him,

> . . . the child . . . the dream or the joke are all, among many other things, figures for an alternative to passive acceptance; for the possibility of remaking, for revision as a way of protecting our pleasures (1998:5).

When assessing a humorous communication, we are therefore mostly interested in its quality, in whether it is an attempt to communicate, even through displacement, anxiety and concerns, or whether it is an attack, which heralds forth no resolution. Humour, then, may have quite destructive and defensive qualities, but not invariably so. Indeed, it may be more apposite to view humour generally as occupying some mid-position of meaningfulness between various bipolarities: pulling towards–drawing back; pain–pleasure; hostile–friendly; serious–playful; destructive–constructive; antagonistic–co-operative and willing–reluctant (Spurling, 1951).[24] The advantage of such a conceptualization is that it emphasizes the role both of the defensive and the adaptive ego functions operating in humour.

---

[24] In his paper Spurling outlines these polarities in relation to teasing. I would like to suggest that we can observe such polarities in all forms of humour.

Chapter 4
Humour and Health

There are people who have a sense of humour and it occurs to me that one root of a sense of humour is the capacity to experience satisfaction about finding out in oneself something that has been repressed. Klein (1961:243-244)

The art of medicine consists in amusing the patient while Nature affects its cure. (Voltaire)

In his youth Goethe traversed a period of deep depression during which he seriously contemplated suicide. Looking back on this time, Goethe observes: 'But as I truly never could succeed I at last took to laughing at myself, threw away these hypochondriacal crochets, and determined to live' (quoted in Alvarez, 1972:209).

When I reflect back on my own experience of how I have coped with difficulties or stresses in my life I can trace one constant in my responses to it – my sense of humour. I do not mean by this that I am funny. Rather, I am referring to a pleasurable cognitive shift in my perspective at times of stress, towards a more playful, imaginative, humorous, state which has enabled me to feel less overwhelmed or persecuted by the events before me and hence more in control of them. Of course, there have also been times when my sense of humour has failed me, or when I really used it to distance myself emotionally from something I should have been attending to. But it has, on the whole, served me well. This is not simply a matter of personal opinion, since there is now some evidence to support the numerous anecdotes hailing laughter as the best medicine. In this chapter, we shall begin by looking at definitions of a mature, or if you like,'healthy' sense of humour and its relationship to narcissism. This will provide a basis for considering the available research evidence for the positive effects of humour on both mental and physical health.

Humour and self-knowledge

Therapists are essentially in the business of self-knowledge and the various obstacles that we erect to protect ourselves from it. Even though we may seek to be understood, we do not necessarily seek self-understanding (Steiner, 1993). This latter implies an active participation and assumption of responsibility in relation to that which needs to be understood. Whether we espouse a belief in a dynamic unconscious or not, most of us would agree that there are aspects of our experience, of our emotional life, that we prefer to put to one side, to keep out of awareness, to suppress or repress. Language games aside, since Freud the notion of a lived deception, resorted to as a protection against the truth glimpsed and quickly disavowed, has been a familiar one. The truth, unacceptable perhaps because of a shrinking from unnameable desires, is relegated to a domain outside of awareness and conscious life is dominated by falsehood. To be human, one might say, is to struggle constantly with an acceptance of who we are, who we are not, and who we may never be. The difficulties inherent in this task are well encapsulated by Woody Allen's observation that his only regret in life was that he was not someone else. We relieve the psychic pain inherent in this struggle in myriad ways, the less adaptive of which are the hallmark of psychopathology. What is negated, however, does not cease to exist. It is merely relegated elsewhere. Within a psychoanalytic framework it is hypothesized to be relegated to the unconscious domain. This is why Freud aptly referred to the 'return of the repressed', to denote the continued influence of such disowned aspects of our experience on our feelings and behaviour. The idea here is that whatever we disavow comes back to haunt us in different guises. Symptoms encapsulate that which has been disowned and so perpetuate a state of ignorance. The symptoms, if you like, précis the story that we do not want to face up to.

Bergson (1956) argued that the comical person is 'unconscious', that is, we laugh at someone who is ignorant of himself. Conversely, someone who is ignorant of himself laughs only at other people. 'It is not the man who falls down that laughs at his own fall', writes Baudelaire,

> unless he is a philosopher, a man who has acquired, by force of habit, the power of getting outside himself quickly and watching as a disinterested spectator the phenomenon of his ego . . . but cases of this sort are rare (1855:148).

We can but agree with Baudelaire as it is the case that most of us laugh at something in others that is a serious matter to ourselves. Comedy creates an emotional distance from our vulnerabilities and uncertainties.

Jacobson suggests that the comic film permits the onlooker, after an identification,

> to quickly detach himself from the suffering hero, again by unloading on him all the inferiority he dreads himself having, the sins and weaknesses of the past which he has long since mastered (1997:59).

A comic character is usually funny as a function of his flaws. The imperfections help to create emotional distance between the character and the audience so that it is possible to laugh at them. They contribute to our perception of the other as 'other'. The skill in writing comedy, however, lies in the ability to create a character with enough flaws so that he is 'other', but at the same time with enough humanity so that we can identify with what we are supposed to find funny. This is because, as Vorhaus (1994) suggests, comedy is 'truth and pain' – we must therefore identify with the pain at some level to also find it funny.

Because our narcissism often overrules our tolerance for criticism, self-awareness quickly translates mirth into seriousness (Hazlitt, 1885). Hence we seldom laugh as freely at our own shortcomings or absurdities as we do at other people's. This is indeed one way of differentiating a mature sense of humour from the comic. In the comic, the butt of the joke is the other person who is the incarnation of what we once were but need to believe we no longer are. Bollas (1995) argues that in its earliest guises, the sense of humour takes pleasure in inadequacy: 'Mum, the clown, regularly deflates the baby's grandiosity by taking the piss out of him and baby's laughter disarms the frustrated mum' (1995, p. 243). The baby's first laughs may be at his own expense but they are to his benefit as the mother thus imparts the rudiments of a capacity to stand back, to be amused by one's own shortcomings, rather than feel overpowered or persecuted by them. In other words, she teaches the baby how to manage narcissistic blows.

The ability to recognize our own shortcomings and a capacity for forgiveness are intimately related to our ability to adopt a humorous attitude towards our predicament. In turn, this rests on the extent to which we can manage the anxieties inherent in the depressive position (Klein, 1935). Klein hypothesized that in the early months the baby inhabits the paranoid-schizoid position, where splitting mechanisms enable him to cope with the fear that he will be destroyed by a malevolent external force. Through splitting, the baby manages to keep apart 'good' from 'bad' feelings. Around six months the infant enters into the depressive position characterized by a reduction in splitting, which throws a completely different light on to the previous subjective experience of a world sharply divided into good and bad. Though the reduction in splitting allows for more integration, this is at a cost: 'The bad is less bad, but by the same token, the good is less good' (Gomez,

1997:42). As splitting reduces and idealization wanes we have to renounce our own omnipotence and that of our objects while gradually acknowledging our separateness from them. We have to reconcile ourselves to our imperfections, to our responsibility for them, without recourse to another person who can contain our unwanted projections. We also have to come to terms with how loving and hateful feelings cannot be kept apart and so confront our fear that our hate will destroy the person we love. Concern for the object therefore replaces fear and gives rise to a new set of depressive anxieties. Mature humour is born out of a successful mastery of depressive anxieties. This is not to imply that the depressive position is a stage that we move on from, once and for all. Rather, we move in and out of the depressive position and its attendant anxieties. There will therefore be times when, in the grip of more paranoid and persecutory anxieties, our habitual sense of humour may fail us.

A survey of the literature on humour suggests an overall consensus on what constitutes a mature sense of humour: healthy narcissism, a 'broadened view of the self' which can rise above anxieties and the demands of our narcissism (Christie, 1994), modesty (Meltzer, 1978) and ego strength. Poland (1994) quite clearly viewed humour as a gift. He refers to sublimated or 'instinctually neutralized humour' as an indication of what I am referring to here as a mature sense of humour. In Poland's view, such a sense of humour implies:

> sufficient skills of mastery for at least a partial taming of drive urgency, together with a moderation of the narcissistic demands of vanity, a respect for the authenticity of others, and a realization of the grander scale of reality beyond oneself. The quality is of acknowledgement and even acceptance of pain and loss without resignation to depressive hopelessness and hatred (1994:4).

Poland's definition therefore underlines the importance of an acceptance of one's own limitations and the 'givens' of existence without being unduly defensive or arrogant as a means of coping with our predicament. In so-called mature humour we laugh at ourselves *with* others (Pasquali, 1986). It conveys a willingness to share and be open about our vulnerabilities. It invites others to support us through laughing with us at what ostensibly concerns us. Humour manages skilfully to convey both self-effacement and self-importance. It fuses a feeling of superiority with an awareness of insignificance. In a similar vein, Roustang (1987) adopts quite an existential stance and links humour to the acceptance of uncertainty, viewing laughter as 'freedom's possibility to escape from itself'.

Narcissism is the key word that stands out in discussions of mature humour. Narcissism is a term that covers a range of patterns of relating with others (e.g. manipulative behaviour and ruthlessness) and is frequently associated with the personal attributes of grandiosity, arrogance and omnipotence. The 'narcissist' can behave in a superior and aloof manner, giving the impression that he feel himself to be the centre of the universe, even though psychotherapy often reveals deep-seated anxieties. The narcissistic trademarks of hating to be alone although finding it intolerable to be genuinely with others as this stimulates envy, are well known to clinicians. The most important feature of narcissism that is relevant to an understanding of humour is its hatred of self-knowledge. In narcissism, self-knowledge is prevented through the projection of unwanted aspects of the self into others (Symington, 1993). Looking inwards, as this requires putting oneself into question, threatens the narcissistic individual. Being able to stand back, to have perspective, to be able to acknowledge limitations and shortcomings are, as we have seen, the hallmarks of a mature sense of humour. The 'narcissistic envelope' (Symington, 1993), however, precludes the discovery of self-knowledge. The narcissistic person cannot experience, as Klein (1961) suggests, pleasure at discovering something that has been relegated to the unconscious. The 'laughter of recognition' (Bloomfield, 1980), which comes about as a result of a sudden insight into an unconscious aspect of ourselves, eludes the narcissistic person. Rather, they feel persecuted by the existence of an unconscious part of the mind as it exposes the limits of their control. The quality of the humour, in individuals with narcissistic personality structures is quite distinct. Although they may well be appreciators and producers of humour the structure of the humour is frequently one where there is a 'butt' of a joke and they are invariably the 'wit'. However, such a propensity may well be disguised behind apparent self-mocking humour used to deflect attention away from their narcissistic fragility and their envy of other people.

Rob is a forty-six year old writer who has had a measure of success but never really received the acclaim of his father, a respected academic. In many aspects, Rob told me when we first met, his life had been 'good'. He had been married for fifteen years and although they had not been able to have children he felt that both his wife and himself were very fulfilled by their careers. Yet, Rob had been referred to therapy because of frequent headaches which his doctor thought were stress related.

Rob depicted a glamorous lifestyle which stood in sharp contrast to the rather austere and 'serious' atmosphere that he recalled in his family. His father had always valued academic achievement above all else and was faint with praise. His mother had also been an academic and was described as a rather cold woman, whom he remembered as often engrossed in books. In our initial consultation I had asked him if his parents were humorous and Rob had laughed stating quite categorically that he had no memories of laughter in their household. In fact, he added, one of the many differences between his parents and himself was a sense of humour which he possessed and they lacked. He told me that his writing was often witty.

When Rob first started therapy he was clearly anxious and concerned with his perception of the imbalance of power in our relationship but covered this up by referring to jokes about psychoanalysis and psycho-analysts. Humour was then used both to manage his anxiety about his vulnerability and to criticize me covertly. He also often used to joke about his own problems. Once, when reflecting on his need to be knowledgeable and to be recognized for his contribution, he remem-bered a line by Woody Allen who observes that he is astounded by people who want to know about the creation of the universe when it's so hard to find one's way around Chinatown. Rob laughed heartily as he told me this witticism and then quickly moved on to describing a piece of writing he was working on. He went into considerable detail and commented, in a somewhat throwaway manner, that it would 'probably be difficult for you to really understand this because it is too detailed'. The Woody Allen quote he had recounted earlier could have been taken as an indication of his recognition of his own need to run before he could walk. This was certainly the case in therapy as Rob could not tolerate being in the position of the one who needed help. However, in the session reported here, the witticism was followed very quickly by an exchange between us that revealed his rather contemptuous attitude towards me. Humour in this instance was therefore not used to acknow-ledge limitations and so come to terms with that knowledge. Rather, it reflected Rob's way of displaying himself so as to be admired as someone who had insight and was funny, while also reassuring himself that he did not need me as he was far superior to me.

The contribution of narcissism to healthy adaptation and achieve-ment has not been treated as extensively as its contribution to psychopathology. Heinz Kohut (1966) is an exception to this. He views the narcissistic self as a 'maturationally pre-determined step' in develop-ment. Kohut understands the grandiose phantasy, which is the hallmark of narcissism, as being phase appropriate and he cautions against inter-ference with the development of the narcissistic self which could other-wise contribute to later narcissistic vulnerability. In turn, he sees the latter as resulting from a repression of the grandiose phantasy which is then no longer available to modification through development. Kohut therefore locates the emergence of narcissistic disturbances in the earliest exchanges between the child and his environment. Kohut (1966; 1971) also devoted attention to the transformations of narcissism into new psychological configurations. He believed that such transform-ations though driven by, and dynamically related to, narcissism repre-sent attainments of the ego and should be considered as achievements of the personality. Amongst these achievements Kohut included humour.

He regarded humour as providing us with a vehicle for mastering the demands of our narcissistic self and of the idealized object:

> The profoundest forms of humour . . . therefore do not present a picture of grandiosity and elation but that of a quiet inner triumph with an admixture of undenied melancholy (Kohut, 1966:268).

Self-directed humour indeed opposes narcissistic indulgencies without falling back into a paralysing nihilistic or masochistic retreat (Sacerdoti, 1992). Humour releases us from the perils of vanity by keeping us alert. It forces us to put ourselves in question. Humour's greatest achievement lies precisely in its ability to confer a sense of narcissistic triumph while allowing us to catch a glimpse of our ultimate insignificance in the wider scheme of things (Rose, 1969). It helps us to stay within the confines of reality while upholding the demands of the pleasure principle (Birner, 1994). Although this represents a narcissistic achievement that is adaptive, it is important to remain alert to the possibility that the triumph of narcissism may be no more than a 'hollow victory' if it merely leads to denial and isolation of the narcissistic ego (Haig, 1986).

At its core, humour is a 'critical' faculty (Skynner and Cleese, 1993) as it involves actively looking for incongruity. Jacobson (1997) views the function of ridicule as offering the 'necessary other voice' in man's argument with conceit. According to him, comedy's primary concern is that of cutting us down to size by reminding us that 'we resemble beasts more than gods and we make a fool of ourselves when we forget this' (1997:242). In other words, comedy puts us in our place and is a great leveller. Koestler was clear that the ability to juxtapose subjective and objective frames of mind was central to the development of a critical stance:

> The sudden realization that one's own excitement is 'unreasonable' heralds the emergence of self criticism, of the ability to see one's very own self from the outside, and this by association of subjective experience with an objective frame of reference is perhaps the wittiest discovery of homo sapiens (1964:63).

The power of comedy as a social agent lies precisely in its potential impact on the audience's capacity to question themselves as they recognize features of their own dilemmas or impasses which the comedian depicts in his routine. In this sense it functions as a corrective to pretentiousness and complacency (Meredith, 1956).

Humour and mental health

It would be an oversimplification to suggest that the mere presence of a sense of humour is an indication of mental health. Humorous communication is, after all, the master of many servants. It can unite or divide, illuminate or cover up. It can declare either love or war and frequently speaks of both, presenting as it does a superbly constructed, disguised communication of ambivalent feelings and conflicts. Its relationship to mental health therefore ultimately depends on its source and intent, that is on its emotional quality in the context of interpersonal and intrapsychic communication. The literature is nevertheless consistent in one respect: the capacity to laugh at oneself benevolently represents an important psychological development and in this sense 'mature' humour can be said to be related to psychological adjustment. Several writers have converged on the observation that psychiatric patients have a lowered appreciation of humour compared to so-called 'normal' subjects (Levine and Redlich, 1955; Harelson and Stroud, 1967). This has been particularly noted in patients whose contact with reality is impaired (Roberts and Johnson, 1958). Unfortunately these studies are quite dated and there is a dearth of more recent research in this area.

Freud, as we have seen in earlier chapters, viewed humour as one of the most sophisticated defensive processes available to us. May (1953) argued that humour served the function of,

> preserving the sense of self. It is the healthy way of feeling a 'distance' between one's self and the problem, a way of standing off and looking at one's problems with perspective (1953:61).

In a similar vein Allport noted that 'the neurotic who learns to laugh at himself may be on the way to self-management, perhaps even to cure' (1968:92). In his view, no one could be said to be in good health unless they possessed the capacity to laugh at themselves (Allport, 1968). A sense of humour has been recognized as a coping mechanism that facilitates the management of the various stresses we all encounter in our lives (Martin and Lefcourt, 1983). Poon et al. (1992) note that all adults who have aged successfully typically reveal a good sense of humour and refer to it as a positive coping strategy. Solomon (1996), in a pilot study of 155 adults aged 20 to 94, also found a positive correlation between humour, ageing well and personal control. She found that the more people created humour, the more satisfied they felt with their lives and this, in turn, reinforced their use of humour. In her study better health was positively related to the use of humour to reduce problems, the recounting of funny real-life stories and the appreciation of satire and irony. The capacity to adopt a humorous outlook on life, we might say, is a particular coping style, a way of protecting oneself from narcissistic blows. Gallows humour is a good example of this since it is a response to a crisis where the problem is not avoided but is made light of through humour. Overall, the literature suggests that the capacity to laugh at a problem shields us against the slings and arrows of misfortune and the exigencies of life, with all its attendant anxieties.

The anecdotal evidence for the beneficial effects of humour has instigated more formal research addressing its moderating impact between life stress and psychological well-being as well as its more direct effects on mood and aggression. In an interesting series of studies Martin and Lefcourt (1983) researched the effect of humour on the relation between negative life events and current levels of mood disturbance (e.g. depression, anger, fatigue). In their studies those participants who scored highly on measures of humour obtained a lower correlation between life events and mood compared to those participants who obtained lower humour scores. The authors conclude that the impact of humour was demonstrated when lower mean mood disturbance scores were obtained by those participants who reported high levels of negative life events alongside high humour scores, than those who had lower mean humour scores. Having a sense of humour is not correlated with less stress but with an enhanced ability to cope with it. Although humour emerged as a critical variable modulating the impact of stress on mood, the precise way in which humour exerts its effects is complex. Merely noticing potentially humorous situations was found to be insufficient in the studies by Martin and Lefcourt. Rather, for humour to modulate the effect of stress the individual needs to place a high value on humour and be capable of generating it in the stressful situation itself.

Generating humour is more psychologically protective than simply appreciating it (Prerost, 1989; Overholser, 1992). Newman (in Clay, 1997), using Martin and Lefcourt's humour scales, explored whether it is possible to teach people to use humour to manage stress. She randomly assigned eighty participants to two groups, both of which were made to watch a silent video depicting a gruesome industrial accident. In one group participants were asked to narrate the video 'seriously' while the other group was asked to narrate it humorously. All participants performed this task in a room on their own. Heart rate, skin conductance and skin temperature were measured before, during and after each individual's narration. Whether they were high or low in a sense of humour scores those participants who had been asked to create humorous narratives showed significantly lower negative affect, tension and physiological arousal in response to the horrific video. Newman acknowledges that the experimental situation in which participants were asked to redefine stress as humorous does not of course exactly mirror an equivalent real-life situation, nevertheless the study does lend some support to the notion that reframing events humorously is adaptive. Perhaps even more reassuringly, Newman observes that 'what matters is the ability to make yourself laugh' (in Clay, 1997:2). As she listened to the humorous narratives, though experienced as funny by the narrators, they were not necessarily deemed funny by her.

Although Martin and Lefcourt's study was one of the first of its kind and is persuasive, its findings have not been consistently replicated. Moreover, the measures of humour which were used consisted of a combination of scales that do not necessarily measure the same construct. In a study attempting to replicate their findings but using a more adequate sample, Porterfield (1987) found that although there was evidence that negative life events were significantly related to depression, there was no evidence that sense of humour moderated that relation. Instead, participants with higher humour scores reported significantly less depression than did those with lower scores, regardless of their life stress levels. This suggests that a sense of humour mitigates depression directly rather than helping people manage stressful situations. Porterfield thus proposes a 'main effect model' of humour rather than the 'buffering model' proposed by Martin and Lefcourt.

Using a prospective design, Nezu et al. (1988) report that even though humour correlates with a reduction of depression following stressful experiences, there is no correlation with measures of anxiety when more complex regression analyses are computed. This is surprising, given that both depression and anxiety are components of stress. Further support for a link between depression and humour comes from a study which found that exposure to humorous stimuli on audiotapes decreased depression induced by observing depressing slides to the base level, an effect that did not occur in a control group that was not exposed to humour (Danzer et al., 1990). However, not all studies support the effect of humour on depression. Safranek and Schrill (1982), for example, in a study of undergraduate students found that neither humour use nor humour appreciation moderated the effects of the life events on depression (measured by the Beck Depression Inventory) and anxiety (measured by the State-Trait Anxiety Inventory). Likewise, Anderson and Arnoult (1989) examined the role of various moderators of stress, including humour, but found that it did not exert any effect on depression in the face of stressful situations. To counteract some of the problems associated with the humour measures used in much research in this area, Thorson et al. (1997) developed a new multidimensional humour scale. They found that scores on this scale were positively correlated to optimism and self-esteem and negatively with depression. In another study, six months following breast cancer surgery, the tendency to use humour as a coping mechanism reliably predicted less distress in women and mediated the relationship between overall optimism and reduced post-surgery distress (Carver et al., 1993).

In addition to an interest in the effects of humour on stress and mood, research has focused on its function as a coping mechanism for the management of anger and aggression. In a study by Singer (cited in Gelkopf and Kreitler, 1996:240) Black adult participants were exposed to material discrimination against Black people. Subsequent exposure to humorous material was followed by a reduction in the participants' levels of aggression and tension, irrespective of the affective content of the humorous material (i.e whether aggressive or neutral). Prerost (1987) used proced-ures to arouse aggression and three stimulus conditions (aggressive humour, neutral humour and non-humorous material) in a sample of undergraduate women. His results suggest, however, that providing an incompatible response to aggression, such as humour stimuli, had no effect on aggression. In a study of the use of humour on a psychiatric ward, a measure of humour as a coping strategy was not correlated with verbal hostility, behavioural hostility or anger in schizophrenic patients (Gelkopf and Sigal, 1995). This indicates that at least in schizophrenic patients a humorous outlook on life does not imply less hostility or anger, and that the multiple occasions for catharsis provided by a humorous outlook on life do not suffice to reduce hostility. Nevertheless, exposing a whole ward of hospitalized schizophrenics to humour during a three-month period reduced verbal hostility in that ward as reported by the nurses (Gelkopf et al., 1993). The authors suggest that these results may be understood as evidence that humour may have exerted its effects on the staff as they were also exposed to the humorous videos through working on the ward. Some evidence supports the latter hypothesis because, in the same study, social support by staff (measured by an independent questionnaire) improved for that ward during the experimental period even though the effects did not generalize to support received from other patients or families. Although some studies do report an effect of humour on aggression, overall the results are inconclusive.

The evidence for the moderating effects of humour on stress and mood is at present somewhat mixed, but more encouraging. If humour does exert an effect on these variables, this poses the question of how this might be achieved. Although there appears to be a relationship between humour and more successful coping, the specific cognitive processes that underlie these effects require elaboration. Intuitively, the mood-altering and stress-moderating effects of humour are easy enough to recognize when we reflect on our own experience. The power of a satisfying comedy film to affect our mood, even if only temporarily, requires no elaboration. Similarly, the emotional release facilitated by humour and laughter during a stressful episode is a common experience. If we are undergoing a personal crisis the opportunity to share our concerns and laugh about them with a friend or partner often alleviates our subjective experience of the stressful event. This may be partly because humour allows us to gain control by reappraising the event as less threatening (Solomon, 1996). Goffman (1967), for example, points out that an embarrassing experience can be reframed as 'not serious' by making light of it and so increases the person's control over an event that was experienced, and is recalled, as aversive. In other words, even if we cannot change or control certain events in our lives, humour allows us to reconstrue that which we cannot alter and thereby increases our sense of being in control. In turn, perceived personal control is associated with better emotional well-being, better health and enhanced ability to cope with stressors (Thompson and Spacapa, 1991). Dixon (1980) proposes that humour involves elaborating alternative meanings and hence serves to reduce their potentially threatening nature. He suggests that humour may have evolved as an adaptive response to stress. Dixon argues that humour increases our ability to deal with stress by achieving a level of arousal appropriate to the task, removing restrictions in cognitive processing and facilitating the generation of new solutions. This may, in phantasy or in reality, diminish the threat posed by the stressor. The suggestion is that humour gives us perceptual flexibility through increasing our cognitive control.

The stress-buffering effect of humour may well be a function of humour's relation to coping mechanisms (Gelkopf and Kreitler, 1996).[25] One study involving undergraduates found that their scores of a sense of humour were related to particular coping styles, that is, they were positively correlated with minimization and suppression, and negatively correlated with blame, mapping and reversal (Rim, 1988). The most likely pathway for humour's effects is through the cognitive reappraisal of the stressor, which facilitates a reattribution, or reframing, of the problem. Mishkinsky (1977, quoted in Gelkopf and Kreitler, 1996) defined humour as an attitude enabling us to modify concepts, beliefs, situations and objects and reorganizing their meaning in more than one dimension. Responding to a stressful event with humour depends, therefore, on the individual's capacity to entertain different perspectives on a problem, detecting the presence of possible incongruities. Perception of incongruity and its resolution, as we saw in Chapter 1, has been identified as an essential component of a sense of humour. Because incongruity includes discrepancies, contrasts, and even conflicts, dealing with incongruity actually involves problem-solving.

Another important process involved in humour is 'shifting'. This refers to the transformation of the cognitive process or content which is salient at the time (e.g. changing an attitude or point of view) (Gelkopf and Kreitler, 1996). Kreitler et al. (1988) showed that understanding a humorous stimulus involves different types of shifting. The most significant shift is from the habitual meaning of the stimuli to a new sphere of contents which, in turn, facilitates the assumption of alternative perspectives on a situation or problem. This is accompanied by a relatively smaller shift in evaluating the major protagonist(s), usually from neutral or positive to less positive, which provides a more immediate emotional gratification leading to catharsis. The shifts are responsible for both the production of the incongruity and its resolution.

---

[25] I should like to acknowledge the very thorough review by Gelkopf and Kreitler (1996) as this provided me with numerous reference sources.

Nilsen et al. (1987) concluded that humour forces the mind into modes of thinking that are highly suited to effective problem-solving since they are investigative in orientation and concerned with trial and error. The quality of humour productions is correlated positively with creativity and ideational fluency (Brodzinsky and Rubien, 1976; Ziv, 1984) and humour comprehension is correlated with factors of general and verbal intelligence (Feingold and Mazella, 1991). Moreover, a sense of humour has been related to specific cognitive processes and contents. Humour comprehension and appreciation have been related positively to mental flexibility (Morreall, 1991), as manifested also in the positive correlation between rating of jokes as funny and speed of mental rotations (H. Johnson, 1990).

Effective problem-solving ultimately relies on a capacity to be receptive to new ideas. It also involves being able to recognize that we can 'get it wrong' without being discouraged by this. Likewise, using humour effectively rests not only on some of the cognitive skills mentioned above but also on a capacity to be open to feedback and criticism. As Sypher put it:

> No society is in good health without laughing at itself quietly and privately; no character is sound without self scrutiny, without turning inwards to see where it may have overreached itself . . . so the comic spirit keeps us pure in mind by requiring that we regard ourselves *sceptically*' (1956:242, my italics).

A rigid maintenance of the sceptical approach to oneself and to life may of course reflect an unduly suspicious disposition or a difficulty or fear in committing oneself to any one idea or pursuit in life. However, at its best, the sceptical attitude allows for some distance between that which may concern us and our own needs and preoccupations. The creative use of humour enables us to manage a state of not knowing, which does not represent a rejection of knowledge *per se* but rather represents a genuine quest for knowledge (Sacerdoti, 1992). To be able to question, to doubt, requires a degree of emotional disengagement or 'distancing'. It reflects the capacity to shift into a different mental gear, which facilitates a qualitatively distinct appraisal of situations, or experiences, that are often highly emotionally charged. The ability to be humorous requires a degree of disinhibition, a loosening of linguistic associational activity, an open-minded cognitive and emotional stance. The value of humour rests on its ability to tap 'multiple levels of meaning' (Richman, 1996). As du Pre put it:

> Like the popular optical illusion in which one can see a vase or two faces, but not both at the same time, humour may have a Gestalt effect that leads us – if only momentarily – into perceiving the situation in a radically different way (1998:183).

Humour is undeniably the hallmark of a particular attitude to life. Thus, it has long been noted that humour reflects a playful attitude, 'involving 'non-seriousness' and light-heartedness (Arieti, 1976; Bateson, 1958). 'The extent to which our sense of humour', writes Mindess,

> can help us maintain our sanity is the extent to which it moves beyond jokes, beyond wit, beyond laughter itself. It must constitute a frame of mind, a point of view, a deep-going, far-reaching attitude to life (1971:10).

Humour has indeed been related to specific attitudes. Of particular note is 'distancing', which denotes a capacity to stand back from issues pertaining to the self thereby allowing a more dispassionate view of them and so enables us to transcend more automatic and habitual ways of responding (Goldstein, 1976). In a study of humorous exchanges amongst adolescent girls, Fine (1984) found that humour, through its distancing properties, provided a means for exploring the meanings and boundaries of identities and situations.

It is generally held that laughter accompanies the dissociation of the experience of distress. Dissociative phenomena are best thought of along a continuum that covers states such as day-dreaming or distraction to more severe changes in memory and identity. The humorous space we can enter at times of distress represents a mild form of dissociation. Keltner and Bonanno argue that laughter accompanies:

> the dissociation from potentially distressing arousal brought about by a positive reinterpretation of the source of distress . . . studies of differences in humour proneness consistently find that people predisposed to humour do indeed dissociate from distress (1997:688).

Interestingly, in a study comparing comedians and non-comedians, Salameh (1983) found that comedians were more likely to elaborate comic themes when asked to make up stories about tragic pictures they were shown, thereby displaying a tendency to translate the tragic into the comic.

Using humour in stressful situations may also be beneficial to us because it serves to enlist social support from others (Nezu et al. 1988). Those who generate humour are generally well-liked. Gelkopf and Kreitler (1996:241) point out that 'a funny individual will receive more support, be more popular, and is more likely to assume a position of leadership'; (see also Goodchilds, 1959; Dixon, 1980; Ziv, 1984). It is often observed that though we may be inclined to confess to all sorts of crimes and misdemeanours, few of us would own up to lacking a sense of humour (Bergler, 1956). This reflects an acknowledgement that humour is an attractive quality that reaps interpersonal benefits. If through humour we are more attractive, then people are likely to seek out our company and this may make them more likely to support us and so lessen the experience of stress. Moreover, it may preclude a withdrawal into a depressive state by ensuring the availability of interpersonal support that has been shown to be so critical in the recovery from depression (Klerman et al. 1984). In a very interesting and methodologically sound study, Keltner and Bonanno (1997) researched the intrapersonal and interpersonal correlates of laughter during bereavement. Their guiding hypothesis, confirmed by their results, is that Duchenne laughter (see Chapter 2) accompanies dissociation from distress and enhances social relationships. They found that discrete episodes of Duchenne laughter relate to a behavioural measure of dissociation from distress,[26] even though the correlational nature of the study does not permit an elucidation of the underlying mechanisms that account for the observed relationship. Furthermore, the authors found that Duchenne laughter was associated with reduced ambivalence towards a current significant other, with more positive emotions in observers and with observers' judgements that the bereaved participant was healthier, better adjusted, less frustrating and more amusing, thereby lending support to the notion that laughter enhances social bonds. Keltner and Bonanno further emphasize:

> These findings are particularly noteworthy when one considers that laughers and non-laughers differed neither in their personality nor in the other emotions that they displayed, and that observers had only participants' expressive behaviour, and not their speech, on which to base their inferences and responses (1997:698).

The humour response may in fact be understood as a kind of positive mood. Moods are:

> affective states that differ from emotions (which are usually more intense), are involved in the instigation of self-regulatory processes and are capable of changing a broad range of our affective, cognitive and behavioral responses, many of which are unrelated to the mood-precipitating event (Gelkopf and Kreitler, 1996:247).

It is something of a truism, with considerable research to back it, to say that positive mood has a range of effects on our functioning. It has been found to contribute to increased feelings of self-esteem and sense of self-efficacy (Kavanagh and Bower, 1985; Salovey, 1987, quoted in Gelkopf and Kreitler, 1996), enhanced positive evaluation of the enjoyment of activities and events (Carson and Adams, 1980), more optimistic outlook (Mayer and Bremer, 1985), enhanced positive predisposition toward others including strangers (Veitch and Griffitt, 1976), and heightened

---

[26.] When relatively little negative emotion is reported despite indications of threat-reactivity in other response domains, such as physiology (e.g. heart rate), emotion-focused, avoidant coping processes, such as emotional dissociation, are inferred.

likelihood of helping others (Dovidio, 1984). Gelkopf and Kreitler suggest that these and similar effects of mood are explained 'by means of the congruence between affective states and cognitive processes: mood elicits concepts and memories related to it associatively' (1996:247). Humour may therefore exert its effect by inducing a positive mood.

Even though the actual effects of humour may themselves be short-lived they may nevertheless set in motion a series of cognitive and emotional shifts which accrue more significant benefits for the individual. The nature of the broader implications of using humour as a coping strategy is an interesting and related question. For example, Overholser (1992) noted an effect on self-esteem. He found that high scorers on the 'Coping Humour' scale also reported higher self-esteem. In a study of the self-concept in adolescent humorists, Ziv (1981) did not find any differences between the humorist and non-humorist boys on self-concept measures. Of note, however, were the significant differences he found between the self-concept of the girl humorists as opposed to the non-humorist girls. The former's self-concept emerged as male oriented (according to prevailing stereotypes). It would then appear that for girls at least, humour was a characteristic of liberation from the female stereotype. A study by Kuiper and Martin (1993) lent some support to the notion that the effective use of humour enhances our view of the self leading to a more positive self-concept. Using discrepancy between ideal and actual self-concept as an indicator of well-being they found that greater levels of humour are linked to a more positive and healthier self-concept. More specifically, they demonstrated that increased humour was significantly related to:

* reduced actual–ideal self concept discrepancy
* greater temporal stability of the actual self-concept
* increased positive self-content (sociability) and decreased negative self-content (depressive personality)
* reduced endorsement of extreme and rigid standards for evaluating self-concept.

Although these results confirm our expectations, the results are purely correlational. Consequently, they need to be considered in light of the difficulty in ascertaining whether it is humour *per se* which contributes to self-esteem or a more positive self-concept, or whether people with high self-esteem are more likely to feel, and to be, humorous. It is therefore not possible to determine humour as a causal factor in the development of a positive self-concept or whether the latter is a necessary prerequisite for the development of enhanced humour.

Notwithstanding the shortcomings of the research reviewed in this section, and our partial understanding of how humour exerts its effects on psychological well-being, the evidence overall is encouraging. Moreover, there is also evidence to suggest a moderating influence on physical well-being, and we shall now turn our attention to this.

Humour and physical health

The healing properties of laughter have long been recognized. In the thirteenth century laughter was used as an anaesthetic for surgical procedures. Five hundred years ago it was prescribed as a treatment for colds and depression (Erdman, 1993). In the seventeenth century the physician Sydenham observed that a good clown exerted a more benefi- cial influence upon the healing of a whole village than 'twenty asses laden with drugs'(quoted in Adams, 1994). In the nineteenth century the physician Spencer conceived of laughter as a restorative mechanism acting through the release of excess tension. In one South American rainforest community a 'festival of laughter' is held when one of its members is ill in the belief that this will enhance healing (Holden, 1993). Ferenczi was also familiar with the belief that laughter possesses healing qualities:

> In classical times, doctors whose teachings were held in esteem for a thousand years quite seriously recommended that patients should be stimulated to laughter in order for their diaphragm to be shaken and their digestion promoted (1911:332).

The ancient Biblical maxim that 'a merry heart doeth good like a medicine' (Proverbs, 17:22) has indeed gained increasing support within medicine. Ellis (1978) described humour as the 'wonder drug'. Hunter 'Patch' Adams, the unusual American doctor whose life story has been recently represented in a film (*Patch Adams*, Universal Pictures, 1999), pioneered the medicinal value of humour. A subversive figure amongst the medical fraternity, Adams believes that compassion, humour and empathy are as essential to physicians as the physical treat- ments they dispense. His personal style is provocative and his own background as a former psychiatric patient on the verge of suicide is possibly significant in the development of his tenacious interest in laughter therapy. Such speculations are inevitable and will undoubtedly lead some people to question his approach, which is truly 'alternative'. Personal psychopathology and unconscious motivations are, however, not sufficient grounds for discrediting someone's vision. If it were the case, the views of some quite brilliant therapists would also be questionable.

Adams is an important figure because he dared to challenge medical orthodoxy, which takes itself far too seriously. In so doing it overlooks the very reason for its existence, namely to care for patients whose humanity and need for compassion should never be secondary to the technical procedures they may also require. In other words Adams' approach emphasizes the importance of remembering that doctors along with all other healthcare professionals are treating people and not diseases. According to him, laughter and humour are ways in which the doctor's and the patient's shared humanity can be actualized (Adams, 1994). In addition, Adams' venture, the Gesundheit Institute, is a laudable attempt to provide a free, full-scale, hospital and healthcare community, where formal treatments will be offered alongside alternative therapies and humour. Not surprisingly, Adams admits that:

> The focus on humour in medicine at Gesundheit Institute has often been declared a major deterrent to our getting funds. Still, I insist that humour and fun (which is humour in action) are equal partners with love as key ingredients for a healthy life (1994:66).

Adams' work has inspired that of others such as Joel Goodman, founder of the Humour Project in America. Goodman emphasizes that it is not the case that doctors should be comics or clowns but rather that,

> humour as a health intervention is not about gags, jokes or punchlines. It's an attitude, a way of being open, a gentle embracing of reality. We encourage professionals to invite smiles and laughter, not to try to make patients laugh (quoted in Holden 1993:48).

Perhaps the best personal account of humour and laughter's healing qualities was offered by Norman Cousins' (1979, 1985) experience of recovery from a serious collagen disease (ankylosing spondylosis). In his book, Cousins describes how ten minutes of belly laughter had an anaesthetic effect which enabled him to have at least two hours of pain-free sleep without recurrence to any analgesic medication. He also reports a drop of at least five points in the erythrocyte sedimentation rate (ESR), an indicator of the severity of an inflammation or infection, during laughter. Cousin's self-medication of Marx Brother's films may provide only anecdotal evidence. His account was nevertheless enthusiastically embraced by the medical fraternity, so much so that even though he was not himself a physician he was offered a position within UCLA as an Honorary Professor of Medicine, Law and Human Values (Buckeley, 1990, quoted in du Pre, 1998). Cousin's account captured the interest of researchers who have attempted to study the psychophysiological function of laughter and its impact not only on psychological, but also on physical, health. This interest comes as no surprise since contemporary understandings of physical disease do not ignore the contribution of psychological factors both to the aetiology and outcome of physical disease (Erskine and Judd, 1994).

In a purely physical sense, laughter leads to the activation of muscles, an increase in heart rate, and an amplification in respiration with a concomitant increase in oxygen exchange. Following laughter, relaxation occurs, blood pressure falls to pre-laughter levels, digestion is enhanced, muscle tension decreases and pain is reduced in response to endorphin release. Some of these physiological changes mirror some of the benefits accrued through physical exercise. Fry and Savin (1988) estimate that the impact on the heart of twenty seconds of laughter is comparable to three minutes of rowing, and laughing one hundred times per day is roughly equivalent to spending ten minutes chugging away on a rowing machine.

The belief in humour's healing properties lies behind the growth of so-called 'laughter clubs' which have mushroomed throughout India. In March 1995 Dr Kataria invited a handful of people in Bombay to start laughing together. At first each would take it in turns to tell a joke so as to start off the communal laughter. The participants reported feeling better – though this has not been formally measured – after 10-20 minutes of laughter every morning. This small group soon grew in numbers; presently laughter clubs contain 25-80 people. There are around 300 such clubs throughout India. One factory in Bombay organizes laughter clubs first thing in the morning for its workers. Nowadays, participants no longer use jokes to start laughing – they just start, capitalizing on laughter's contagious nature. Each laughing session starts with a deep breathing exercise similar to Pranayam in Yoga which helps in increasing the vital capacity of the lungs and assists laughter. Then, everyone chants 'ho, ho, ha, ha' gradually increasing the speed of the chant and looking at each other's faces. The chanting exercise is called *kapalbhati* and is characterized by the rhythmic movement of the diaphragm and abdominal muscles. In addition to the actual physical relaxation that the communal laughter promotes, the clubs are also exploiting the well-recognized interpersonal benefits of laughter. Laughter enhances social relations by producing pleasure in others through simple contagious processes (Provine, 1992).

Before you decide not to renew your membership of the local gym and just watch re-runs of *Fawlty Towers* or start up your own laughter club, it is advisable to read on, since the relationship between humour and physical health is intricate. To begin with, it is important to bear in mind that studies, on the whole, are evaluating the impact of the behavioural response of laughter but frequently write about laughter and humour interchangeably. Clearly, most laughter is a response to something perceived to be humorous. Nevertheless, we may perceive something to be funny and yet not laugh out loud and it is unclear as to whether this in itself produces beneficial physiological changes. Although the more direct beneficial effects of laughter on the body are important, if humour does exert an effect on physical well-being it is likely that it operates in a more complex manner which needs to take into account some of the cognitive effects that were reviewed earlier. For example, people who perceive a humorous aspect to a situation are less likely to appraise it as threatening and therefore may not respond with a great increase in sympathetic-adrenal arousal. It may also be that even if experiencing stress, if people are able to derive humour from other aspects of their lives, the positive emotions associated with humour may counteract the negative emotions engendered by stress, thereby minimizing any stress-related arousal increase (Martin and Dobbin, 1988). It would appear, as mentioned earlier, that it is not just laughter but the capacity to produce humour under stressful situations that is important.

The use of humour to reduce stress and improve health by producing changes in the immune system has been the subject of more recent research. The enhancement of immune system functioning has been hypothesized to be one of the possible mechanisms for the reported health-related effects of laughter. There is now evidence that psychological factors exert an effect on the resilience of the immune system and therefore our resistance to disease. Immunoglobulin A (IgA) is a natural substance that allows the body to fight virus. It represents the body's first line of defence against upper respiratory viral and bacterial infections. Studies have shown that IgA can act to immobilize or inhibit the adherence of antigens, which may reflect its primary mode of protective action (Dillon and Totten, 1989). Taking saliva samples can test IgA levels. Several studies have shown that IgA levels are increased when participants (both adults and children) have been made to watch a humorous film (e.g. Martin and Dobbin, 1988; Lambert and Lambert, 1995). Dillon and Totten (1989) found that 'coping humour' (as measured by a scale of both humour production and appreciation) was related inversely to the incidence of upper respiratory infections in mothers and newborns and that this was correlated with IgA levels in the saliva and breast milk of mothers. Martin and Dobbin (1988) found decreased IgA levels during stressful life events in people termed 'low humour users' compared to 'high humour users' whose levels of IgA remained constant even in the midst of a crisis. More recently, in a more comprehensive study using larger samples, and with a variety of humorous and control films to test the generalizability of their results, McClelland and Cheriff (1997) demonstrated that humour arousal increased IgA levels significantly in college students exposed to humour films. In their study, a good sense of humour, measured as a trait, was associated with higher baseline levels and with greater increases in IgA levels in response to a humour-arousing film. They propose that:

> The most likely explanation of why and how humour affects IgA is that one or more positive emotional experiences, created probably in several ways, but not sensitively reflected in self-reports of moods, serve to enhance IgA through release of a hormone (1997:343).

Using psychoneuroimmunology as a framework, Berk et al. (1989) found that exposure to a humorous video was associated with a reduction of serum levels of cortisol, epinephrine (adrenaline) and growth hormone, all of which have implications for the reversal of the neuroendocrine and classical stress hormone response. M. Bennett (1994; 1997) used a slightly bigger sample to study the effects of a brief period of mirthful laughter on stress and natural killer (NK) cell cytotoxicity. Thirty-three healthy adults were randomly assigned either to a group which viewed a humorous video, or to a control group which viewed two short video tours. Those who laughed more revealed greater decreases in self-reported stress following the humorous video. Stress scores decreased significantly more in the humour group than in the distraction group. The study, though limited by a comparatively small sample, also showed that merely viewing a humorous video did not significantly affect NK activity. However, mirthful laughter significantly correlated with increases in NK cytotoxicity over baseline values. The relationship between lower stress levels and higher NK activity was demonstrated in all participants regardless of which group they had been assigned to.

In addition to the effects on NK cell activity, other researchers point to the effects of laughter as a relaxant and argue for its analgesic properties. Albeit limited by a very restricted sample, Kelley et al. (1984) found that two children suffering from burns reported reduced pain after exposure to cartoon humour. Other studies have benefited from larger samples. Hudak et al. (1991) found that undergraduate students who watched a humorous video maintained or increased their discomfort thresholds for transcutaneous end-nerve stimulation compared to those who were exposed to a non-humorous video, who decreased their thresholds, especially if they had a weak sense of humour. Aiello et al. (1983) reported that students exposed to an overcrowded situation in limited space suffered less discomfort and reported less fatigue and more vigour when exposed to humorous material than not. In a study of elderly patients suffering from chronic pain Adams and McGuire (1986) found that they requested less pain relievers after watching a series of humorous videos over a six-week period. They also found that the participants reported more positive affects. Dental patients who use more laughter and joking immediately prior to dental procedures also report less stressful subjective experience than those who do not use humour (Trice and Price-Greenhouse, 1986). In this latter study, however, the nature of the surgical procedures the patients were subjected to was not controlled for. It is therefore possible that those patients who did not laugh were expecting far more invasive procedures and their anxiety was more elevated to begin with. Overall the research indicates that those individuals who report using humour as a coping strategy also report fewer health problems (Simon, 1990; Carroll and

Schmidt, 1992). The relationship is unlikely to be straightforward since it is very difficult to isolate the use of humour as the only variable mediating health outcomes.

Laughter: the best medicine?

This review of the research literature could reasonably lead to the conclusion that the results from both psychological and medical research are not only interesting, but also lend some support to the therapeutic value of humour. I would propose that they are, and they urge us to take humour seriously. However, a note of caution should be heeded. Taken as a whole, it is fair to suggest that once the methodological limitations of several of the studies on the psychological benefits of humour are taken into account, the link between humour and depressive affect, for example, is modest. An endemic problem throughout the research in this field is posed by the measures of humour that are used. Most studies rely on self-report measures that focus primarily on the positive aspects of humour (i.e. non-hostile, facilitative rather than negative humour at the expense of others) and they do not always distinguish the ability to appreciate humour from the ability to generate it. Furthermore, many studies use relatively small samples, predominantly constituted by undergraduate students. This begs the question of how generalizable the results are. Several of the studies also rely on the elicitation of humour in an enforced experimental situation that is far removed from the generation of humour in every day life. Research in fact suggests that people have more difficulty making jokes in laboratory studies, and they laugh less heartily than in naturalistic studies (Chapman 1983). More naturalistic observation of spontaneous humorous behaviour, which reflects the multidimensional nature of humour as a construct, is needed. An important consideration is that even the positive results provide us only with purely correlational data. In addition, most studies do not include adequate 'emotion-evoking' controls to allow for a distinction to be drawn between the effects of humour and those effects generated by positive emotions in general (Gelkopf and Kreitler, 1996). For instance, watching a documentary about Mother Teresa was also found to enhance IgA levels when compared to watching a documentary on Fascist activities during World War II. Of interest was the finding that even though participants reported an increase in negative moods following the Mother Teresa documentary, their reaction – positive or negative – did not distinguish between those whose IgA levels increased or decreased. Differences in IgA gains were, however, predicted by high scores on a measure of 'Affiliative Trust'. High scorers on this measure write about co-operative, friendly, trusting, relationships between people (McKay, 1992, quoted in McClelland and Cheriff, 1997). Affiliative Trust expressed after an arousing film is the only psychological state measured to date which is associated with gains in IgA, whether the film is humorous or depicts 'caring' (McClelland and Cheriff, 1997).

A more conservative assessment of the available research suggests that the beneficial effects of humour are most probably more general than specific (du Pre, 1998) and short lived rather then exerting longer-term effects except, possibly, indirectly. In a review of the research on the relationship between humour and physical health, Saper (1987) justly emphasizes the complexity of physiological systems as well as the inevitable variation in people's responsiveness to humour stimuli and differences in severity of the illness reported in the various studies. Such factors need to be borne in mind when we consider the research data and any inferences we draw from them. Where significant effects have been found, the evidence is 'positive but weak' (Gelkopf and Kreitler, 1996) and points to humour as a 'background factor promoting physical health'.

Send in the clowns: humour in healthcare settings

Although the effects of humour on physical and psychological well-being merit further research before we can make more confident assertions about the supposed beneficial effects, this is not sufficient reason to dismiss the therapeutic function of humour in healthcare. This is because humour's function may be most apparent and effective when considered in the interpersonal context of the patient-carer[27] relationship. Indeed, a measure of the current interest in humour within healthcare settings is the development of 'humour programs' in hospitals and other agencies in America (du Pre, 1998) as well as in England (Oppenheim et al., 1997). In Britain, Labour's 'New Opportunities Fund' is to spend £300m over a three-year period on alternative medical therapies such as laughter therapy. Patch Adams has even been invited to speak at a medical conference on this subject (Harlow, 1999). Between 1988 and 1992 the Humor Project in New York awarded grants to launch 125 humour programmes in various healthcare settings. In such programmes carers are encouraged to use humour with patients when it seems helpful and appropriate. Some programmes provide patients with a selection of humorous tapes, books and puzzles and invite clowns or comedians to visit the wards. Overall these projects foster the development of a particular culture where staff are encouraged to engage with patients in a humorous manner.

Intuitively, most healthcare professionals would emphasize the connection between positive attitudes, such as humour, and their relationship to

---

[27.] I am using the term 'carer' to denote any professional involved in the physical or psychological care of patients.

both physical and psychological health. Although research on the application of humour in healthcare settings is sparse, there are encouraging indications that it allows patient and carer to reveal their identifications with each other (Beck and Ragan, 1992), that it helps reduce embarrassment, facilitates rapport and encourages attentiveness (Smith-du Pre, 1992). The use of humour in palliative care has been advocated (Herth, 1990; Dean, 1997) as well as for patients with cancer (Erdman, 1993). There are now reports in the literature, for example, of patients' adaptive use of humour in cancer wards. The use of humour in the context of people faced with death or other losses is not, however, appreciated by everyone. A case in point is the example reported by Erdman (1993) of a young woman who had to undergo a hysterectomy. She describes how this woman approached her predicament with humour. Before the surgery she sent out invitations to friends to her 'coming out party', reassuring them that there would be 'plenty of womb for everyone' and announcing a sale of her contraceptive items. When I shared this account with a few friends and colleagues the response was mixed. Some, like myself, found the account funny *and* poignant. Others described it as 'sick' or as indicating a denial of her predicament. In truth, it is impossible on the basis of the reported vignette to reach any conclusions about the specific use this woman made of humour. We do not know, for example, if she had been able to confront the serious implications of her condition at a young age or whether she was in a state of complete denial, buttressed by humour. Or was her use of humour a constructive way of managing her distress by voicing her feelings in a manner that enabled her to retain some control? Moreover, by using humour to deal with the inevitability of her predicament she may have enabled her friends and family to stay close to her and support her. It is often the case that we create distance between ourselves and those who remind us, through their predicament, of our own vulnerability. If someone can laugh about their predicament it may indirectly also help others to approach what is feared. Given the impossibility of knowing what was really happening in this particular patient's situation, the instinctive responses I obtained to the vignette reflect the very idiosyncratic ways in which we all react to the depicted circumstances. Not everyone is able to metabolize emotional pain into a humorous perspective. Many of us, particularly in certain cultures, are conditioned to respond with sobriety to certain situations. Illness and death are considered to be subjects that need to be approached with sensitivity and seriousness. Indeed they are, but this does not mean that humour has no place in settings where illness, despair and death have to be faced.

The available research, invariably of a qualitative or purely anecdotal nature, describes the use of humour to engender hope, offer perspective and establish a sense of connectedness with self and others. Looking at fourteen terminally ill individuals, Herth (1990) reports that twelve of them identified humour as engendering hope. Other benefits reported

by the participants included a sense of belonging fostered by the experience of shared laughter, physical relaxation and an altered perspective of
otherwise overwhelming situations. Humour can make a valuable contribution in influencing the prevailing culture in institutional settings by
creating a feeling of intimacy in otherwise impersonal and austere
environments which affect the very quality of the interactions between
staff and patients (Kaplan and Boyd, 1965). The emphasis is on
'laughing with' rather than 'laughing at'. In a classic study of the relationships amongst medical staff and between medical staff and patients in a
hospital setting, Emerson (1969) found that humour was used to
address difficult or sensitive topics. For example, it was used by patients
to talk indirectly about their feelings towards staff or the likelihood of
their own death. By using humour, patients referred to these topics
obliquely but the staff, on the whole, grasped their serious import and
responded accordingly. In this sense, humour serves as an effective
'transitional device' (Mulkay, 1988) which smoothes the introduction of
awkward topics:

> Adoption of the humorous mode gives participants a degree of protec-
> tion against the negative consequences of their potentially deviant
> actions and gives recipients a chance to indicate how far they are willing
> to co-operate before either party has become seriously involved (Mulkay,
> 1988:83).

The belief in the therapeutic[28] value of laughter lies behind recent
schemes that have introduced clowns on children's hospital wards. It
would be easy to dismiss the function performed by the clowns purely as
some distraction activity or a noble attempt to introduce a measure of
fun within an otherwise depressing and/or threatening environment for
children who are undergoing medical interventions. Such an assumption is too simplistic, and is contradicted by the available research. Over
the last few years a charitable organization, the Theodora Trust, has
started to introduce clowns in two British children's hospitals. The
clowns, referred to as 'Clown Doctors', visit children on the wards. In
consultation with doctors and nurses they focus on individual children
who have been identified by the staff as needing attention, as well as
contributing more generally to the atmosphere on the ward for all the
children, their families and the staff. They strive, wherever possible, to
see the children at the same time each week in order to introduce a
degree of predictability to their visits, which are eagerly awaited by the
children. Such has been the success of this scheme that it is expanding
world-wide and recently received attention in the *Lancet*. In this article

---

[28.] I am using 'therapeutic' in its broadest sense to include both the psychological
and physical benefits of humour and laughter.

Oppenheim et al. (1997) highlight a number of the important functions performed by the Clown Doctors.

- Firstly, they draw attention to the way in which the clowns help children become integrated into the ward.
- Secondly, the clowns create new places where treatments coexist with fantasy and thereby enhance the children's mastery over what is ultimately a very threatening environment.
- Thirdly, the clowns help the children to transform anxiety. They give the example of how the 'beep beep' of an intravenous drip can be transformed by the clown into a calypso song. The clowns on the wards enact situations, emotions or thoughts that the child may be experiencing so as to help prevent those emotions from being expressed in an uncontrollable manner or being repressed altogether. The clown makes use of the very strategies and modes of communication which are present in the early interactions between mother and baby whereby, through play and fun, anxiety can be successfully worked through (see Chapter 2). Through their clowning performance and their interactions with the children, the clown can assist the child's emotions allowing them to be played out within the boundary of play activity, so that they remain theatrical and playful and not real.
- Finally, the potential positive effects on the families and staff working on the wards should not be ignored since the clowns contribute to the overall atmosphere and culture of the ward.

A comparatively recent study by Locke (1996) emphasizes the therapeutic value of humour in a healthcare setting. She undertook a study of micro-interactional process and emotional displays during professional encounters in a paediatric setting. She focused in particular on 'comedic performances' enacted by the physicians in response to patients' families negative emotions. The performances were not organized around a punchline; rather they consisted of non-verbal behaviour (e.g. playing peek-a-boo or entering a room wearing a stethoscope adorned with fuzzy animals). Locke concludes that these performances generated fun and were incompatible with anxiety, fear and despondence. They fostered a shift towards positive emotions because they acted as cues for optimism. By recruiting more positive feelings, adherence to medical recommendations was also increased. Partaking in moments of fun and laughter also generates a sense of resilience in the patients and their families by reinforcing that they have the capacity to withstand a crisis and still enjoy a moment of fun.

    A qualitative study by Hinds et al. (1987) which looked at fifty-eight adolescent oncology patients emphasizes the latter point. The young patients reported that those nurses who initiated or responded to teasing and entered into playful interactions made them feel more hopeful. In particular they felt that the humour did not distort the reality of their illness; rather they observed that it conveyed to them the nurses' belief in their ability to cope with it.

Not only are there interpersonal benefits to using humour between patients and carers, but research looking at the effects of various types of distracting activities, such as music or occupational activities compared to humour, also suggests quite specific effects (Banning and Nelson, 1987; Gaberson, 1991). Gaberson (1991), for example, found that patients in a preoperative waiting period who listened to humorous audiotapes showed a non-statistically significant trend towards lower anxiety levels compared to patients exposed to tranquil music or no intervention. In the most methodologically sound study of this type, Cogan et al. (1987) were interested in the suggestion made by Walsh (1928) that laughter could assist the healing of wounds and reduce pain after surgery. They demonstrated that laughter acts as a pain antagonist and works as effectively as relaxation training in increasing discomfort thresholds. This study is of note since its design was such that it was able to show that it was laughter *per se* and not simple distraction that contributed to a reduction of discomfort. The research evidence, even though some of it does not reach statistically significant results, at the very least suggests that we should take seriously clowning or the value of more humorous interactions between staff and patients on children's wards. This is an area that warrants further research.

The research, along with the anecdotal evidence emerging from the study of humour on children's wards, is very encouraging. Could such results transfer to settings caring for adult patients? Anyone working with children will testify to how 'natural' it feels to interact with them in more playful ways, even in a professional context; it is indeed difficult to refrain from doing so. In adult settings such exchanges might not seem so appropriate. The more intimate exchange that humour implies may feel at odds with the more formal types of interactions typically sanctioned within the professional context of a relationship between the patient and the nurse/doctor/psychologist. Locke (1996) suggests that in adult settings more adult forms of theatrical displays might be instrumental in engendering positive feelings. Yet such performances would most likely rely on verbal humour that may, paradoxically, reduce the potential efficacy of humour. This is because, as Locke points out,

> The threat-rigidity hypothesis intimates that other forms of expressive displays which require considerable cognitive processing may have difficulty engaging adults who are preoccupied with anxiety and fear (1996:55).

Indeed, a study of laughter in a psychiatric ward for schizophrenic patients found that patients showed a consistent and meaningful preference for non-humorous interventions (Rosenheim et al., 1989). Gelkopf et al. (1993) found that schizophrenic patients who were exposed to humorous videos preferred 'easy' comedy or slapstick to 'complicated' comedy such as Mel Brooks, the Pink Panther or the Marx Brothers. Given some of the hypothesized difficulties in cognitive processing which have been associated with schizophrenia it would appear that the exposure to humour which relies on more complex cognitive processing may create more anxiety, misinterpretation and lead to avoidance rather than having therapeutic benefits.

Moreover, there is some evidence to suggest that our response to humour is affected by how well members of the audience know each other. Pollio and Edgerly (1976) found that comedy which contains more hostility and derision may be enjoyed only if watched with a group of people we know relatively well and with whom we feel relaxed, rather than with a group of people whose 'friendliness' is a matter of ambiguity. Gentler forms of humour (in the study this was comedy performed by Bill Cosby) could be enjoyed either with strangers or with friends. In an acute psychiatric ward setting, where aggression may be prevalent and people do not know each other well, certain types of humour may well be contra-indicated. However, this does not preclude the potential effectiveness of encouraging more humorous exchanges between carers and patients. It may well be that what is largely responsible for the positive effects of humour reported in paediatric settings is not simply the experience of laughter – though this does act as a pain antagonist and may alleviate anxiety – but, more significantly, humour and laughter are effective because they contribute to qualitatively different interactions between carers and patients. The study mentioned earlier by Gelkopf et al. (1993) would indicate that the introduction of humour on a psychiatric ward led to patients reporting higher levels of support from the staff who in fact perceived the patients as less hostile. A plausible hypothesis put forward by the authors is that the humorous films may have had a therapeutic effect on the staff, whose attitudes towards the patients shifted.

A study by Tennant (1990) reported a direct impact of humour on older patients' behaviour. When humour was provided on a regular basis to a group of older adults in supported accommodation, this was associated with a reduction in agitation, compared to a control group who received no intervention. The level of agitation in the participants in the control group actually increased during the experimental period along with decreases in their morale scores. The author notes that this change may have been attributable to the inclement weather which restricted the participants' levels of activity during that time. During the three-week experimental period different forms of humour were offered twice weekly. The preferred forms were a live comedian and situation comedies such as *I Love Lucy*. In addition to the effects on agitation, those exposed to humour reported a decrease in feelings of loneliness and dissatisfaction, though this effect was not statistically significant. Tennant speculates that the humour programme exerted its effects by promoting group cohesion and stimulating social relationships. In other words, humour can alter relationship dynamics.

Laughing matters

Humour is not only of potential benefit to patients – it also helps staff manage the inherent tensions, contradictions and ambiguities of the carer role and function. Humour is a potentially useful strategy for staff whose work may be rewarding but is also, undeniably, emotionally taxing. Staff need good support systems but these are not always available and burnout is a significant problem, especially in nursing (Lemma, 1993; 1999). Humour can provide an effective way of 'letting off steam' under stressful working conditions. The now classic television series *M*A*S*H* illustrates well the use of humour in a medical setting during wartime. It highlights how it is possible to maintain therapeutic attitudes under stressful conditions. Humour, as Kuhlman notes, provides '. . . an emotional language with which . . . staff mark the sense of incongruity that characterises their work' (1988:1085). A study by Coser (1960) revealed that humour was used in particular by more junior staff working in a psychiatric hospital as a way of managing hostile feelings which could not be articulated. Humour is a suitable medium to express conflict because it allows for the expression of aggression without the consequence of more overt behaviour (Stephenson, 1950). Wolf (1988) studied the use of nurses' humour on a ward for terminally ill patients. Much of the recorded laughter was in response to the perceived incompetence of novice nurses. This suggests that the hostility was displaced on to relatively junior staff whose vulnerability became the butt of the joke, thereby relieving the inevitable tensions and anxiety generated by working in such close proximity to death. When the nurses laughed about their patients' predicaments they were poking fun at their own human frailty and at the intimate mixture of the sacred and the profane in their work. Addressing the use of humour amongst occupational therapists, Vergeer and MacRae (1993) note that it facilitates team cohesiveness, deepening and sustaining of interpersonal relationships, enhances job satisfaction and provides an outlet for stress, helping the staff to deal with their frustration.

    In a work context, humour does appear to enhance collaborative practice by functioning as a status equalizer (Dean, 1997) and helps to build teamwork by fostering trust, deflecting anger and defensiveness and increasing tolerance for imperfections. A sense of fun at work in healthcare settings has indeed been proposed as a key factor in worker productivity and resourcefulness (Robinson, 1991). Humour aids communication but also acts as a bridge to 'emotional bonding' among colleagues working in demanding settings such as psychiatric units or emergency wards (Rosenberg, 1991; Buckwalter, 1994; Moran and Massam, 1997). Where the nature of the work offers little opportunity for a sense of accomplishment, humour can act as the vehicle through which staff support each other in solidarity against the odds, as it were (H. Johnson, 1990). Summarizing the function of humour in psychiatric settings Kuhlman notes that 'It proposes an illogical, even psychotic response, to irresolvable dilemmas and offers a way of being sane in an insane place' (1988:1085). As a clinician working in an NHS psychiatric unit, I can but agree. Gallows humour facilitates a symbolic mastery where little or no actual mastery is possible. For this reason it is especially prolific in situations where the very nature of the work presents staff with an insoluble incongruity. To return to the example of the television series *M*A*S*H*, Kuhlman (1988) points out how the doctors were working to treat soldiers injured in the war only to then return them to the battlefield. This incongruity was managed through humour. Although there are several papers emphasizing the value of humour in healthcare settings, its relationship to burnout and, more specifically, to the tendency towards depersonalization of the recipients of care, has not been examined. An interesting question is whether the proverbial gallows humour reflects heightened or reduced sensitivity to crisis situations (Moran and Massam, 1997).

This brief account of the importance of humour in interactions among staff and between patients and staff is no more than a reminder of the importance of good communication skills. There is now ample evidence to suggest that better communication between staff and patients not only improves patient satisfaction, but also benefits the psychological care of patients (Davis and Fallowfield, 1991). The evidence emerging from the relatively embryonic field of humour and health would suggest that humour should be afforded a place in any teaching on effective communication skills between patients and staff. The way sensitive subjects in psychology, medicine or psychiatry are taught may also benefit from being taught in a humorous manner. There is some anecdotal evidence that this can be very effective and models a way of handling sensitive issues in a humorous manner (Watson and Emerson, 1988; H. Johnson, 1990).

Humour, used judiciously and for the benefit of the patient and not our own self-aggrandizement, is a very powerful, yet subtle, form of communication which may ease the difficult exchanges that take place in healthcare settings between staff and the recipients of our care (Warner, 1991; Wormer and Boes, 1997; Isola and Kurki, 1997; du Pre, 1998). As humour is first and foremost a tool for communication, it may enhance relationships and mediate the effects of work-related stress, partly at least because effective communication enhances the likelihood of peer support. The ambiguity of humour lends itself well to interpersonal negotiation in settings that are typically laden with the anxiety both of the patients and of the staff who have to contain the patients' multiple projections.

Chapter 5
The Analytic Double-Act

The natural thing is playing, and the highly sophisticated twentieth century phenomenon is psychoanalysis. Winnicott (1971:41)

But where reality is inconceivable, because it is so monstrous, or the ego is so weak, the only approach may be through the glancing thrusts of the theatre of the absurd . . . or the humour that, like some love, touches the truth lightly to avert madness. Rose (1969:927)

It's no laughing matter

As I embarked on writing this chapter I was faced with an interesting question: would I have ever contemplated publishing my views on the use of humour in psychotherapy if I had still been in training as a psychoanalytic psychotherapist? The answer came to me with little hesitation: no. My primary motivation for holding back would have been my concern about the reception of such views by those responsible for assessing my suitability as a potential psychoanalytic psychotherapist. What might 'they' have thought if they really knew what I thought: 'You do *what* with patients?' This might give you the misleading impression that my training was an Orwellian nightmare, with the 'psychoanalytic thought police' monitoring my every intervention. Alternatively, you may be expecting a confession to the use of some outrageous techniques or you may simply think that I am of a paranoid disposition. On all counts, I think, I shall disappoint you. It is nevertheless fair to say that British psychoanalytic training institutions, although striving to embrace plurality, ultimately take positions on certain theoretical and technical matters. Any student, in any discipline, soon learns what is acceptable and what might be considered less so. And humour and laughter in psychotherapy are often considered to be in the 'less so' category.

My anxiety at the prospect of sharing my views on humour needs to be considered in the prevailing climate conveyed by much – but by no means all – of the psychoanalytic literature. I am referring here to the literature on the nature of the therapeutic relationship in particular, with its emphasis on the interpretation of transference. With regard to the literature dealing with humour explicitly it is of note that of all of the analytic literature I refer to in this book, only six of the references are British. The sparseness of the publications is perhaps a measure of the lack of interest in this area but it may also reflect a shared anxiety about their fantasized reception.[29] As Baker (1993) – a UK-based psychoanalyst – remarks:

> The paucity of the literature on the subject is noteworthy and we might well conclude that this is an area where analysts prefer privacy as in other areas where they might attract criticism (1993:952)

This anxiety was mirrored in the attitudes of therapists asked to comment on their use of humour and laughter in psychotherapy.[30] When I approached 20 therapists who described their orientation as psycho-dynamic about their experiences, 60% reported that they laughed with their patients. Of these, only 10% had ever shared a joke with their patients. Their use of humour was largely restricted to the use of a more light-hearted, playful manner, word play or irony, and their inclination to laugh with a patient if they said something funny. However, of those who made use of humour, the vast majority (80%) said that they would be very reluctant to share such interventions with their supervisors. When asked what would hold them back their replies fell into the following three broad categories reflecting specific expectations of responses from supervisors:

- It would not be considered 'work'.
- Such interventions would be interpreted as attempts to avoid painful affects by both therapist and patient, thereby reinforcing defences and resistance rather than contributing to the analytic process.
- The supervisor viewed the task of psychotherapy as being primarily to interpret the transference and this required the maintenance of as 'neutral' an attitude as possible.

---

[29]. In general, group analysts have written more favourably about humour in psychotherapy (Bloch et al., 1983; Lewis, 1987). Herbert Strean (1994) has also edited a collection of papers broadly supporting the use of humour in psychotherapy.

[30]. These data represent the result of a very small-scale, qualitative, pilot survey carried out by myself. An important limitation of this study, besides its relatively small sample, is the absence of any control for the kind of analytic training received by the participants or any other control group. Its aim was solely to get a flavour of practitioners' attitudes in this field and whether any trends might be apparent.

Of the 40% of therapists who reported never having used humour, two reported that it was because an opportunity had never presented itself and four because they did not feel that there was any advantage in using humorous interventions over standard psychoanalytic interpretations. Only one therapist said they were strongly against the use of humour because it was 'incompatible' with an analytic attitude, though the latter was not defined or expanded upon. Another therapist felt that humour could very easily be misconstrued by the patient and was therefore best avoided.

The small survey I carried out gives at least a flavour of what appears to be happening. Some therapists do use humour but seem reluctant to disclose openly their use of it for fear of disapprobation from colleagues, especially those who are in a relatively more senior position to them. Using humour is somehow not felt to be a legitimate, or useful, part of analytic work. The way in which clinicians write about the analytic encounter confirms this impression. As Pasquali notes:

> I found that the literature does indeed contain descriptions of analytic work which can give rise to the notion that a good analyst does not feel anything beyond a uniform and mild benevolence towards his patients (1986:231).

Likewise, Gedo observes:

> It has been customary to disavow much of the activity that takes place in a successful analysis that is not directed to the analysand's unacceptable wishes or to the unconscious defences against becoming aware of these (1979:35).

Pasquali adds:

> We feel more at ease when we share with our patients what is painful and makes us suffer than what is pleasant and could possibly make us laugh (1986:231).

This point of view is echoed by Bloomfield (1980) who acknowledges therapists' tendencies to 'avoid sharing feelings especially if what is to be shared is amusing, pleasant or laughable' (1980:135).

There does certainly appear to be a primarily suspicious attitude towards humour within psychoanalysis. This is consonant with the prevailing emphasis on the rules of anonymity and neutrality along with a concern to avoid colluding narcissistically with patients or to act out the therapist's own conflicts. It may also be, as Bader speculates, that the observed avoidance of the subject of humour within psychoanalysis reflects that:

> . . . a certain percentage of people drawn to doing analytic work tend to
> have inhibitions about the spontaneous expression of feeling, including
> passion and humour and a certain propensity for depression (1993:48).

It is not difficult to think of practitioners who would certainly fit the
profile depicted by Bader. My own experience of the analytic world is
nevertheless that I would not describe most practitioners as being either
more likely to be depressed or as having difficulty with the expression of
their emotions than one would expect to find amongst therapists of other
orientations. Furthermore, I have not found them to be any more or less
humorous than the average person we are likely to meet outside the field
of psychoanalysis or even in the general population. However, even
though most of the therapists I have in mind do have a sense of humour
they are frequently loath to employ it in the context of psychotherapy as
they feel it challenges the prime neutral stance of the therapist. The
question is therefore not so much whether psychoanalysis attracts
depressed, humourless, people but rather whether psychoanalytic
training and mainstream practice encourage the avoidance of humorous
exchanges as one of several potential ways of 'being with' patients.

In this chapter I consider the prevailing analytic view of the therapeutic relationship in some detail, in order to try to understand the
relative neglect of humour as a valuable communication, and potentially
mutative exchange, between therapist and patient. This will then allow
us to consider its use. It is important to start with an examination of the
assumptions surrounding the notion of the therapeutic relationship
because any consideration of the use of humour in psychotherapy
inevitably raises fundamental questions, such as what are the aspects of
the relationship which are conducive to change, what are the characteristics of an effective therapist and what are the mutative factors in
psychoanalysis. Nowadays, in particular, there is a strong tendency to
uphold the interpretation of transference as the main mutative intervention. The attitudes to humour in psychotherapy are intimately related to
the assumptions practitioners make regarding those processes believed
to be mutative. It is worth noting that these assumptions are sometimes
held with degrees of conviction matched only by the lack of research
evidence to uphold them. I am not suggesting that these assumptions
are necessarily erroneous. Rather, I am suggesting that it is important to
retain an open mind as we endorse concepts that are no more than
hypotheses, however helpful they are to us in understanding our
patients. This, of course, applies in equal measure to the personal views
I shall outline in this chapter.

In the shadow of the transference[31]

Psychotherapy unfolds in a relational context: patient and therapist
meet with both explicit and implicit aims and expectations. Both bring

to the relationship their personal motivations and needs. The analytic literature in particular offers a rich framework that allows for an understanding of the vicissitudes of this unique encounter. Notwithstanding significant differences between the schools of psychoanalysis regarding its aims as a therapeutic treatment and the techniques used to achieve these aims, all schools subscribe to the importance of the patient–therapist relationship. They differ nevertheless in the features of the relationship that are emphasized and held accountable for therapeutic progress and outcome.

The outcome of therapy is held by many, if not most, contemporary psychoanalytic practitioners, to be related to the successful elaboration and re-evaluation of patterns of relating which become accessible through an analysis of transference phenomena, that is, the enactment in the present of implicit schemata or dynamic templates of self–other relationships (Sandler and Sandler, 1997). In this theoretical climate the interpretation of the transference has become the cornerstone of mainstream analytic technique, cutting across theoretical divides (Hamilton, 1996), overshadowing other potentially mutative interventions or interactional processes. In particular, the therapeutic functions of the so-called 'real relationship' have been neglected. This neglect partly explains why humorous exchanges between therapist and patient have also received scant attention. This is so since such exchanges reflect a therapeutic style which conflicts, in some respects, with received wisdom about the analytic persona that is internalized during training. This so-called 'ideal' typically undermines the importance of the real person of the therapist viewing her as the receptacle for the patient's projections and hence distortions.

In referring to the real relationship, I have in mind two aspects 'which must be carefully differentiated, although both are inherent in the concept: first, the realistic nature of the communications between the therapist and the patient; and second, the personality of both therapist and patient as real persons' (Couch, 1979:2). Both aspects are part of the real relationship, which might best be described as:

> The realistic communication between therapist and patient when they are functioning as their real selves; that is, relatively free from transference or counter-transference influences (Couch, 1979:2).

Most therapists readily acknowledge that a 'real' human relationship between therapist and patient is central to the therapeutic enterprise. However, Couch (1979) points out that, starting with Freud himself, clinicians have taken this for granted thereby precluding a theoretical

---

[31.] I should like to acknowledge my gratitude to Dr A. Couch for letting me have sight of one of his unpublished papers on the therapeutic relationship, which greatly assisted me with a review of the literature and influenced the first part of this chapter.

elaboration of its significance as part of the therapeutic process. The 'human foundation' of psychoanalysis is largely underplayed in the literature. This appears to be partly because this awareness is to some extent in:

> a covert and possibly subversive conflict with the explicit conceptual formulations and 'rules' of the analytic process: that is, with the primacy of interpretations, transference and counter-transference reactions, and the concerns for analytic neutrality, anonymity, acting-out, unresponsiveness, and so forth (Couch, 1979:1).

Although the more realistic aspects of the patient-therapist relationship have not been emphasized within psychoanalysis, the importance of the transference relationship most certainly has. As Freud's understanding of the variables that facilitate change in psychoanalysis evolved, the relationship between therapist and patient gradually took centre stage. Freud first used the term 'transference' in 1905b when he was reporting on his own attempts to elicit verbal associations from his patients. He noted changes in the patient's attachment to him developing in the course of treatment that involved strong emotional components. These feelings were regarded as transferences coming about as a consequence of a 'false connection'. He came to see transferences as new editions of old impulses and fantasies aroused during the process of psychoanalysis, with the therapist replacing some earlier person. At first this new discovery disturbed Freud. He saw it as an unwanted complication in his new technique. But he soon capitalized on his former so-called 'error' to formulate the major pillars of psychoanalytic technique: namely, the analysis of transference and resistance. In 1909 he remarked that transference was not just an obstacle to psychoanalysis but might play a positive role as a therapeutic agent. Later he concluded that it was in fact necessary for any psychoanalytic cure. Patients who were unable to develop a transferential relationship were not thought to be treatable by psychoanalysis.

Since Freud, there has been a strong tendency within psychoanalysis towards a widening of the concept (Sandler et al., 1973). Some therapists view all aspects of the patient's relationship to the therapist as transference (see for example Joseph, 1985). Often accompanying such a position is the belief, expressed originally by Strachey (1934), that the most effective interpretations are transference interpretations. There appears to be a continuum along which therapists broadly situate themselves on this question. This ranges from those who believe in the 'total transference' and who focus almost exclusively on the here-and-now transference interpretation, and those who draw a clear distinction between real and distorted aspects of the relationship and whose range of interventions includes so-called 'extra-transference' interpretations (Hamilton, 1996).

Although the analysis of transference is considered nowadays to be at the heart of analytic work, it is also a powerful dynamic. It is believed to be part of what drives the relationship. A patient can therefore also be a transference object for the therapist and can arouse in her feelings that are inappropriate to the present relationship. Countertransference, the phenomenon accounting for the therapist's reactions to her patient, has been variously defined. At first Freud used it to denote the therapist's 'blind spots' and own transference to the patient. Subsequent formulations broadened the concept to the inappropriate emotional responses created in the therapist by the patient's transference material and role expectations. In more contemporary, especially Kleinian, usage, it denotes all of the feelings aroused in the therapist by the patient. In other words, there has been a shift from seeing countertransference as something which interferes with technique, to viewing such responses by the therapist as a means of understanding the patient's unconscious communications, thereby acting as a direct guide for analytic interpretations of the current material.

The concepts of transference and countertransference represent one of Freud's most important and inspired contributions. He was the first therapist to recognize emotional involvement with the patient. He was also the first to theorize on it. However, it has been suggested that he was frightened by that involvement and thus tended to defend himself from it (Carotenuto, 1986; Smith, 1991; Langs, 1976). This is, of course, only speculative. However, it is the case that Freud's original concepts admit the therapist's emotional involvement but at the same time distance it by transforming it into a therapeutic instrument and, more importantly, considering it in some way 'inauthentic'. This inauthenticity is signalled by the term 'transference', which implies diverting an emotional current from its normal destination and redirecting it to a false address. This, in turn, implies an external origin for what occurs in the patient-therapist relationship. This way therapists, in theory, can act within that relationship as observers who have no responsibility for the emotional dynamics of the patient (Smith, 1991). Although many therapists are very sensitive to the dynamics that evolve with their patients, the emphasis is on an acknowledgement of how the patient projects certain roles on to the therapist, who at times will enact these roles. The acknowledged effect is thus from patient to therapist and not vice versa, even if the therapist's potential for 'role responsiveness' is recognized.

Underpinning more contemporary views of transference continues to be a basic, and all too rarely challenged, assumption that can be traced throughout psychoanalytic theorising, namely the existence of an objective reality known by the therapist and distorted by the patient (Stolorow and Attwood, 1992). One important implication of this position, with clinical ramifications, is a view of the process of psychotherapy as one in which the impact of the observer on the observed as an ever-present influence on the therapeutic dyad is minimized:

> When the concept of distortion is imposed, a *cordon sanitaire* is established, which forecloses the investigation of the analysts' contribution in depth (Stolorow and Attwood, 1992:92).

Szasz (1963) in fact argued that transference interpretations are a defensive measure to protect the therapist from too intense, affective and real life involvement with the patient:

> For the idea of transference implies a denial and repudiation of the patient's experience qua experience; in its place is substituted the more manageable construct of the transference experience (Szasz, 1963:353).

Gill (1979) also stressed the non-transferential element in any therapeutic dyad in describing how the patient may experience the therapist in a particular way because of an actual event in their relationship. The patient's selective attention to this particular event is a manifestation of transference but does not necessarily involve a distortion of reality. It is not so much a question of whether transference occurs – it does in all relationships in so far as we all bring past experience to bear on all our present interactions and this colours our interpretation of what we perceive to be 'out there'. Rather, the question is whether in the specific context of the therapeutic relationship the transference colours and distorts all aspects of the relationship with the therapist. Couch (1979) draws attention to the way in which the real relationship has been overshadowed by the emphasis on transference, its presence seen as 'a kind of contamination or interference' with the transference rather than an essential feature of the multi-layered relationship each patient–therapist dyad elaborates.

Within mainstream practice the emphasis is on the interpretation of the transference relationship but the literature is most certainly not devoid of references to the clinical usefulness of the therapist's 'real' emotional responses (Winnicott, 1947; Heimann 1950; Little, 1951). On the whole these contributions fail to articulate explicitly the distinction between the real and the transference relationship. A paper by King about affect in psychoanalysis does offer an important qualification in this respect:

> I do not, however, assume that every communication between patient and therapist relates directly to transference, and it becomes important to differentiate those feelings and moods which are related to the operation of the transference, from those related to my reactions as a human being working with another human being . . . (1977:33).

Many so-called 'modern' therapists who are unduly convinced that most of their emotional reactions in therapy are responses to the patient's unconscious, frequently overlook the distinction drawn by King (Couch, 1979). In a critique of 'modern' technique Couch (1979) offers an alternative perspective. He argues that the vast majority of the therapist's reactions (feelings and thoughts) are best understood as quite 'ordinary responses' to what the patient reports about his inner and outer life. Some of these responses can assist the therapist in an empathic understanding of the patient and may therefore establish a 'foundation' for eventual interpretations. However, many of the therapist's reactions are best understood as genuine reactions to important aspects of the patient's life as a fellow human being:

> These natural interchanges on this ego level are probably essential for creating an analytic atmosphere of real human engagement where the full personality of the patient can emerge without constriction and be fully analysed. The absence of these natural responses by the therapist in the real relationship, especially when called for by actual tragedies, losses, failures, successes, disappointments and significant events in the patient's life, can be the cause of the most serious errors in an analysis – namely, the professionalised creation of an inhuman therapeutic situation, divorced from real life (Couch, 1979:19).[32]

Therapists are frequently inclined to inhibit the natural responses Couch refers to, or to feel somewhat guilty, for example, if they laugh with a patient. The inhibition of such responses is linked to a belief that they would compromise the transference. Although such responses are worthy of examination as they are occurring in the context of a relationship and may therefore throw light on what is happening between patient and therapist, they need not necessarily be avoided. Moreover, I suspect they are avoided less often than reports of clinical work might suggest. Rather, they are most likely left unreported either out of concern about what others will think, or because they are viewed as inconsequential to the process.

The therapeutic alliance

The value of humour in psychotherapy is most evident when we consider the nature of the therapeutic alliance. As we shall see later, humour can be used to forge, consolidate and repair ruptures in the

---

[32.] Although I am in broad agreement with Couch (1979), it is nevertheless important to acknowledge that it is difficult to operationalize the way in which we can reliably distinguish the 'real' responses that he advocates, from the so-called countertransference.

alliance. Few would dispute the central importance of a bond or alliance between patient and therapist as a *sine qua non* of therapeutic work. This is another way of saying that the relationship is a reciprocal one to which both parties contribute. The notion of a therapeutic or treatment alliance has its origin in Freud's writings on technique, although he never designated it as a distinctive concept. Originally it was encompassed within the general concept of transference. In 1913 Freud referred to the need to establish an 'effective transference' before the full work of psychoanalysis could begin. The essential distinction made by Freud at this time was between the patient's capacity to establish a friendly rapport and attitude to the therapist on the one hand and the emergence, within the framework of treatment, of revived feelings and attitudes which could become an obstacle to therapeutic progress.

Some psychoanalytic theorists have been concerned with differentiating the treatment or therapeutic alliance from transference 'proper' (Sandler et al., 1973) – a trend reflected in the work of Greenson and Wexler (1969) in the way they regard the core of the alliance as being anchored in the 'real' or 'non-transferential' relationship. They argue that in order for patients to develop healthy ego functioning and the capacity for full object relationships, the analytic situation must offer them the opportunity for experiencing in depth both the realistic and unrealistic aspects of dealing with objects. That is, both the treatment alliance and the transference are considered important for therapy. Zetzel (1956,1970) made a notable contribution to this issue by introducing the notion of the 'therapeutic alliance' which she felt was closely related to the real doctor–patient relationship. Zetzel (1970) states that the presence of a real object relationship is necessary for the therapeutic alliance to develop, and, significantly, that these conditions are necessary for the psychoanalysis itself to proceed. Her position reflects a more general position, which proposes that a part of the patient's ego is identified with the therapist's function and aims, and another part is engaged in resistance. The therapeutic alliance reflects the operation of the so-called observing ego which works alongside the therapist. Humourous exchanges encourage the observing ego as both patient and therapist enter the humourous space within which an alterative perspective on the patient's predicament, or an impasse in the therapy, can be elaborated.

There is now considerable evidence to support the contention that the quality of the therapeutic alliance is important in the successful outcome of psychotherapy across different therapeutic modalities. It is beyond the scope of this chapter to review this research, but influential reviews of this type of literature emphasize the importance of interpersonal factors as prominent ingredients of change in all therapies (Saltzman et al., 1976; Marziali, 1984; Lambert et al., 1986; Horvath and Luborsky, 1993; Castonguay et al., 1996; Krupnick et al, 1996; Roth and Fonagy, 1996).

Mirror, mirror, whose reflection do I see?

Focus on the quality of the therapeutic alliance brings to the fore the reciprocal nature of the therapeutic relationship. The person of the therapist emerges as a critical, if neglected, variable that should be researched. The systems-oriented approaches to psychotherapy have always stressed the circularity of human relationships and there is no reason to believe that the patient–therapist relationship should be an exception. Research that devotes attention to the patient and therapist as an interactive, mutually determining system may eventually lead to the possibility of specifying which styles of interaction contribute to effective (i.e. curative) emotional exchanges. There is indeed a dearth of research offering a detailed phenomenology of the patient–therapist system or of its boundaries and frame.

Lambert (1989) observes that even though research has been increasingly concerned with the agents of change, this has included everything but the contribution of individual therapists to the outcome. This is consonant with the general impression one gets when reading the psychotherapeutic literature with its focus on technique and operationalizing treatment protocols, to the comparative neglect of the impact of the therapist's own personal psychology. Such a bias colludes with the prevalent analytic ideal of therapist neutrality, with only lip service being paid to the notion of the therapist as a *participant-observer*. There still appears to be a failure to articulate a systematic account of the *fact* of the therapist's subjectivity. Subjectivity is surreptitiously allowed for in many contemporary writings, but objectivity is lauded as the ideal therapists should strive towards, as if the former did not necessarily compromise the latter. The therapist's ineluctable subjectivity is problematic, but we run the risk of allowing it to become a real obstacle only if we fail to research its modulating effects (Renik, 1993; 1998). It is imperative in therapeutic work that we do not place our perceptions beyond critical appraisal. We do not necessarily need to slip into a postmodernist relativism, which can render thinking virtually impossible, in order to account for subjectivity, but we do need to acknowledge and monitor the subjective factors that impinge on our perceptions (Cavell, 1998) and hence influence our behaviour.

The pre-eminence of the interpretation of transference phenomena is reflected in the analytic persona many therapists model themselves on: a relatively unobtrusive, neutral, anonymous, professional who sacrifices her so-called 'real' personality to receive the patient's projections, thereby providing fertile ground for the development of the transference. The notion of the therapist as a blank screen for the patient's projections is difficult to uphold. This was, of course, Freud's (1912) own ideal as he described how the analyst should function as a 'mirror' to the patient's projections so that the reactions to the therapist could then be analysed to throw light on the patient's relationships more generally. Freud was aware of the limitations to this process imposed by the analyst's own 'blind spots'. His emphasis, however, was narrowed to the impingement on the therapeutic space by the therapist's own emotional difficulties rather than an examination of the variation in personality and hence in therapeutic style, as determinants of the process. The notion that the 'real' person of the therapist might introduce an important variable into the treatment was not explored. Balint and Balint (1939) noted that the viability of the mirror-like attitude was gradually challenged. Gitelson (1952) and Heimann (1950; 1960) were amongst those theorists who drew attention to the notion of a 'fit' between patient and therapist whereby some might fit together better than others. The 'fit' can be said to be a function of technique or skill only in so far as these are 'conditioned' by the therapist's personality.

Klauber (1986) challenged the notion of neutrality, arguing that the therapist's efforts to sustain this illusion were in vain and merely reflected a failure to 'give credit to human intelligence and the human unconscious' (1986:130). He adds:

> Alongside the distorted image of the analyst due to the patient's transference, which is modified by treatment, goes a considerable perception of his realistic attributes, with the result that the patient identifies with the analyst's real personality and value system (1986:136).

Although advocating that therapists should monitor their contribution to the analytic relationship, Greenberg notes that:

> The suggestion that we can be blank screens or reflecting mirrors seems a kind of conceit; the idea that we can judge and titrate abstinence appears arrogant and evenly hovering attention seems both epistemologically and psychologically naïve (1996:212).

The dangers of adhering too rigidly to the analytic rules imparted to many contemporary therapists in training are elaborated by Lipton:

> Paradoxically, modern technique can produce just what it may have been designed to avoid, a corrective emotional experience, by exposing the patient to a hypothetically ideally correct, ideally unobtrusive, ideally silent, encompassing technical instrumentality rather than the presence of the therapist as a person with whom the patient can establish a personal relationship (1977:272).

The central theme that pervades Lipton's position is straightforward: the therapist as a person is a variable that cannot and should not be ignored. Moreover, it is a variable that – even if it were possible – we need not try to eliminate as it contributes to the analytic ambience of collaborative work which provides the essential backdrop to analytic work. Without this we might as well recount our sorrows to a computer. Lipton is not just referring to such qualities as warmth and respect for the patient, which are of course important. Rather, he is suggesting that patients live in a real world as well as in their phantasy world and that the exchanges with the therapist's humanity involve confrontations with their limitations as much as with their strengths. In other words, an important aspect of the therapeutic relationship is that it involves a confrontation with the reality of the therapist as real person, capable of spontaneous responses and, hence, inevitably fallible. The negotiation of disappointments and frustrations with a therapist who is real, in the sense just outlined, provides a potentially mutative interpersonal experience as long as this can be worked through. Just as a therapist compromises her potential effectiveness if she remains too fully a real person with no sensitivity to the distortions of projection, she will be equally ineffective if she remains solely a 'symbolic object' (Szasz, 1963). The therapeutic situation requires of the therapist that she functions as both real and symbolic, and of the patient that he perceives the therapist as both. Relative neutrality and anonymity – 'relative' insofar as they can never be absolute – are important components of the therapeutic stance towards which the therapist should strive, without which the analytic work is compromised. This does not, however, preclude an empathic, authentic, warm and sometimes humorous attitude.

It is impossible to sustain neutrality and anonymity if by this we mean the withholding of personal information – whether verbalized or enacted – or the inhibition of the therapist's 'real' personality, beliefs and values. In outlining these views I am not advocating self-disclosure by the therapist – in the vast majority of cases I can see no good rationale for doing so from the vantage point of the best interests of the patient. Rather, I have in mind here the *inevitable* disclosures of the real person of the therapist through the way they dress, talk, decorate their room, how much or how little they intervene, what they choose to focus on and whether and what they may or may not laugh about. Moreover, the therapist's *considered* disclosure, for example, of her vulnerability and uncertainty through the use of self-deprecating humour, can promote a climate where an acceptance of limitations can be faced without fear of being admonished, as well as helping to demystify the therapeutic process itself (Bloch et al. 1983). The use of humour represents a way of conveying this humanity without having to be more explicitly self-disclosing. Humour is an expression of the therapist's personality and reflects a way of 'being with' patients which appears antithetical to the classical rules of analytic technique. Nevertheless, it is neither an obstacle nor irrelevant to the process, as exemplified in the following two clinical vignettes.

Mary is a forty-seven year old single woman referred because of social anxiety, though this masked a far more complex range of difficulties. She described feeling paranoid at times and avoided going out as much as possible even though she had managed at least to hold down a job. In therapy she was very cautious with her disclosures and was preoccupied with questions of confidentiality. She set up a kind of hide-and-seek game with me, speaking in an unnecessarily convoluted, vague manner as if she wanted to guarantee my attention but also to remain in control of what she told me. This had the effect of getting me to work very hard to understand her. I was often reminded at such times of the young child who hides but wants to make sure that he will be found by the mother.

As a child, Mary had been brought up by her mother. Her father had left her mother when Mary was only three years old. She had an older sister, who had been sent to live with an aunt, with whom she had limited contact. Mary's mother was described as a very needy woman who had relied on Mary to provide her emotional support. She recalled her mother restricting her movements, seldom allowing her to play with other children. Her mother used to enquire as to who was her 'best friend', only then to ask Mary for reassurance that she loved her more. Mary described how her mother would reassure her that if they remained together everything would turn out right. Although they had been very close, Mary had never managed really to understand what had happened to her father or why her sister did not live with them. When she asked her mother these questions her mother used to reply that she need not worry herself with such upsetting thoughts. This seemed to sum up best the intolerable position Mary had been placed in since she knew both that there were unanswered questions about her family history and that she could not know the answers. Her knowledge could not be processed, since thinking was denied in the very merged relationship with her mother. As an adult Mary was especially preoccupied with knowing what other people thought and, in particular, what other people thought she thought. I think this reflected her hope that through knowing another's mind she could come to know her own and recover all the lost knowledge of her own history.

Mary conveyed a suffocating relationship with her mother which she sought to recreate with others but which she also dreaded. Mary was therefore always seeking quite intense, exclusive relationships in which she would then become very controlling. She found it intolerable not to know the other person's whereabouts and she could become very jealous and suspicious. Her only relationship with a man had been short lived and she had no close female or male friends since she quickly drove people away by her intrusive behaviour. Mary had lived with her mother until she (Mary) was forty-two, having then been re-housed following her one and only admission to hospital triggered by a suicide attempt shortly after her mother's sudden death.

In the sessions, Mary would very frequently ask me if I understood what she meant in a rather anxious and, at times, hostile manner. Silences were intolerable and she frequently demanded to know what I was thinking. One function of this behaviour was to reassure herself that I was 'with her' all the time. As a child Mary reported a heightened fear of the dark and she continued to sleep with a light on. Her anxiety about being 'left in the dark' about what was happening in another's mind compelled her to have to control my every thought. She desperately wanted me to throw some light on her internal confusion. Being separate felt intolerable to Mary; yet a constructive 'togetherness' was attacked by her need to control. Most of my interventions in response to this particular dynamic were usually received with contempt, and highlighted her paranoia. She felt I was only trying to catch her off guard and she believed I was often withholding information from her. For example, she became at times suspicious that I was having a relationship with her psychiatrist and that we were both talking about her together in derogatory terms.

Although Mary was not psychotic in the psychiatric sense of the term, she was enslaved to a psychotic part of her personality which led her to feel unduly suspicious and hence persecuted by others. This would translate in hostile and at times quite grandiose behaviour which was Mary's way of protecting herself from the disappointments she antici- pated in her relationships. Some months into the therapy Mary came to her session feeling highly paranoid. She described in her typically tortuous manner an incident at work which had clearly made her feel suspicious about a colleague's intentions. She was visibly distressed as she related to me how she felt marginalized at work. It was hard to follow her story as Mary's speech was very pressurized. On this occasion I did feel quite confused, as though I had also become caught up in Mary's difficulty in separating external and internal reality. She asked me, without really leaving me any space to comment, what I thought was happening. She asked me this several times and eventually clearly expected a reply. I felt under pressure to release her from her persecutory anxiety, yet I could not really think about what was happening between us. At that point I found myself thinking about the expression 'the blind leading the blind'. I did feel genuinely confused and I said somewhat self-mockingly: 'As soon as I actually understand what is happening, rest assured, you will be the first to know'. As I heard these words I felt anxious about the response they would evoke. Much to my surprise, Mary's facial expression relaxed and she sat back in her chair. She smiled and, punctuating her response with a laugh, she said 'I do always feel I am going to be the last one to know, don't I? I know it can't always be the case but I feel as if I am not part of things and then I just don't know what's going on'. Mary was smiling but now there were also tears in her eyes. She then went on to talk about her mother's paranoia and how she felt 'contaminated' by it.

The use of a somewhat more spontaneous intervention on my part, which Mary perceived to be funny, appeared in this instance to draw Mary back from her psychotic stronghold into reality where she could stand back and take some perspective on her predicament. This transformed her paranoia into a more depressive reaction as she realized how lonely and confused she felt. It is difficult to pinpoint exactly, or with certainty, what changed the trajectory of this session. I would like to propose, however, that my intervention conveying my own uncertainty and confusion provided a model for how to manage the anxiety of not knowing, and allowed us to create a space for thinking about the meaning of what she had been trying to communicate. The intervention also indirectly implied that she assumed I would withhold information, whereas I was assuring her that I would share my thoughts with her – I was thereby indirectly reminding her that we were in a collaborative relationship. This, in turn, allowed Mary to address her own difficulties and so retreat from her paranoid position where others were always to blame for leaving her in the dark. Some patients would find it even more anxiety-provoking to have a therapist declare their confusion, and this may unduly tax the patient. It is the therapist's responsibility ultimately to manage their confusion. However, used judiciously, a more light-hearted recognition of the therapist's fallibility can be used to therapeutic effect.

A more humorous stance may be especially important if the emergence of the patient's aggression in the transference might otherwise give rise to counter-aggressive reactions in the therapist (Kernberg, 1982), as was the case for me in my work with Paula. The use of humour in such instances may offer an opportunity for repairing ruptures in the alliance. Paula had been in once-weekly psychotherapy for about one year, at which point I announced that I would be leaving my then post in the NHS a few months later. Paula had always adopted a rather aggressive stance towards me, which I had understood to be her first line of defence against any attachment figure who might then disappoint or indeed abandon her. Many of the patients we see in NHS psychiatric settings come with complex and often tragic histories of abandonment and loss. In psychotherapy we encourage them to trust us and to develop a relationship with us, but patients in NHS settings are more likely than those in the private sector to have to contend with a high rate of therapist turnover and changes in the very structure of the services delivered, so that they can end up feeling that they have, once again, been let down after they had started to trust someone. The system all too often recapitulates their earlier trauma. Paula was no exception.

Paula had been brought up in institutional care from the age of three and had experienced difficulties in most of her placements in foster care. As a child she was described as hyperactive and as an adolescent she had become involved in delinquent activities. She was referred because of her eating problems and self-harming behaviour. When I first met her she was twenty-five years old and lived in bed and breakfast accommodation. She worked as a prostitute and occasionally dealt in drugs. She was a bright and lively young woman who was very streetwise. She never minced her words and she was often involved in disputes and physical fights with people and other workers who, in the main, found her very difficult and abrasive.

I liked Paula but at times I also 'hated' her (Winnicott, 1947). Working with her in therapy was hard but she had made some progress as evidenced in her resolution, six months into her therapy, to stop working as a prostitute, where she often placed herself at risk, and she gradually started to look into college courses. Paula was never herself explicitly appreciative of the help offered to her. On the contrary, she was frequently verbally abusive, as on those occasions when she stormed out of our sessions calling me a 'fucking bitch'. I was therefore dreading having to announce to her that I would be leaving my post. I knew she would be very angry and would feel cheated but that she would be unable to acknowledge that she had become attached to me. To protect herself from this painful realization she would have to devalue our work together and rubbish me. Paula did not disappoint me in this respect. She was furious and I think I bore the brunt of all her previous disappointments. She managed to make me feel very guilty about leaving. Following the session in which I announced my news she cut herself quite badly and was admitted to hospital. The following week, when she told me what she had done, Paula denied that this had anything to do with me. My interpretations to this effect were met with accusations that I 'fancied myself as important' and that I should 'get a life'. It was impossible to talk with her about her feelings towards me. Aggression and violence were the means through which Paula managed her emotional experiences.

Feelings were running high in the session following the news of my departure. I also felt angry as all my attempts to engage Paula in an exploration of what was happening between us were attacked. In this same session she told me that a few days previously she had found a useful book in the local library about women who 'loved too much'. She spoke in some detail about the book. She had in fact stolen it from the library as it was small and fitted in her coat pocket. She was planning to give it to one of her colleagues who had been 'on the game' for too long in her opinion. Although the subject matter of the book was significant, given our impending separation, I sensed that through this story Paula was perhaps also giving expression to her unconscious recognition that I had offered her something of value (like the book) but that somehow these good things did not belong to her, that is, she could only steal them. Also, I think that this communication reflected her experience that through leaving her *I* was stealing something of value to her. However, I sensed that it would not be productive to draw attention to my formulation through a more formal transference interpretation. Paula was at that point still too angry and volatile and I felt that she would not really hear what I had to say. I had been struck by her description of the 'pocket-sized' book, small enough to carry with her all the time and I felt that this expressed a wish to be able to have me all to herself. I therefore said, 'I have never read this book but it sounds a hell of a lot more handy and reliable than me'. Paula burst out laughing and looked at me: 'It fucking well is, you fucking cunt, but it's not as funny'. I smiled and she laughed some more. She then spoke of her friend about whom she was worried. She was able to agree with me when I then interpreted that she was worried about what would happen to her after I left, in particular whether she would be able to leave prostitution or would be drawn back into that world without my help.

My impression was that my humorous intervention dissolved Paula's angry stance. My comment implicitly and succinctly acknowledged that as far as she was concerned I was unreliable and that she would need to replace me in some way – this was an internal 'fact' but also a reality as I was leaving well before our work should ideally have come to an end. My intervention aligned me with her perception of me as unreliable. It also helped to reassure Paula that I had not been destroyed by her attacks, simultaneously allowing me to give expression to some of my aggression through the use of humour. The outcome was that we were then able to talk more directly about her anxieties. In this exchange the transference ramifications of what Paula was saying were not ignored, but what I believe shifted the session was the use I made of myself in a more real and immediate manner by engaging with Paula through the use of humour. The aim was to repair a painful rupture in our relationship before a deeper exploration could take place. It is important to emphasize that there had been a rupture at different levels of our relationship. Firstly, at the level of the real relationship as I was a human being unable to continue helping another who needed the help. Secondly, at the level of therapeutic alliance in so far as we had made a contract that we would work together for eighteen months and this was being curtailed. Finally, these 'real' disappointments then found their painful echo in the transference.

One of the most important developments in psychotherapy is the lived experience of a relationship within which feelings experienced by the patient to be destructive can be safely contained and understood. The therapist's capacity to withstand the patients' attacks is critical in this respect. The therapist's survival provides a template through which future relationships may be experienced as resilient and thus available for creative use. Winnicott (1971) believes that the therapist's capacity to survive is itself mutative. In this respect Rappaport observes:

From the continual cycle of destruction and redefinition of the analytic couple comes the potential for the patient to find in the analyst the objects he needs and to trust they can be aggressively handled (1998:371).

The use of humour is one of several ways in which the therapist may convey to the patient that she has survived and that difficulties in a relationship can be surmounted. I am not advocating ridiculing a patient by ignoring or laughing at their attacks or criticisms. Rather, I am suggesting that humour can both grasp the painful reality and let the patient know that the therapist can withstand this, and the relationship can transcend such ruptures. Humour provides a very effective medium for establishing, solidifying and repairing ruptures in the therapeutic alliance. The therapeutic alliance needs to be maintained and repaired after occasional inevitable breakdowns so as to ensure the patient's continued co-operation. Moreover, Safran et al. (1990) suggest that the outcome of psychotherapy is strongly associated with the successful repair of ruptures in the alliance. Moments of shared laughter and humour are important markers of the human encounter between patient and therapist and of a more robust alliance (Poland, 1994) which aims to create the conditions of safety necessary for the understanding of another person's unconscious. Attempts to analyse transference-based resistances to change are rendered all the more arduous if they occur, as Bader suggests,

> . . . in an atmosphere that the patient can construe as sombre and humourless, because the therapist's insights get drowned out by the meanings that the patient attributes to the affective tone of the interpretation (1993:43).

Humour may enable the patient to view the therapist as a less formidable figure. Barry (1994) even suggests that the therapist's appreciation of jokes at his expense may further the therapy. He does not view such a response as a violation of neutrality; rather he views a serious or grave response to such exchanges as potentially replicating the parents' inability to tolerate ridicule. On one occasion, when I was unusually tired during a session with a patient I saw face-to-face, I was conscious of trying to hide the fact that I was yawning. My patient, a very perceptive young woman with a talent for mimicry, smiled and then observed that my attempt to disguise the yawn was so skilful that she felt I deserved an Oscar for my performance. I found this very funny and I laughed in response adding that, much as she appreciated my efforts and I was glad they had not been wasted on her, I felt she was also letting me know she would appreciate my undivided attention much more. My patient laughed and acknowledged that she had thought I was looking tired and felt I was bored. We were then able to examine her fear of criticizing me even though she had felt angry as she interpreted my yawn as evidence of my lack of interest in her. We were thus able to negotiate a potentially difficult juncture in a humorous manner which validated her accurate observation, reflected my capacity to tolerate her criticism without feeling admonished by it and conveyed my acknowledgement of the underlying aggression in her communication. This led to a fruitful exploration of her experience in her relationship with her depressed mother whom she felt she had always needed to protect.

Although I am in broad agreement with the sentiments expressed by Barry, it remains incumbent on us to consider our response to a patient's ridicule carefully, since in the patient's experience it may serve to undermine the therapist's capacity to manage this. A humorous response may well convey that the attacks can be survived, but it could also express the therapist's inability to take the attack seriously. The therapist's humour may itself be used to retaliate against the patient.

So, what about the 'real' relationship?

Although Freud (1911-1915) never explicitly theorized on the use of humour in psychotherapy, his manner with his patients is renowned for departing from his written technical prescriptions (Greenberg, 1996; Couch, 1979). He is reported, for example, to have used joking in his work with patients (Loewenstein, 1958). Freud did not shy away from being a 'real' human person in the analytic situation; he revealed, through his conversational manner, far more of himself than many therapists would feel comfortable doing nowadays. This quality is apparent in many of Freud's published cases (Couch, 1979), as well as in his patients' reports about their analyses with him (Grinder, 1940; Doolittle, 1956; Blanton, 1971). For example, in his account, Sterba observes:

> Freud did not hesitate to transcend the so-called classical or orthodox behaviour of the therapist as it was prescribed by training institutes. He freely deviated from the straight and narrow path of 'impersonality' and indulged in 'parameters' that would have met with an outcry of indignation by the adherents to a strict and 'sterile' attitude of the therapist which is supposed to present the classical model of the therapist's behaviour. (1982:123).

He adds that when he met one of Freud's former patients, the Wolfman, the latter described how 'free and easy-going' Freud was in the therapeutic situation and Freud's willingness to discuss subjects other than the patient's analytic material.

It is unfortunate that the most important lessons to be learnt from Freud about 'how to be' with a patient were contained in his natural style, conveyed in his patients' accounts of him, which he never articulated in more theoretical terms. One consequence of this is that therapists without much imagination have, all too often, adhered, all too literally, to those aspects of technique that Freud wrote about (Couch, 1979). This has contributed to cardboard cut-out therapists who are at worst inhibited and, at best, uncertain or uncomfortable with the possibility of more spontaneous, humorous, exchanges with their patients. I am, of course, generalizing. The therapist as a mirror is the model of 'how to be' with patients that is internalized by many, but by no means all, therapists. It is more commonly observed in less experienced therapists. Indeed, it is of note that rigidity in attitudes about 'how to be' with patients is seldom encountered in more experienced practitioners – irrespective of their psychoanalytic allegiances – and even less so amongst those who were themselves analysed or supervised by Freud's more immediate descendants. Although this is but a personal impression, these therapists seem much more comfortable in their analytic skin and are able to relate in a more genuine manner, within analytic boundaries, than their less experienced counterparts.

The analytic persona I have been describing is not outmoded. Take, for example, a paper published in a contemporary British psychoanalytic journal in which the author discusses the two main attitudes to psycho-analytic assessment. This paper describes one approach whereby the assessment is carried out:

> . . . in a way that approximates at first technically to an ordinary analytic session. The patient is greeted courteously but *gravely*, and subjected from the outset to an intense scrutiny, with the minimum of instruction, *or measures that might be described as 'putting one at ease'* . . . .*no automatic social responses are given, for example smiles* (Milton, 1997:48; my italics).

The rationale usually given for such an approach is that it very quickly brings to the fore the patient's more primitive anxieties. This is indeed often the case. Possibly armed with little understanding of what is likely to transpire in an assessment, the patient coming to meet a therapist they have never seen before, who welcomes him 'gravely' and actively avoids the usual social responses he might reasonably expect from a professional person, will quickly feel anxious and possibly a little paranoid. There are no surprises here, and I am far from convinced that this represents the most effective way of understanding another person's emotional difficulties.

It is interesting to speculate as to who benefits from the adherence to the kind of approach just outlined. The analytic frame and its prescrip-tions of neutrality, abstinence and anonymity exist not only for the patient's benefit but also for the therapist's – a fact frequently overlooked. The prevailing analytic persona may provide a safe screen for therapists' own apprehensions about more spontaneous exchanges, as it legitimizes a more withdrawn, grave stance. Working analytically generates anxiety for both participants since any such exploration is an invitation to enter the uncharted territory of our own unconscious as well as that of our patients. In using humour we are also exposing our own unconscious. This provokes anxiety, not only because of an appropriate concern with safeguarding the therapeutic space from the impingements of our own difficulties, but also because it can make us feel exposed and vulnerable. By keeping a careful reign on our spontaneity we protect ourselves from the anxiety inherent in the analytic enterprise, viewing ourselves more as receptacles for the patient's projections than as active participants in the process. Through the highly prescriptive rituals that surround the therapeutic relationship we have found a way of sustaining the illusion that we are observers, onlookers into another's unconscious, meanwhile keeping our own neatly in check.

Lipton's (1977) classic article on Freud's technique made a significant contribution to the criticism of the 'overly rigid, technical impersonality of the post-Freudian developments' (Couch, 1979) which he termed 'modern' technique. Lipton argued that Freud excluded a substantial personal relationship with patients from his technique, which was nevertheless implicit in his own personal style. He held that it was this 'excluded characteristic' which differentiated so-called 'classical' from 'modern' techniques. In Lipton's formulation the 'personal relationship' between patient and therapist is a necessary part of therapeutic work that it is both outside technique and 'subject to individual variation'. Lipton proposes that a technical style that includes a personal relationship confers advantages over the 'modern' technique that tries to exclude it.

In a similar vein Anna Freud made the following remarks:

> With due respect for the necessary strictest handling and interpretation of the transference, I feel still that we should leave room somewhere for the realization that therapist and patient are also two real people, of equal adult status, in a real personal relationship to each other. I wonder whether our, at times complete, neglect of this side of the matter is not responsible for some of the hostile reactions which we get from patients and which we are apt to ascribe to 'true transference' only. But these are technically subversive thoughts and ought to be handled with care (1954:618-619).

My own experience concurs with Anna Freud's assessment of the *status quo*. Discussing the 'real' relationship can feel at best of little import, that is, 'of course there is a real relationship but what really matters is the transference' and, at worst, it can feel as if one is being subversive by mentioning that there is more to psychotherapy than the interpretation of transference. To an extent I am of course exaggerating – few therapists adopt such polarized positions. Yet it seems important to emphasize the relative neglect of the multifaceted nature of the therapeutic relationship and the therapeutic functions of the real relationship in particular. Indeed Viederman advocates the direct expression at certain times of the real person of the therapist not rigidly hidden behind the 'orthodox' façade of anonymity, neutrality, and abstinence:

> My intent . . . is to place the relationship at centre stage as an aspect of the therapeutic process that leads to change, to examine the reluctance of therapists to acknowledge its role, and to explore the manner in which it manifests itself in the psychoanalytic process that leads to change . . . By 'real' person of the therapist I refer not only to his outward traits, but also to his unique characteristics as a person and to his behaviour in the analytic situation which goes beyond interpretation and clarification (1991:452).

To speak of being more 'real' or more 'human' may either sound trite or evoke a twinge of discomfort as it triggers visions of the excesses of those therapists who commit many sins in the name of 'being real' with their patients. The maintenance of professional boundaries is integral to the therapeutic enterprise. This does require the therapist to exercise a degree of inhibition of some of her more natural inclinations. A therapist is not a friend and you don't go to see one with the explicit intention of having a good laugh. If, as the therapist, you have a naturally humorous or ironic slant on life, this manner of relating will benefit from being monitored in the therapeutic interaction as it will not always be appropriate. The 'wear and tear' (Malcolm, 1981) of psychoanalytic work partly arises precisely because of the struggle to keep ourselves from doing the things that we might otherwise do with family or friends. In analytic work we are forever carefully balancing the requirements of the analytic attitude with the need to convey enough humanity so that the patient will feel that they are engaging with an alive and thoughtful person in whom they will bestow their trust. Tarachow (1963) argues that the therapist imposes a 'therapeutic barrier' to safeguard the analytic space from the pull to respond to each other as real objects towards which both patient and therapist are drawn. Humorous exchanges pose a threat to this delicate balance. Because humour fosters intimacy and is so revealing of oneself, it propels both patient and therapist into potentially hazardous territory ripe for acting out. The danger is that it will seduce both parties away from the analytic task of understanding the unconscious.

Ferenczi stands out as one of the more controversial figures in the history of psychoanalysis (Stanton, 1990) precisely because his bold attempt at 'mutual analysis' provides a good example of how total immersion in the 'real' relationship between patient and therapist is not necessarily therapeutic. Ferenczi genuinely struggled with the difficulty in reconciling the professional role with a more personal, humane involvement with patients which he believed was integral to the therapist's function. There are lessons here for us all, since his attempts at 'mutual analysis' were problematic, to say the least. Nevertheless, the notion that the therapist's real affective responses may at times be of therapeutic benefit to the patient, even when they transgress the classical analytic stance, resonates throughout Kohut's (1984) work. He argues that such responses may be mutative and provide the patient with conditions of safety. Likewise, Fairbairn (1958) concluded that interpretation was insufficient for psychical change but that the therapist as a 'real' person played a significant part in bringing about a beneficial change in the patient's 'endopsychic' state. According to him, a real relationship between therapist and patient has to be established. To meet every demand of the patient, and to partake in the relationship as if patient and therapist are equal participants, is clearly not only 'impossible but also dishonest' (Mitchell, 1993). This does not mean, however, that affective exchanges transcending the roles of patient and of therapist have no place, even if they are more revealing of the therapist's personality. It is indeed apposite to ask ourselves, along with Stone, as to whether the transference is seriously compromised if the patient knows:

> whether one takes one's vacations in Vermont or Maine or indeed (let me be really bold!) that one knows something more about sailing than about golf or bridge (1961:48).

The transference is undoubtedly a very important dynamic, which, as it unfolds in psychotherapy, enables the therapist to get a more immediate experience of the patient's unconscious dynamics. However, it can take root and be understood only in the context of an analytic atmosphere that addresses the real as well as the transference relationship. We ignore the therapeutic functions of the real relationship at our own peril. Paolino offers an insightful perspective on these functions:

> The real relationship is just as important to the psychoanalytic process as the other aspects of the therapeutic relationship. If the real relationship is not actively recognized and utilised in the therapy sessions then the patient is exposed to a relationship with the therapist that is interpersonally sterile and lacking the opportunity for the patient to develop a meaningful and therapeutic object relation. (1982:232).

The neglect of the real relationship, and consequently of the real person of the therapist, has important clinical implications since a failure to respond in a humane and reasonable manner at a critical juncture can undermine the therapeutic alliance (Couch, 1979). If a patient relates a funny incident and I feel confident that I am not being drawn into a collusive dynamic, I feel it quite natural to laugh with the patient as I would do if I were having a conversation with a friend or a colleague. With a few patients, humour has been a prominent feature of our relationship without in any way detracting from, or compromising, the analytic task and the elaboration of the transference. With other patients I never laugh, and some have even described me as 'overly serious'.

One of the main therapeutic functions of the real relationship is to provide a human framework for the emergence of the unconscious structure of the patient's transference potentials. 'With absolute neutrality and mirror-like impersonality and un-responsiveness', writes Couch,

> the transference imagoes would appear like abstract projections in a human vacuum, put on to a therapist who was only a 'cloth and wire' figure of a mother or father (1979:21).

Thoma and Kachele (1987, quoted in Stern et al., 1998) also underline the necessary function of a more authentic way of relating, which provides the backdrop without which transference is not perceivable. The important real qualities of a therapist, such as warmth, sensitivity *and sense of humour*, create the essential human backdrop for the patient's articulation of their experiences. If a sense of humour is as central to our nature and adaptation as I have been proposing throughout, then this type of communication and way of 'being with' the patient should not be excluded from the therapeutic relationship. However, inasmuch as humour is always revealing of the therapist's personality, its use is antagonistic to the ideal of therapist neutrality and anonymity. Humour is one of several ways of relating to a patient that are open to the therapist, which encourage the development of a lively and supportive atmosphere conducive to an understanding of the unconscious.

Mutative encounters

We cannot begin to understand the relative neglect of humour as a valid communication in psychotherapy which has therapeutic potential, unless we view it in the current climate of the primacy of transference interpretation as the mutative intervention *par excellence*. This becomes quickly apparent in clinical forums where practitioners discuss their work. The mutative effects of interventions other than transference or reconstructive interpretations have received scant attention. Nevertheless, as Bader observes:

> Clinical experience challenges us to account in our theory for those instances in which the spontaneous and deliberate action of the analyst,

such as using humour, has the effect of deepening that analytic process and outcome (1993:27).

More recent psychoanalytic contributions cast a different light on the pre-eminence of transference interpretations. This challenge is presented by those theoreticians and clinicians influenced by both dynamic and systemic ideas who emphasize the importance of the co-construction of new contexts by the meeting of two subjectivities (Sameroff, 1983; Stern et al., 1998; Beebe and Lachmann, 1988, 1994). The underlying assumption in these accounts is that both patient and therapist contribute to the regulation of the exchange, even if their respective contributions cannot be regarded as equal. From this perspective regulation is an emergent property of the dyadic system as well as a property of the individual. In this way the thorny question of subjectivity is not avoided or underplayed. Rather, it is embraced as an unavoidable 'given' which needs to be understood. More importantly, such perspectives enable us to elaborate hypotheses about the nature of the therapeutic process where both therapist and patient contribute to the creation of a unique relationship. Within this context there is room for a variety of interventions, other than transference interpretation, which may have mutative potential.

The research which has inspired these perspectives originates from the field of developmental psychology. A notable contribution from this field has been the description of interaction as a continuous, mutually determined process, constructed from moment to moment by both partners in the mother-infant dyad. Approaching the question of the patient–therapist relationship from the standpoint of infant research, Lachmann and Beebe (1996) propose three organizing principles of interactive regulation: ongoing regulation (a pattern of repeated inter-actions), disruption and repair (a sequence broken out of an overall pattern) and heightened affective moments (a salient dramatic moment). In the therapeutic situation, ongoing regulations range from postural and facial exchanges to greetings and parting rituals. According to Lachmann and Beebe (1996), the way these are regulated promotes new expectations and 'constitutes a mode of therapeutic action'. In other words, they are suggesting that interactions, even if not verbally articulated, are nevertheless potentially mutative. The therapeutic action of 'disruption and repair':

> lies in the organisation of a greater flexibility in negotiating a range of co-ordination and miscoordination in the process of mutual and self-regulation (1996:8).

They suggest that these principles serve as metaphors for what transpires between patient and therapist. Moreover, they believe that:

At every moment in a therapeutic dyad there is the potential to organise expectations of mutuality, intimacy, trust, repair of disruptions, and hope, as well as to disconfirm rigid, archaic expectations (1996:21).

I should like to draw attention, in particular, to the notion of 'heightened affective moments' as this is especially pertinent to the use of humour in psychotherapy. Pine (1981) originally described particular interactions between mother and baby, which were characterized by a heightened affective exchange, of either a positive or a negative nature. This might denote respectively, for example, the experience of united cooing by both mother and baby, or moments of intense arousal in the absence of gratification. Pine suggests that such events are psychically organizing, that is, they allow the infant to categorize and expect similar experiences and so facilitate cognitive and emotional organization. Beebe and Lachmann (1994) propose that heightened affective moments are organizing because they trigger a potentially powerful state[33] transformation that contributes to the inner regulation. If the regulation is experienced positively as, for example, when the mother and baby are engaged in facial mirroring interactions in which each face crescendos higher and higher, subsequent experiences of resonance, or of being on the same wavelength with another person, are organized around such a heightened moment. The notion of heightened affective moments is by no means new and most therapists would agree that such exchanges are essential in evolving an emotionally meaningful relationship with their patients.

Stern et al. (1998) elaborate some of the above ideas, grappling with the notions of the 'real' relationship and 'authenticity'. They observe – and this may ring true for anyone who has had the personal experience of therapy – that what we often remember as patients of our therapeutic experiences are 'moments of authentic, person-to-person connection' with the therapist:

> When we speak of an 'authentic' meeting, we mean communications that reveal a personal aspect of the self that has been evoked in an affective response to another. In turn, it reveals to the other a personal signature, so as to create a new dyadic state specific to the two participants (1998:917).

They refer to these particular exchanges as 'moments of meeting'. Amongst the general examples offered of such moments the authors refer to 'the moment when free play evolves into an explosion of mutual laughter' (p. 908). Lachmann and Lichtenberg (1992) also highlight

---

[33.] 'State' is used to denote arousal and activity level, facial and vocal affect and cognition (Lachmann and Beebe, 1996).

moments of humour. These 'moments', in a general sense, are not only potentially pleasurable interpersonal events, but they also serve an important function as they provide opportunities for new interpersonal experiences (Lachmann and Beebe, 1996). Stern et al. (1998) propose that they rearrange 'implicit relational knowing' for both patient and therapist. This rests on an important distinction drawn by the authors between 'declarative knowledge', which they hypothesize is acquired through verbal interpretations, and 'implicit relational knowing', which is acquired through the experience of actual interactions between patient and therapist. They suggest that moments of meeting contribute to the creation of a new intersubjective environment which directly impinges on the domain of 'implicit relational knowing', thereby altering it. Such interventions are therefore believed to be *mutative*. They bring about change through 'alterations in ways of being with' which facilitate a recontextualization of past experience in the present, 'such that the person operates from within a different mental landscape, resulting in new behaviours and experiences in the present and future' (Stern et al., 1998:918).

Unlike transference interpretations, such exchanges bring into play the person of the therapist and not their analytic role. Although they may be said to transcend the analytic role, they do not abrogate the professional relationship. It is, of course, debatable whether the distinction drawn by Stern et al. between a more personal engagement with the patient and the act of interpretation proper, is tenable. Some clinicians take issue with this (see Williams, 1999). I do not think that the act of interpreting necessarily conflicts with the notion of the therapist as a 'real' person. The manner in which an interpretation is offered to the patient can be very enlivening and engaging. Interpretations cast in a humorous light are a prime example of this as they bridge the gap between 'being real' and interpreting: they convey understanding, while revealing the shared humanity of both therapist and patient. However, many interpretations are offered to patients in ways that can feel rather distant and impersonal.

The striking feature of the accounts of both heightened affective moments and moments of meeting is that their hypothesized features mirror the very nature and quality of humorous communication. Lachmann and Beebe (1996), for example, note that the key features of heightened affective moments are as follows: they are a mutual and unique creation of the particular dyad; they are characterized by a transformation of the expectation of both therapist and patient of how the interaction will unfold and this results in a dramatic transformation of the patient's state. Stern et al. (1998) also note the 'improvisational' nature of these interactions that can occur only when the therapist allows into the relationship something personal in addition to any technical considerations. The affective immediacy is the hallmark of these exchanges. The spontaneity that is a property of such exchanges surprises both patient and therapist and such moments are therefore imbued with creative potential. Reik (1936) draws attention to the element of surprise in wit which produces a jolt. He likened this to the realization of insight in psychoanalysis, which he felt shared a similar quality of surprise. This point is echoed by Baker who cautions that 'the humorous comment [in therapy], if it is to be effective, must emerge with a degree of spontaneity, as does a good interpretation' (1993:953). The structure of humour, as we have seen, is built upon incongruity and its resolution. Its delivery relies on timing so as to maximize the element of surprise already set in motion by the incongruous presentation. Both these aspects raise our expectations and lead us to a climax with a punchline or an actual exchange that is unexpected. Humour therefore essentially transforms the original expectation and takes us to a new space and, even if only temporarily, our affective state is altered. When we engage in humorous exchange with another person, whatever is mutually created in the exchange moves the two partners into a new 'humorous space' which has been jointly co-created; hence the connecting and transforming power of humour. Humorous exchanges between patient and therapist therefore provide one of the richest opportunities for the experience of moments of meeting and, I would like to propose, are essentially mutative. Stern et al. (1998) in fact note that moments of meeting create 'an 'open space' in which a shift in the intersubjective environment creates a new equilibrium, a 'disjoin' with an alteration in or rearrangement of defensive processes' (1998:915).

Since 'moments of meeting' are not planned, Stern et al. (1998) emphasize how easy it is to miss the opportunities that they present us with. They call upon the therapist to respond

> with something that is experienced as specific to the relationship with the patient and that is experienced as expressive of her experience and personhood, and carries her signature (1998:917).

It is all too easy to fail to seize the opportunity to interact with a patient in a more spontaneous fashion if we are focusing too hard on making the correct or clever interpretation or, indeed, if we believe that the only valuable interventions are those that focus on the transference. Therapy provides numerous opportunities for humorous exchanges but we do not always seize them. As therapists we are confronted with a difficult challenge since we have to contend with the analytic superego that we all internalize through our training experiences. Kubie (1971) notes that therapists who use humour often do so with a guilty conscience. Some therapists respond to patients' expressions of humour by remaining demure even if they subsequently acknowledge that what the patient had said was funny. In supervision they report lapses into laughter as 'confessions' awaiting some reprimand. Such a reaction is striking and we can only speculate as to why such a natural response should need to be suppressed. Is a more neutral, sober response to a patient's use of humour more helpful? Furthermore, what might be the consequences of actually inhibiting such responses? In a discussion about the relative merits of therapists' openness with patients about their reactions, Friedman highlights the dilemma experienced by many therapists:

> The attempt to conceal something one would ordinarily reveal has consequences apart from, and far more important than, what is concealed. Conversely if the therapist is frank about himself he is choosing to make the odd relationship seem more like an expectable relationship, and that conceals something about the therapist that concealment would reveal, namely his peculiar role (1988:440).

We are faced with a familiar catch-22: how do we reconcile the personal and the professional without sacrificing the unique space afforded by the therapeutic relationship? The inherent ambiguity of the therapist's role is a familiar one. As was suggested earlier, in order to protect the uniqueness of this role we inhibit certain responses that threaten to make the therapeutic relationship more similar to social or intimate relationships. In so doing we run the risk, however, of standardizing the relationship to such an extent that it becomes insensitive to the needs of individual patients. Bader alerts us to the potential pitfalls of inhibiting humorous responses:

> For some patients, a serious, emotionally restrained analytic ambience with a therapist who modulates his or her affective expressiveness in order to convey analytic neutrality can reinforce certain pathogenic expectations and fantasies rather than help the patient face and work through them (1993:43).

The potential in humour for disconfirming expectations is important since for some patients the more aloof, serious therapist may be experienced as a repetition of interactions with a withdrawn or depressed parent who was unable to engage in a lively manner and stimulate the baby or child. In therapy with such patients, *how* the therapist is with the patient may be as important as *what* the therapist interprets. Being humorous and playful in psychotherapy is as much an expression of a particular way of 'being with' the patient as it is an actual verbal intervention. Let us now therefore turn more explicitly to the question of humour in psychotherapy.

Humour in psychotherapy[34]

By this point I hope you will feel at least open to the possibility that humour in psychotherapy has a place as a legitimate vehicle for communicating with the patient and that it represents a powerful intervention.

Let us then look more closely at its use and contraindications for it. I do not wish to imply that we should, or even can, use humour prescriptively. For its use to be effective it has to be spontaneous. That is its essential quality, without which it no longer holds open the potential to become a moment-of-meeting. So much depends on the particular patient-therapist dyad, the point of intersection in their relationship when humour occurs and the unique meanings that its rejection, interpretation or mutual enjoyment will hold for both. How the therapist responds is perhaps less important than whether the patient and therapist can come to understand what has happened if there has been a failure to respond, for example, to the recounting of a funny incident or a joke.

Greenson (1967) observed that the best therapists have a good sense of humour, but he cautioned against its use for exhibitionistic or sadistic purposes. Therapists who have used humour will recognize the emotional connection that a well-timed joke or humorous vignette can facilitate. Rosten (1961) beautifully encapsulates the therapeutic potential of jokes when he describes them as 'the affectionate communication of insight'. Humour can bridge the conscious and unconscious concerns of a patient. Its indirectness can help to bypass defences thereby allowing the patient to hear something they might otherwise be more inclined to dismiss or ignore if presented to them in the guise of a more 'serious' interpretation. In an atmosphere of trust, humour can affectionately expose defences, illuminate the transference and strengthen interpretation. Some painful observations can be rendered digestible by slight leavening. Bloomfield (1980) points out that humorous comment, rather than avoiding painful affect, may in fact be helpful to show up a patient's intellectualization and make a more immediate communication possible.

A patient's favourite joke and response to humour have been assumed to be revealing of a core emotional conflict and have therefore been used by some therapists as a diagnostic tool (Redlich et al., 1950; Zwerling, 1955). People reveal their unconscious both by the jokes they tell and by what they find funny. Likewise, Dana (1994) advocates paying attention to a child's ability or difficulty in appreciating jokes. She believes that this is diagnostically significant in understanding the child's

---

34. This discussion focuses only on the use of humour in psychoanalytically oriented psychotherapy. Although the arguments and questions raised are equally relevant to other types of psychotherapy, I am restricting the discussion here to the views of psychoanalytic psychotherapists on the matter. There is, however, ample literature within the fields of some approaches to family therapy, cognitive-behavioural and humanistic approaches discussing the use of humour (e.g. Frankl, 1965; Ellis, 1977; Ravella, 1988) where it is considered far less controversial. Frankl in particular invoked the use of 'paradoxical intention' by inviting the patient to 'will' their symptoms which would then produce laughter at the absurdity of the situation.

cognitive style and potential learning disabilities. Although the content of jokes deemed funny is revealing of a person's emotional attitudes, I would not advocate eliciting a joke in an assessment consultation. I would nevertheless pay close attention to the spontaneous recounting of jokes. More importantly, I tend to view a patient's capacity for humour as prognostically encouraging and its absence as significant (Searles, 1979; Sands, 1984; Poland, 1994). If humour is not used predominantly as a sadistic attack on the other or to inflate the narcissistic self, its presence indicates some degree of readiness to reveal the thoughts and feelings which it attempts simultaneously to disguise. It is a kind of communication that what is hidden is clamouring for expression. The capacity to use humour relies, as Kris points out, on the person's ego development and control:

> One is reminded of persons to whom the comic in general is unknown. They fear regression in all comic pleasure, they lack the faculty of letting themselves go. One finds in analysis that this is due to a lack of strength in the ego. If patients of this type acquire or reacquire the faculty of humour in analysis, it is only after the dominating power of the ego has been restored, and thus regression to comic pleasure has lost its threatening aspect (1952:203).

In my own work I look for evidence of humour not only in the obvious sense of the recounting of funny stories but also the relaying of events in one's life in a more humorous, light-hearted manner (to be distinguished from denial and minimization of something emotionally significant). In those cases where the patient's presentation suggests an inability to play or an inhibition in spontaneous responses, I often enquire whether humour was used in the family or ask for any specific recollections of humorous exchanges between family members rather than elicit actual jokes. Sometimes patients are quite surprised by this question and it often acts as a trigger for recollections of disputes or critical incidents which were either managed successfully through being made light of, or were experienced as significant ruptures in communication without any opportunity for repair. The therapist's use of humour with patients who have grown up in quite humourless environments and where depressive withdrawal was the solution to interpersonal problems, may model an alternative way of managing conflict without avoiding it.

Searles (1979) suggests that humour is the avenue through which disillusionment is sublimated throughout development. He views its appearance in therapy as an indication that the patient and therapist have begun to integrate disillusionment in their relationship.

A year into his therapy John – himself a stand-up comedian who had been referred because of depression – started to express covert disenchantment with the lack of progress in the therapy. Although he had related to me how successful he had been as a comedian in an earlier part of his life he was now in fact unemployed, only occasionally doing manual work. The therapy was devoid of any laughter even though his manner of describing events indicated a capacity to turn things on their head and a witty disposition. Such a perspective was, however, lost in his predominantly depressed demeanour where hopelessness loomed large.

John harboured a deep sense of grievance towards his mother whom he recalled as unavailable to him but 'married to the bottle'. However, he was more aware of his guilt than his rage. His father had been experienced as an absent figure both physically and most certainly emotionally. His diluted anger was directed largely towards the father for abandoning his mother. John remembered poignantly wanting to make her laugh and felt admonished when he failed to amuse her and she would turn, as he saw it, to drink instead.

Nine months into the therapy I collected John five minutes late from the waiting area. I apologized for my lateness, to which he replied that it had not been a problem since it had given him time to get himself a coffee. Coffee could really perk him up and he had wanted to be alert for the session, having reached my office feeling rather tired. 'Just one shot and I can be revived', he told me, as he continued to discuss the effects of caffeine on his system for the next ten minutes. As I listened to him I found myself becoming quite irritated at the detail he was giving me about the coffee. I felt he was wanting to communicate to me his rage at being kept waiting, yet I knew how difficult he found direct expressions of anger. John had never reconciled himself with his mother's suicide when he was in his early twenties. It had followed a heated argument during which he had told her she was 'nothing more than a drunk bitch'.

In the session, John appeared to be telling me that the coffee (not insignificantly a drink) had provided him with the gratification he needed when I had failed to be there for him on time. As he spoke I had the image of coffee advertisements going through my mind and said to him; 'I guess the only instant thing around here is coffee'. John, for the first time, burst into laughter. The atmosphere in the room between us changed. He looked at me and said: 'That's funny! And yes, I am pissed off with you for being late'. He laughed some more. He then became more thoughtful and his eyes, for the first time, filled with tears, as he recalled an incident from his childhood. He had come home from school with a picture that his teacher had praised. He had wanted to show it to his mother. He remembered always wanting to show her his good work, hoping that this would make her happy. On this particular occasion he found her stretched out on the floor with a bottle by her side and he withdrew into his room. He observed that he must have felt very angry but he had not cried or shouted. I said that when he had arrived for his session he had wanted me to be available to him, to share with him what had been on his mind, but that he had found me involved in something else and he had felt neglected. He had soothed himself by turning to coffee, the effects of which he could at least control. John agreed, observing that that must have been his mother's reason for turning to alcohol.

This particular exchange illustrates how humour was able to resolve an impasse and give permission for feelings that had felt too dangerous to articulate. However, the use of humour did not preclude an elaboration of the feelings that had been defended against and the tone of the remainder of the session reflected this. By responding in a more humorous manner I think that I also conveyed to John that I could survive his hostile attacks. His laughter was therefore not only laughter of recognition but also of relief. Fenichel is reported to have said that a patient's response of laughter to a therapist's interpretation is evidence of its correctness (quoted in Levine and Redlich, 1955). This certainly concurs both with my own experience as a patient and with my own patients. In the patients' laughter – reminiscent of the child's laughter while playing as he discovers a new-found skill – there is an element of surprise and an acknowledgement that something once hidden can now be revealed (Reik, 1936).

Rose (1969), Bloch et al. (1983), Haig (1986), Satow (1991), Bader (1993), Heuscher (1993) and Poland (1994) outline the varied benefits that can be accrued through the use of humour in psychotherapy. I shall synthesize their views as there is a degree of overlap between them. These authors suggest that humour:

- encourages the observing ego
- facilitates interpretation by bypassing resistance
- strengthens the therapeutic alliance
- highlights issues which are anxiety provoking
- builds ego strength
- modulates anxiety
- contributes to the internalization of a model of intrapsychic communication which modulates mood and anxiety
- soothes, while respecting the power of inner conflict and outer hurt
- lifts repression
- modifies the superego by mobilizing its benign aspects
- conveys the therapist's ability to tolerate and master certain affects and roles induced by the patient via projective mechanisms
- conveys the therapist's capacity affectionately to appreciate the patient's hostility and recognize their attempts, however neurotic, to establish mutuality
- undermines fixed or habitual views and attitudes by introducing alternative or unexpected options.

All of the above are important effects of humour. I should like to draw particular attention to the last point. A good analytic interpretation is one that highlights and then pulls together conflicting aspects of experience. It presents these psychic events to the patient as somehow related. The juxtaposition of psychic events that emanate from different unconscious motivations or needs, can be experienced as a surprise and can jolt the psychic landscape. Similarly, an important aspect of humour is the juxtaposition of incongruous images or ideas. A humorous story which contains a vivid image may then be used by the patient at other points in the therapy as a reference to code a particular behaviour or experience (Bloch et al., 1983). In my second analysis I vividly recall my analyst telling me in a humorous manner the story of Peter Rabbit who was so impatient that he could barely wait for the carrot that had been planted in the garden to grow. Consequently he used to pull it up prematurely and its roots would never take. The story amused me and touched me because I am a lot like that! Since being told this story, each time I find myself to be responding impatiently, I recall it and it makes me laugh. I see myself as Peter Rabbit with a rather sorry-looking carrot that leaves me invariably unsatisfied. Had my analyst responded to my characteristic impatience with a more sober interpretation about my difficulty in containing my anxiety while in waiting, rather than humorously encoding it through an amusing story, I think that I would not have been able to access the intervention so readily, and so effectively, each time this particular dynamic presented itself in my life. My analyst's affectionate understanding, conveyed through her choice of this story, was itself helpful in allowing me to feel not only alert to this dynamic, but also more compassionate to the needs that lay behind my impatience. In other words, it served to activate a more benign superego.

Bader draws attention to the needs of some patients who may require 'a more visceral and affectively undeniable demonstration from the analyst that the relationship [is] safe-enough to risk analytic exploration' (1993:27). He refers to humour as a 'metacommunication' to the patient about the therapist's internal psychological state which fosters safety and confidence in the patient. It conveys to the patient the therapist's mental state which discomfirms inhibiting expectations and so increases the patient's ability to be self-reflective and confront painful affects.[35] Overall, most authors agree that humour facilitates the alliance with the observant ego, whereas humour's more critical side is directed towards the resistances. Rose (1969) illustrates how, through its reliance on negation, humour can help to lift repression. Many humorous statements are predicated on the negation of whatever they are aiming to illuminate. As Freud (1925) observed, when we use negation the ideational content of repression is uncovered, even if this is not tantamount to an acceptance of it. Yet, as Rose, reminds us:

[35.] This will of course depend on the therapist's underlying intentions in making the humorous comment.

Such a modest accomplishment should not be despised. Humour, making use of negation, may introduce into consciousness the intellectual possibility that such-and-such might be true. This can be an essential first step (1969:934).

Jack was a thirty-five year old scientist. He was a highly intelligent man who had started therapy somewhat reluctantly, following the break-up of a longstanding relationship. His ex-partner had accused him of being 'detached, aloof and unresponsive'. His presentation in therapy gave me a flavour of the roots of these accusations. Jack was indeed rather distant. Intimacy raised the spectre of contempt as it served to remind him of his dependency which he strove hard to deny. In therapy, Jack was quite critical of my interventions. Whenever I implicitly invoked in my interpretations an unconscious mechanism, he was quick to launch into a well-practised admonishment of psychoanalysis and the notion of the unconscious in particular. The hostility towards me that was embedded in these intellectual onslaughts was barely disguised, yet Jack vehemently denied it.

According to Jack, psychoanalysis was the prototypical catch-22 situation: he could not win since anything he said I could take to mean its opposite. This was highly relevant in the context of his own relationship with his mother whom he had experienced as always 'going back on what she said'. For example, he had various recollections of his mother denying that she had agreed to something. In addition, she appeared to have used Jack as the receptacle for her unwanted projections and had attributed to him feelings that he felt did not belong to him, though he could never be sure, hence his perpetual internal confusion. He was therefore suspicious that I might similarly brainwash him and tell him what he thought and felt. His need to protect himself from the intrusion of another was palpable. It also represented a significant resistance in the therapy, since in the first sixteen months it was impossible to get him to free-associate, use the couch or bring his dreams. I often felt as if he experienced me as the enemy and he had to safeguard his threatened psychic territory. Although we met for psychotherapy three times weekly it did not feel as though we were working together.

A year into the therapy, Jack was once again criticizing in a session the notion of the unconscious. He presented an elegant argument which would have made any critic of psychoanalysis very proud. On this occasion he also spoke of how he could put the money he paid me to much better use since he was not deriving much benefit from psychotherapy. Although the content of what he said was by no means novel, I was struck by the impassioned way in which he was speaking, which was qualitatively different. I felt more connected with him at that point and, within myself, I felt somewhat amused: here was this man vociferously telling me that what I practised was a sham, yet, a year on, he was still in quite an intensive therapy. I commented, in a light-hearted manner, 'You know I was doubtful at first about psychoanalysis but you make it sound so interesting I feel I must go away and read up more about it. It looks as if it's me who is getting a good deal here'.[36] Jack stalled. His riposte was usually prompt, yet this time it was a few seconds before he laughed and said: 'I guess I do spend so much time talking about this and reading about it that even I, the great sceptic, am driven to conclude that *this* (his emphasis) must be significant!'. For the remainder of the session we were able to examine his resistance a bit more freely. This exchange did not resolve the resistance once and for all but it marked a turning point insofar as it created an opportunity for experiencing a more collaborative and lively exchange. Furthermore, in subsequent sessions, when a similar dynamic emerged he would at times laugh, observing that he was going into 'lecture mode'. This became a helpful shorthand for his tendency to cut off emotionally, placing me in the vulnerable position of the one needing help or tutoring.

Humour encourages a freer, more playful interaction between patient and therapist which can contribute towards a loosening of an impasse. Since humour contains an implicit message about serious matters, underlying a humorous exchange there is a negotiation about whether to transpose the communication into a more serious discussion (Emerson, 1969). In its ambiguity lies the power of humour since it allows both the patient and the therapist to take interpersonal initiatives that might otherwise feel too risky. When used by the therapist it also allows the patient to 'run if he needs to' (Greenson, 1967) should he not yet be ready to confront the emotional weight of the interpretation. This is possible since, through using humour, the therapist extends an invitation to think about something serious but allows the patient to overlook it by merely laughing and not taking it any further. It is a way of knocking on the door of the defensive edifice without forcing entry. Explorations that produce more psychic pain than the patient can bear can be returned to at a later point. Generally speaking, in psychotherapy, less is often more. Tarachow observes that:

> An interpretation should rarely go as far as possible. It should, by prefer-
> ence, fall short even of its immediate intended goal. This gives the patient
> an opportunity to extend your interpretation, gives him greater share in
> the proceedings and will mitigate to some extent the trauma of being the
> victim of your help (1963:49).

Most of the available literature, with the notable exception of Kubie's (1971) contribution, reflects an interest and a belief that humour can be used to therapeutic ends. Many authors underline the need to use it

---

[36.] Rose (1969) describes a similar example, though I had not yet read his paper when I was seeing this patient.

cautiously and for therapists to monitor its possible countertransferential motivations. Although I am also of the opinion that the judicious use of humour has a place in psychotherapy, the available literature supporting its use is almost exclusively anecdotal. I have been able to find only a handful of studies that have more systematically addressed the use of humour in psychotherapy. Killinger (1977) asked eleven therapists to tape-record sessions with two patients respectively. The tapes were then rated for the presence of humorous exchanges, the direction of the communication (other- versus self-directed), the manner of the delivery (non-defensive versus defensive) and the humorous content (relevant versus irrelevant). The aim was to determine whether humour was facilitative, that is, whether it led to further patient exploration of the topic and more positive attitudes towards the therapist. The study concluded that the use of humour acted in most instances as a stimulus to further exploration and to more positive attitudes. Unfortunately the paper does not report detailed results or how the positive attitudes were measured, and consequently it is not possible to draw firm conclusions from it. A study by Golub (1979; quoted in Saper, 1987) examined the effect of counsellors' use of humour. In this study videotapes based on a detailed script enacted by actresses were used. The data did not reveal any significant differences in the participants' evaluation of the counsellors who used or did not use humour.

A far more methodologically sophisticated study was attempted by Golan et al. (1988). They looked at patient preference for humorous versus non-humorous interventions. In their study they asked sixty female patients classified under three separate personality types (obsessive, hysterical and depressed) to rate twelve tape recordings of simulated therapy sessions. The therapists in the study had been asked to use humour to achieve three different functions: anxiety reduction, perspective building and emotional confrontation. The results indicate that non-humorous interventions were consistently favoured over humorous ones and this effect was independent of the patient's personality. Nevertheless the *extent* to which the non-humorous interventions were preferred was contingent on an interaction between personality and type of humour. For example, obsessional patients were the most vociferous critics of the use of humour when it was employed in the simulated sessions to confront patients, especially when compared to the reactions of the hysterical patients. The latter rejected humour only when it was aimed at reducing anxiety (a finding that is counterintuitive). The depressed patients were less significantly opposed to the use of humour when employed to reduce anxiety but were critical of its use as a means of confrontation. At face value such results would discourage most therapists from invoking humour. However, there are significant limitations to this study. Firstly, the sessions were simulated and it is therefore likely that the spontaneous quality of humorous exchanges is lost and hence the exchanges are more contrived. Secondly, patients were asked to rate sessions of which they were not a part. Taken out of the context of a particular relationship where both participants have some knowledge of each other, the use of humour may indeed seem insensitive or inappropriate. Had the patients been asked to rate their own therapists for their use of humour the results might well have been different. This point is acknowledged by the authors. Moreover, they found that when the patients were asked two open questions regarding what they liked or disliked about the humorous interventions, their responses suggested that humour aroused more positive feelings than the replies to the quantitative, closed questions had initially suggested.

The study by Golan et al. stands alone as an attempt to evaluate the use of humour empirically. The results emphasize the need to use humour cautiously and also highlight that its potential benefits can be meaningfully assessed only in the context of a real relationship between a particular patient and a particular therapist. The research also alerts us to the question of which humour to use, when and with whom, that is, we cannot make generalizations.

When humour is out of place

The expression of humour is of course both 'cause and effect' of the interactive field between patient and therapist (Lewis, 1987). Its effect, according to Lewis, will therefore also depend on a number of contingencies that are hard to predict in advance and even control. Hence humour is best used with caution. Kubie (1971) contributed one of the most forceful papers on the contraindications of humour, emphasizing its potential for destructiveness. He points out that it is often used to mask hostility behind a façade of camaraderie or to blunt the sharpness of a disagreement. He also thinks that it serves as a defence against the therapist's own anxieties as well as those of the patient. Finally, he views it as the most seductive form of 'transference wooing'. He concludes his rather sobering account by stating that 'Humour has its place in life. Let us keep it there by acknowledging that one place it has a very limited role, if any, is in psychotherapy' (1971:103). It is difficult to disagree with most of what Kubie says, insofar as he alerts us to the perils of using humour in an unthinking manner. Although there are no shortages of advocates of the use of humour in psychotherapy, as we saw earlier, some of the reported accounts on the use of humour may leave one with a distinctively uncomfortable feeling. For example, Roncoli (1971) uses 'bantering' with obsessional patients, which involves caricaturing them. It is not difficult to imagine how such an intervention could very easily backfire and simply serve to discharge the therapist's own hostility. Masochistic tendencies in the patient may also apparently lead them to welcome humour in therapy, as the hostility it may convey could collude with their masochism (Dooley, 1934). Using humour with patients who are paranoid, or who have a history of being given very contradictory messages in childhood, should also be very carefully considered (Sands, 1984) – as indeed was the case in my work with Jack – since the ambiguity of humour may be difficult to tolerate.

Any communication we make as therapists with our patients requires thoughtful consideration. It is incumbent on us to reflect upon the meaning and underlying unconscious determinants of all of our interventions. Humour is no exception. However, this is the limit of my agreement with Kubie's ultimately rigid stance. His arguments nevertheless invite us to look more closely at the thorny question of whether or not a therapist should gratify a patient's wish or request (Mitchell, 1993). If a patient tries to make us laugh, should we respond? The classical analytic position is that the analytic relationship is essentially frustrating. The analytic work consists of coming to terms with the frustrations it presents the patient with – frustrations that are the essence of what it means to be human. The anonymity of the therapist and the regressive aspects of being in the therapeutic situation all arouse and intensify the deep desires that have silently shaped the patient's life. The analytic situation is intentionally set up to stir such regressive wishes and to deny them gratification so that they can be articulated and then renounced. Some might think this is indeed the paradigm of a bad joke. The analytic rationale is, however, that to gratify these desires would be tantamount to acting out rather than thinking about what is happening, thereby preventing the patient from discovering his 'style and his conditions for loving and hating' (Menninger, 1958:57).

The patient's wish for an idealized relationship belongs to the transference realm and is much more a product of the patient's past than a realistic reaction to the therapist as a real person. The gratification, instead of interpretation, of such transference wishes would, in my view, constitute a fundamental error with the vast majority of the patients we see. The patient's use of humour as a way of recreating a symbiotic, narcissistic relationship with the therapist needs to be interpreted and not colluded with. Being amusing and inviting laughter can be very seductive, and it is easy to be lured into a relationship with the patient in which an insidious complicity undermines the therapeutic work.

Nowadays, however, there is recognition of the particular needs of a group of patients who are more disturbed and who often have histories of quite severe deprivation. In these cases the patient's explicit request for a deviation from the analytic frame are understood as 'ego needs' rather than instinctual wishes seeking gratification (Winnicott, 1954; Balint, 1968). With such patients some therapists are more inclined to meet their demands as the only way to move beyond a therapeutic impasse. It is not easy to distinguish between a patient who shares a joke with us in an attempt to seduce us, from the patient who needs us to appreciate their attempt to 'make a joke' and so share in the laughter and their developmental achievement. This is partly because, as Hoffman argues,

> A patient's desires generally involve a complex shifting hierarchical
> arrangement of needs and wishes . . . it is virtually impossible to formu-
> late an assessment of their relative weights and positions in that instant . . .
> the analyst's actions are themselves embedded in, and even partially
> constituting of, his perpetually fluctuating arrangements of desires'
> (1987:212).

Hoffman's remark will no doubt ring true with many therapists, but our
task, though certainly difficult, is not 'virtually impossible'. Our formulations can never be more than attempts to frame our perceptions in a
particular meaning context so that they may guide our behaviour. They
are, nevertheless, all we have and we should not dilute their potential
correctness by withdrawing into an apparently noble, relativistic, stance
which underlines the difficulty in knowing another person's reality. In so
doing we are abrogating our capacity to think. Of course it is difficult to
track what is happening between therapist and patient; we can only do
our best. But it is possible, on the basis of our knowledge of the patient's
developmental history, of their transference configurations, of their
patterns of relationship, to formulate a hypothesis – and to treat it as
such – about how they may be using humour, for example, at any point
in time, and so adapt our response accordingly.
    Mitchell argues that:

> The patient's acceptance of the traditional structure of the analytic situ-
> ation and the patient's efforts to transgress these structures can both
> carry many different meanings that can have very different kinds of
> impact on the analyst (Mitchell, 1993:181).

Some of our patients' wishes have a sense of freshness about them which
accounts for our cautious willingness to go along with their request or
invitation to be different, to step out of the usual analytic frame. In these
situations we have the sense of someone who has never had the kind of
experience they are inviting us to share. Alvarez (1992), in her discussion of work with children, points out how a 'depriving' type of interpretation in response to, say, a question such as 'Do you like animals?' may
be experienced by a deprived child as cruelly rejecting of what may be a
first overture of friendliness. She also argues that we need to view
defences in a developmental perspective as achievements rather than
merely impediments. Likewise, with patients' use of humour. For some,
the capacity to adopt a humorous perspective on their predicament,
even if it involves a degree of denial, may nevertheless represent a developmental advance. As Mitchell describes it:

> There is a sense of something happening for the analysand that has never
> happened before, a use of capacities, an opening up of a dimension of
> the self, a kind of connection never thought possible (1993:183).

Such experiences in the therapeutic encounter may contribute to significant changes. Within developmental psychology, changes in the baby are
conceptualized as being partly a function of the adult's interpretation of
the baby and the tailoring of their response on the basis of this understanding:

> Organisational change from within the infant and its interpretation by the
> parents are mutually facilitative. The net result is that the infant appears
> to have a new sense of who he or she is and who you are, as well as a
> different sense of the kinds of interactions that can now go on (Tronick,
> 1989:9).

A similar process can occur in therapy as a result of the therapist's
responsiveness to the patient's needs, thus allowing for a new experience which challenges existing templates of self–other relationships.
With some patients, the quality of therapist's response to, or interpretation of, the patient's invitation to laugh with them can contribute to a
re-working of internal models of relationships. I am not, therefore,
proposing that change emanates solely from the mutual participation in
such novel experiences. It rests also on an understanding of the conflicts
and inhibitions that may have prevented therapist and patient from
having such experiences before.

The humorous mirror

Therapy is a privileged space within which the patient not only
expresses his pain, frustration and disappointments but can also share
with the therapist his excited plans, aspirations and sense of humour.
Although the humorous façade will at times conceal psychic pain, if we
hear only the fragility or pain of the communication we may miss the
patient's valuable resilience that has kept their humorous sublimations
intact (Russell, 1991) or that represents an attempt to relate differently.
Humour can act as a way of managing an unbearable reality in a manner
that injects new life and meaning. We are often, however, held back in
our inclination to partake in our patients' apparent pleasure when they
are humorous out of fear that we may produce too much excitement,
which may distract or collude with the patient's need for gratification. It
is of course important that we guard against using humour in an
inauthentic manner or to serve our own defensive needs in an attempt
to ward off an anxiety-provoking interaction with the patient, or to invite
the patient's admiration of our wittiness. As Poland reminds us 'An
analysis is the patient's show, not the analyst's' (1994:22). Caution is
indicated, but we need not be deterred by this. As Coltart notes, 'A
humorous remark by a patient which can be responded to in kind may
cover a lot of ground and have more impact than the most careful, fully
serious, longer interpretation' (1993:93).

The invitation to be humorous is an invitation to something quite specific by a patient and is therefore embedded in a dyadic field in which the patient and therapist are either able to find and connect with each other or to deflect and miss each other. The process of negotiation of the meaning of such an invitation is the critical variable (Mitchell, 1993). With patients who use humour to distance or to seduce, for example, it would be unhelpful to collude with our laughter. In such situations it will be important to point out the way in which they are using humour. The use of humour may well change during the course of a therapy and we need to remain alert to these changes, as mutual laughter at a later stage might communicate the important recognition that change has taken place.

Psychoanalysis is a rich, complex and stimulating theory and application but it does not present a unified view of the mutative factors in psychotherapy (Hamilton, 1996). The current interest in the 'something more than interpretation' (Stern et al., 1998) will, it is hoped, pave the way for research into other mutative factors in psychotherapy beyond the interpretation of transference. Although the interest is current, these ideas are by no means new. There have been several other notable contributions emphasizing the importance of non-interpretative influences to the outcome of psychotherapy (Ferenczi, 1928; Balint, 1968; Winnicott, 1965; Freeman, 1998). We have much to learn yet about the more specific interactions which promote a good alliance between therapist and patient, and whether these vary depending on the patient's own preferred mode of relating.

Even though the ideal of a neutral, opaque, mirror-like therapist no longer holds sway as powerfully as it did in the past, the notion that the therapist should guard against more revealing ways of 'being with' the patient is embedded in the predominant culture of analytic training. Transference interpretation remains the mainstay of analytic practice and in some analytic circles, dare I say it, it has become almost fetishized. Listening to some case presentations can at times leave one feeling distinctly uncomfortable as virtually everything the patient says is reduced to the 'You mean me' type of interpretation. It is as if the actual content of what the patient says is subordinate to its transference implications. Such interpretations sometimes appear very clever indeed, but it may be worth asking ourselves whether they represent the main pathway to psychic change.

We can only gain in our understanding of how psychotherapy, in its broadest sense, works if we become more aware of the hidden functions of the real relationship that is always present in the background of every psychotherapy. As with the transference relationship, the real relationship should be seen as essential for the therapeutic process. Although published and oral reports of clinical work suggest that many therapists work mainly through the transference, and that successful outcome is attributed to the working through of the transference relationship, I do wonder if this reflects the reality of day-to-day practice behind closed doors. My hunch is that therapists do and say far more than offering transference or reconstructive interpretations to their patients. Maybe they even laugh or relate humorously far more than they report to colleagues. We do not yet know the relative contribution of therapists' different interventions to the ultimate outcome of psychotherapy. It would in fact be interesting to research whether better outcomes are associated with therapies where transference interpretations are central and, if so, whether this is the case for only particular types of problems or patients.

If we are prepared to go beyond transference interpretation and grant the real relationship and other so-called 'non-specific factors' mutative potential, this will allow humorous exchanges between patient and therapist the serious attention they deserve. In an effort to train therapists to take their patients seriously we may have, as Pierce suggests 'too often taught them to take them soberly and humourlessly' (1994:105). Sometimes sharing a humorous anecdote illuminates an interpretation in a way that brings it to life for the patient in a far more emotionally immediate and accessible manner. The use by the therapist of their own sense of humour is important because it can dramatically and forcefully point to a psychological truth and lead to a clarification, rather than avoidance, of unconscious communication. Coltart (1993) argues that the therapist should respond to a patient's humour. Not to do so would be, in her opinion, 'churlish and affected'. She notes that even if the therapist responds with laughter this does not preclude the possibility of subsequently analysing that exchange as it may throw light on novel views, feelings and attitudes. This is indeed the point made by Stern et al. (1998) insofar as they emphasize the importance of examining moments-of-meeting in therapy once they have occurred.

Perhaps we are all too ready, as Sands put it,

> to expect, and sometimes encourage the expression of the patient's anger and facilitate the expression of sadness with a box of Kleenex left carefully within reach, but the expression of humour is usually left to accident (1984:441).

Just as we are often firm believers that in order to cope with difficulties in life we need to have shared some positive, enjoyable experiences and developed secure attachments that steel us for the more challenging times to come, such positive exchanges are equally important in the patient–therapist relationship (Pasquali, 1986). It is helpful for the patient to have in mind the recollection of a moment of shared laughter which indicated a mutual understanding – a moment of meeting – when he is grappling, at another point, with a more difficult exchange with the therapist. This may be especially important for those patients who enter therapy with little capacity to play. 'If the patient cannot play', writes Winnicott, 'then something needs to be done to enable the patient to become able to play after which psychotherapy may begin' (1971:54). Humour can foster a more playful atmosphere while retaining a serious focus. The emergence of humour in therapy in a previously humourless patient is one of the greatest achievements and more significant outcomes in psychotherapy that I have had the privilege to be party to. Psychoanalysis is, as Fonagy and Target (1996) aptly describe, a 'pretend experience' in which play is central. Moreover, if we overlook the more playful and funny aspects of psychoanalysis, Friedman (1994) reminds us that we are not only doing a disservice to our patients but we also deprive ourselves of some of the pleasure inherent in our work.

'Sanity' writes Rose, 'requires a critical mirror, but where reality tolerance is low, the mirror had better be tinted or funny' (1969:928). Whether we choose to hold up the humorous mirror to our patients will depend, as with any other intervention, on our tact, judgement, and sensitivity to the transference and countertransference matrix operating at any point in time. Although humour is a valuable intervention it is best conceived as presenting moment-to-moment benefits as opposed to an 'overall strategy or goal' (Saper, 1987:362). The art of therapy lies in knowing not only when, but how, to present material that can be grasped affectively by the patient.

Chapter 6
Why Humour?

Perhaps a sense of humour is essential to human survival. Amusement in the self and in the other may be a vital constituent part of a comprehensive perspective on life. (Bollas, 1995:243-4).

Laughter and humour, as we have seen, are universal. This invites the question of why such a particular type of communication, along with the physical response of laughter, may have evolved. Although Koestler (1964) referred to laughter as a 'luxury reflex' there are those such as Alexander (1986), Weisfeld (1993) and Fry (1994) who are clear that laughter and humour were selected for in evolution. Indeed, the evidence for the effectiveness of laughter and humour in moderating stress and improving immune functioning that was reviewed in Chapter 4, though still comparatively limited, is usually invoked as evidence for an evolutionary account of the cognitive, behavioural and affective response of laughter.

Evolutionary accounts attempt to explain the reproductive advantages conferred by a particular behaviour. In one of the first accounts on the functions of laughter, Hayworth (1928) argued for a social function rather than a fundamentally biological one. He thought that laughter was originally a vocal signal to other members of the group that they may relax in safety. Along similar lines, Ramachandran (1998) suggests that laughter and humour involve the build-up of a particular expectation or 'model' followed by a twist or anomaly that entails a change in the model but only as long as the model is non-threatening. Laughter is produced to inform others that there has a been a 'false alarm' to which they need not attend. Much laughter does indeed convey a sense of reassurance that all is well. It is also the case that we are less likely to laugh with others unless we feel relatively safe. However, we also laugh out of anxiety or employ gallows humour precisely at those times when we feel most vulnerable and the risk is real. So, Hayworth's and Ramachandran's hypotheses account for only some laughter and therefore they are not satisfying as more general theories of why laughter may have evolved.

Some theorists have proposed that laughter corrects deviant behaviour (see Chapter 1). This explanation is usually cast in terms of the welfare of the group in so far as the group is said to benefit from this method of social control (Fine, 1983). Although criticisms served up as humorous comments or observations may be easier to digest, it is difficult to see why such a complex behavioural system would have evolved for an apparently restricted purpose (Weisfeld, 1993). If the theory of social correction is correct, it presents difficulties when we then try to accommodate such humorous expressions as wordplay or the incongruity element of humour. Although humour may be used as a signal to others that certain behaviours are unacceptable, the social control effect of humour may be an incidental by-product of its original function(s).

Provine (1998) has demonstrated that the underlying structure of laughter in humans is always the same. This suggests that laughter is instinctive and is designed, according to Provine, to help us to co-operate socially. In his studies he found that once people are taken out of their social context and brought into a laboratory situation to be shown humorous videos, laughter is subdued or disappears altogether (Provine and Fischer, 1989). Laughter evolved, according to Provine, because it facilitates social bonding. He argues that laughter is an ancient mode of pre-linguistic vocal communication that has evolved into an additional skill – a sense of humour – processed in a more advanced area of the brain. In other words, he is suggesting that we are seemingly programmed to laugh with others. In this respect, tickling is a very interesting interpersonal phenomenon since we seldom laugh if we tickle ourselves. Blakemore (1998) studied self- and other-initiated tickling and found a differential response in brain activity. Other-initiated tickling produced, as expected, far more laughter. On the other hand, when the person could predict a tickle, that is, when they were tickling themselves, the brain suppressed the sensation as evidenced using brain-scanning equipment. Our capacity to differentiate the source of tickling appears to be hardwired into the brain. If this is so, then why? Blakemore argues that there is no evolutionary advantage in laughing at our own tickle but it is important to respond to someone else's tickle. As tickling produces laughter it may have evolved to allow us to relate to others and this would also be the case for verbal forms of humour. If we are pre-programmed to respond in this manner, this suggests that a possible evolutionary function of laughter, and at a more advanced level of a sense of humour too, is the facilitation of social bonding and co-operation, as Darwin originally suggested.

Alexander (1986) discusses humour in the context of his views on the function of 'ostracism'. He views the latter as a social tool for manipulating 'conflicts and confluences of interest' through adjusting access to resources. This is a problem that is specifically human since we live together as large groups of people with long lifespans. The paradox of our human predicament is that the greatest threats, but also our supports to us as individuals and as a group, come from other humans rather than any other species. The challenge, from an evolutionary point of view, is how to manage successfully conflicts and confluences of interest with others. Alexander (1986) frames his argument around the notion of 'indirect reciprocity'. By this he means those rewards and punishments that come from individuals or groups other than those directly involved in an interaction. It includes, for example, public or private opinions and is the foundation of moral or ethical systems:[37]

> Indirect reciprocity is the reason that very few things are more relevant to our individual social success than the ability to see ourselves as others see us and respond appropriately (which means, I think, to cause them to see us as we wish them to, and not otherwise) . . . humor is a principle according to which the evolved abilities and tendencies of people to see themselves as others see them, to use ostracism to their own advantage, are manipulated so as to induce status shifts . . . humor has developed as a form of ostracism and . . . historically, at least, ostracism has tended to affect the reproduction of the ostracised individual (or group) deleteriously . . . by restricting access to significant resources (1986:255).

Alexander's thesis is interesting and finds echoes in the theory of humour as degradation (see Chapter 1). The function of degrading another is understood by Alexander to be a means of shunning those who are our competitors. He gives several examples of how jokes serve to elevate the status of the joker while lowering that of the butt of the joke and increasing camaraderie between members of an in-group by identifying the butt of the joke as a common object of ridicule. Although this is clearly only speculative, it is not an unreasonable proposition. However, it does beg the question of how we might then account for the more positive aspects of humour. Alexander suggests that we can understand this as reflecting humour's group-unifying purpose that originally gave us pleasure because it contributed to the more competent functioning of the group in inter-group competition. The reason we may seek out humour and comedy as more individual pursuits (when we buy a humorous book, for example) reflects, according to Alexander, attempts to practice a skill which is necessary in social situations.

It is also true of course that we can increase our fitness, as it were, through knowledge about salient matters. Weisfeld (1993) proposes that

---

37. Alexander views morality and justice as predicated not on the idea of 'justice for all' but rather of ostracism and exclusivity: 'They represent either gestures or convictions with respect to some kind of equality within a group, but explicitly not beyond it and in fact for the purposes of excluding some others' (1986:265).

preference for particular types of humorous content (for example, sex or aggression) may reflect a wish to learn more about a subject that is pertinent to our survival. His overall thesis is that humour evolved to induce us to seek out 'informative social stimulation' and laughter rewards others for obliging by providing us with the relevant information about psychosocial matters. His position is closely related to Pugh's view of humour as 'nature's way of motivating the social sharing of counterexamples' (1977:329). Fine (1976) argues that the content of the jokes of adolescent boys, such as penis length or standards of sexual performance, expresses both curiosity and anxiety. He suggests that by exchanging jokes the boys acquire additional knowledge. This point is echoed by Apte (1985) in his cross-cultural study of humour. He notes that sexual and scatological humour among children provides a channel for satisfying curiosity about the body, its functions and sexual intercourse, while also providing an outlet for aggression through competition. Although sharing jokes may facilitate the exchange of sexual information, the disadvantage of this means of dissemination of knowledge is that it is incumbent upon the recipient to disentangle fact from fantasy (Mulkay, 1988). Some jokes, if misunderstood, may only further obfuscate an anxiety-provoking subject.

Weisfeld's thesis is to an extent consistent with Bergson's theory of humour as corrective, since it implies that we may find funny, for example, the caricature of an obsessional person, because it alerts us to the inherent problems in this predicament and is thus instructive. Although I agree with Weisfeld that we are more likely to find funny, and possibly to actively seek out, jokes or humour pertaining to subjects which are personally salient, I am less convinced that, as he suggests, we are primarily driven to do this because of a desire to acquire further knowledge about a subject. Rather, we are drawn to humour relating to a particular topic because it gives us an opportunity to explore safely and give expression to some unresolved conflict pertaining to that area without having to process it consciously. Indirectly, of course, we could say that this provides us with a learning experience of sorts, but this is less about acquiring factual knowledge and more about learning ways of managing internal conflict constructively. Dixon (1980) points out that humour involves the expression of emotion related to the threat so that:

> . . . The situation that invites amusement must be one that touches on some underlying emotionally charged ambivalence towards the stressor in question. . . . In other words humour is powered by the very threat that it serves to demolish (1980:285).

Freud's own theory is of course a further example of attempts to account for humour within an evolutionary framework insofar as his emphasis on the economy of psychic expenditure afforded by jokes represents the management of instinctual forces which would otherwise threaten our emotional equilibrium and hence our adaptation. It is also important to note that the pleasure afforded by this strategy acts itself as an incentive to seek further comical solutions. Barchilon speculates that the pleasure we derive is so intense because we are creating out of conflict 'new and syntonic solutions which prepare the way for real, structural changes' (1973:29).

Morreall (1987) outlines, in my view, another very interesting account of the possible evolutionary function of humour. He suggests that our enjoyment of incongruity, evident in so much humour, is a response to our need to seek variety in our cognitive stimulation. Such variety is important since we quickly habituate to stimuli. The survival value of stimulus variety is that it makes us curious and so we are more likely to explore our environment which, over time, enhances our ability to cope with it and hence our chances of survival. However, our hunger for stimulation must not place us in situations that are potentially dangerous. The optimal novelty, Morreall suggests, is therefore novelty that does not pose a threat:

> What is desired is freshness in experience where one's overall control is maintained. And here is where humour comes in, for it involves a kind of novelty – incongruity – under the desired circumstances (1987:202).

Dixon elaborates a similar argument :

> The relationship between arousal, curiosity, exploratory behaviour and the ability to discern multiple meanings in a potentially threatening situation would have high survival value for an organism with more brain than brawn (1980:287).

In other words, we are organisms better equipped to respond to threat by cerebral rather then physical strength. Jonathan Miller indeed suggests that, like sex, the pleasure associated with humour is such that this indicates a 'biological payoff'. In a televised lecture, Miller argues that in humour we engage in an exercise of perception which results in a broadening of our categories and encourages more flexibility in our thinking:

> It has to do with a cognitive rehearsal of some sort . . . the more we laugh the more we see the point of things, the better we are, the cleverer we are at reconsidering what the world is like' [We use] the experience of humour as sabbatical leave from the binding categories that we use as rules of thumb to allow us to conduct our way around the world' (Miller, quoted in Palmer, 1994).

Fry (1994) states that laughter and humour are among those examples of the evolution of originally simple, primitive, but survival-enhancing, characteristics that have, over time, been elaborated into effects which surpass their originally simpler origins. Indeed, it is important to draw a distinction between the more basic biological and psychological behavioural determinants and those that represent their secondary developments, such as artistic or social forms (Palmer, 1994). It may therefore be more accurate to view humour as one such secondary development which affords us advantages that suit our specific needs as human beings. Evolutionary accounts are of course speculative and there is as yet no convincing unitary explanation that accounts for all the varied types of humour. Moreover, even if some of the accounts reviewed here are correct, this does not imply that nowadays humour does not serve more varied functions.

Conclusion
Humour, Truth and
Freedom

If you want to tell people the truth you'd better make them laugh, or
they'll kill you. George Bernard Shaw

Perhaps the mission of those who love mankind is to make people laugh
at truth, to make truth laugh, because the only truth lies in learning to
free ourselves from insane passion for the truth. Umberto Eco

Jack Rollins, the manager at various points to such well-known
comedians as Woody Allen and Robin Williams, describes the talent of
the comedian as residing in their ability,

to illuminate a corner in people's consciousness . . . And when they do
put the flashlight on that little thing, whatever that may be, the feeling is
'Oh yeah, Oh yeah, that's right'. Now it's defined. He's seen it as I have
felt it' (Rollins, quoted in Grace, 1991:9).

We feel recognized and understood by the comedian as he 'unzips his
soul' (Carlin, quoted in Grace, 1991) and holds up to us the humorous
mirror. 'No one is ever more himself', says the American comedian
George Carlin,

than at the moment they are laughing. It is like a perfect Zen moment of
letting go of the world. Right at that point when the joke hits your brain
and your brain understands it, all defences are down. And it is at a
moment like that when a new idea can be best implanted (quoted in
Grace, 1991:21).

In this sense, we might also add, as Skynner and Cleese suggest, that
humour is 'persuasive', 'because if you laugh at a joke you acknowledge
the truth of the point it is making' (1993:80).

If we can allow ourselves to be receptive to the process the comedian
(professional or otherwise) initiates for us we can, at some level, be

172

changed by the experience. This is not necessarily a perceptible change when the show is over, as it were, and we retreat to our respective realities. Yet, an important process will have been set in motion: the beginnings of a shift in perspective. It may come back to us at some later stage as a memory of the laughter of recognition. Essentially, we take away with us a sense of freedom and the acknowledgement that for a while at least we have eclipsed the narrow confines of reality (Pollio and Edgerly 1976). Humour, as Mindess, reminds us, 'offers us release from our stabilising system, escape from our self-imposed prisons. Every instance of laughter is an instance of liberation from our controls' (1971:23).

The goals inspiring the richest comedy are the same steering many performing arts: to say what is usually suppressed and to speak truthfully. What we laugh at during any historical period is a 'soulprint of the age' (Stone, 1997). Charlie Chaplin's underdog victories, Buster Keaton's triumph over the runaway train, Laurel and Hardy's endless struggles, 'all fuel the hopes we entertain of solving our human dilemmas' (Jenkins, 1988). We laugh at their mishaps but we relate to their fragility and their struggle. Humour converts that which is intolerable into something emotionally manageable. Groucho Marx, for example, transmuted his own passive early experience of poverty and discrimination through his sense of humour (Marx, 1959). His comedy is characterized by his expression of discontent disguised as silliness or witticisms as when he observes: 'We were so poor even Mama and Papa had to sleep in the same bed'.

Humour develops out of our attempts to reconcile intrapsychic incongruities but it also reflects incongruities in the social structure. Douglas (1975) emphasizes the direct relationship between humour and social structure. According to her, humorous discourse allows for the expression of the contradictions that are inherent in the organized patterns of social life that typify any given society. Humour affords symbolic expression to the 'structural strains and stresses' (Mulkay, 1988). In so doing, Douglas argues, humour challenges existing social structures by denigrating dominant values. Mulkay (1988), however, views this merely as a 'mock challenge' with no serious consequences. An important question is indeed whether humour is a powerful force that can instigate personal and social change or whether it is no more than entertainment or an outlet for tensions. Booth's (1974) distinction between unstable and stable irony is helpful in this respect. Booth argues that we can observe two types of irony. In 'unstable irony' the truth asserted or implied in the communication is in fact that no stable reconstruction can be built from the ruins revealed through the irony. In other words, we could say that in unstable irony there is an attack which does not lead to any suggestions for resolution – the attack is an end in itself. By contrast, 'stable irony' refers to ironic play which reveals an underlying reality and, in this sense, stable irony can truly be seen to assume communicative significance. It represents an attempt to make a statement about the world and contains a hope that it can change.

Along very similar lines, Britton (1998) draws a distinction between 'truth-seeking' and 'truth-evading' fiction. The power of fiction lies precisely in the 'truth' that it contains. Britton is referring here to a 'psychic truth' based on its correspondence with unconscious psychic reality, rather than evasion of it. Rose aptly observes that:

> Like transference or a work of art, humour may represent a literal lie, but it conveys a truth larger than itself. The truth of living only once, for example, can hardly be grasped affectively. But the remark 'We live only twice', is a surreal statement; it provides an affective glimpse of the enormity of the truth while making a bow towards immortal infantile narcissism (1969:937).

It is certainly true that some comedy veers towards social conservatism, as evidenced in much light entertainment. Such comedy is unlikely to represent a serious challenge to the individual or the social group as a whole. Nevertheless, this is not the case for all comedy or humour. Indeed, Mulkay concedes that:

> The interpretative openness of humour seems more accurately to reflect . . . the multiple realities of the social world. In this important respect, humour seems to be superior to ordinary, serious discourse, which is premised on an implicit denial of the fact that we live in a world of multiple meanings and multiple realities (1988:219).

Elaborating on the function of comedy in society, Jacobson points to the intraspsychic changes that comedy can stimulate, if we are receptive to it:

> . . . a more difficult feat is the overcoming of what is deathly in us while we are still alive. And this it [comedy] does often against our wishes, by dogging us with our shadows, by forcing us into the company of our other selves, by insisting we have another voice to speak with than the one we customarily use (1997:229).

Humour, then, provides us with a vehicle for giving expression to some of our innermost wishes or fears so that we may begin to take the necessary action that may foster change.

Humorous discourse reminds us that the world is an interpreted world which is not exhausted by one set of meanings. From this vantage point nothing is taken for granted, nothing is as it seems and things, people, events are there waiting to be questioned. Humour embraces ambivalence and paradox that cannot be resolved. It accepts that we are split – 'beasts with minds' (Stone, 1997) – and recognizes that our drives and appetites will at times overcome our self-imposed restraints, our attempts to fit into the demands of civilization. Humour conveys the struggle and the hilarity of our attempts to control ourselves and the world we live in. Comedy and humour do not shy away from tragedy. Humorous discourse merely represents another language for speaking about death and loss and the givens that hedge our existence.

The content of much comedy concerns itself with the contrast between appearance and concealment, between surface and essence (Mast, 1973; Fisher and Fisher, 1981). Likewise, psychoanalysis aims to reveal the latent content contained in our manifest behaviour, thoughts and feelings. The similarities between comedy and psychoanalysis do not require elaboration. Of course, psychotherapy will also, it is hoped, set in motion changes similar to those I am proposing humour can facilitate, most of which we will not notice or recognize as such immediately. Yet, over time, what enslaved us to the past loosens its grip and we can begin to see the world in a different light. It is only then that a humorous perspective can flourish.

Freud was clear that humour represented the most distinguished expression of the ego's adaptive mechanisms because it confined our compulsion to 'make a choice between suffering and denial' (1927:166). The humorous perspective is born out of our need to manage the unbearable difficulty of being. The mutative potential of humour, if one has the capacity – that is, the ego strength – to create it and to enjoy it, lies in its grasp of the absurdities of life. Humour thrives on the play of opposites, on conflict, on those aspects of ourselves and the world that do not neatly fit the established order. It is to our credit that we have developed a way of coping with this that can bring us such relief as well as pleasure. Without a sense of humour we are impoverished. Perhaps it is because we implicitly recognize this that we feel so affronted if someone does accuse us of lacking a sense of humour.[38] It is as if we realise that we are at some kind of disadvantage. In evolutionary terms it may reflect an acknowledgement of a lack of 'fitness' compared to other members of the group. There may indeed be much truth in Rosten's succint overview of the value of humour, namely that 'He who laughs, lasts' (1994:271).

[38.] 'Men will confess to treason, murder, arson, false teeth or a wig. How many of them will own up to a lack of humour ?' (Frank Moore Colby, quoted in Rosten, 1994:237).

References

Adams, E. and McGuire, F. (1986) Is laughter the best medicine? A study of the effects of humour on perceived pain and affect activities. Adaptation and Ageing, 8: 157-175.

Adams, P. (1994) Gesundheit! Rochester, VT: Healing Arts Press.

Aiello, J. Thompson, D. and Brodzinsky, D. (1983) How funny is crowding anyway? Effects of room size, group size, and the introduction of humour. Basic and Applied Social Psychology, 4: 193-207.

Aldis, O. (1975) Play Fighting. New York: Academic Press.

Alexander, J. (1969) De l'ironie. Revue Française de Psychoanalyse, 33: 441-450.

Alexander, R. (1986) Ostracism and indirect reciprocity: the reproductive significance of humour. Ethology and Sociobiology, 7: 253-270.

Allport, G. (1968) The Person in Psychology: selected essays. Boston, MA: Beacon Press.

Alvarez, A. (1972) The Savage God. New York: Random House.

Alvarez, A. (1992) Live Company. London: Routledge.

Anderson, C. and Arnoult, L. (1989) An examination of perceived control, humour, irrational beliefs and positive stress as moderators of the relationship between negative stress and health. Basic Applied Social Psychology, 10: 101-117.

Anzieu, D. (1980) Une passion pour rire: l'esprit. Nouvelle Review de Psychoanalyse, 21: 161-179.

Apte, H. (1985) Humor and Laughter: an anthropological approach. Ithaca, NY: Cornell University Press.

Arieti, S. (1976) Creativity: the magic synthesis. New York: Basic Books.

Aristotle (1927) Poetics (trans. Hamilton Fyfe). London: Heinemann.

Bader, M. (1993) The analyst's use of humour. Psychoanalytic Quarterly, 62: 23-50.

Baker, R. (1993) Some reflections on humour in psychoanalysis. International Journal of Psychoanalysis, 74: 951-960.

Bakhtin, M. (1968) Rabelais and his World (trans. Helene Iswolsky) Cambridge, MA: MIT Press.

Balint, A. and Balint, M. (1939) On transference and countertransference. International Journal of Psychoanalysis, 20: 225-230.

Balint, M. (1968) The Basic Fault. London: Tavistock.

Banning, M. and Nelson, D. (1987) The effects of activity elicited humor and group structure on group cohesion and affective responses. American Journal of Occupational Therapy, 41: 510-514.

Barchilon, J. (1973) Pleasure, mockery and creative integrations. International Journal of Psychoanalysis, 54: 19-34.

Barley, N. (1995) Dancing on the Grave. London: Abacus.

Barry, R. (1994) Recognising unconscious humor in psychoanalysis In: H. Strean (ed.) The Use of humor in Psychotherapy. New York: Jason Aronson.

Bateson, G. (1958) The role of humor in human communication. In: H. Von Foerster (ed.) Cybernetics. New York: Macey Foundation.

Baudelaire, C. (1855) On the essence of laughter and generally of the comic in the plastic arts. In: Selected Writings on Art and Literature. London: Penguin.

Baxter, L. (1992) Forms and functions of intimate play in personal relationships. Human Communication Research, 18: 336-363.

Beck, C. and Ragan, S. (1992) Negotiating interpersonal and medical talk: frame shifts in the gynaecologic exam. Journal of Language and Social Psychology, 11: 47-61.

Beebe, B. and Lachmann F. (1988) The contribution of mother-infant mutual influence to the origins of self and object representations. Psychoanalytic Psychology, 5: 305-330.

Beebe, B. and Lachmann F. (1994) Representation and internalization in infancy: three principles of salience. Psychoanalytic Psychology, 11: 127-165.

Bell, N., McGhee, P. and Duffey, S. (1986) Interpersonal competence, social effectiveness and the development of humour. British Journal of Developmental Psychology, 4: 51-55.

Bennett, A. (1994) Writing Home. London: Faber and Faber.

Bennett, M. (1994) The effect of exposure to humorous video and sense of humor on NK cell activity: pilot study. Unpublished paper, Rush-Presbyterian-St Lukes Medical Centre, College of Nursing, Chicago, IL.

Bennett, M. (1997) The effect of laughter on stress and immune function. Doctoral dissertation, St Lukes Medical Centre College of Nursing, Chicago, IL.

Bergler, E. (1956) Laughter and Sense of Humour. New York: Intercontinental Medical Books.

Bergson, H. (1956) Laughter. In: W. Sypher (ed.) Comedy: London: Johns Hopkins University Press.

Berk, L. et al. (1989) Neuroendocrine and stress hormone changes during mirthful laughter. American Journal of Medical Sciences, 298(6): 390-396.

Berlyne, D. (1972) humor and its kin. In J. Goldstein and P. McGhee (eds) The Psychology of Humour, Theoretical Perspectives and Empirical Issues. New York: Academic Press.

Berntson, G., Boysen, S., Bauer, H. and Torello, M. (1989) Conspecific screams and laughter: cardiac and behavioural reactions of infant chimpanzees. Development Psychobiology, 22: 771-787.

Bion, W. (1962) A Theory of Thinking. In W. Bion (1967) Second Thoughts. London: Marefield Library.

Birner, L. (1994) humor and the joke of psychoanalysis. In: H. Strean (ed.): The Use of humor in Psychotherapy. New York: Jason Aronson.

Blakemore, S. (1998) Television interview. 'Beyond the Joke', Horizon, BBC, 5 November.

Blanton, S. (1971) Diary of my psychoanalysis with Sigmund Freud. New York: Hawthorn Books.

Bloch, S., Browning, S. and McGrath, G. (1983) humor in group psychotherapy. British Journal of Medical Psychology, 56: 89-97.

Bloomfield, I. (1980) humor in psychotherapy and analysis. International Journal of Social Psychology, 26: 135-141.

Blumenfeld, E. and Alpern, A. (1986) The Smile Connection. New York: Prentice Hall.

Bollas, C. (1987) The Shadow of the Object: psychoanalysis of the unthought known. London: Free Association Books.

Bollas, C. (1995) Cracking Up. London: Routledge.

Booth, W. (1974) A Rhetoric of Irony. Chicago: University of Chicago Press.

Borbely, A. (1998) A psychoanalytic concept of metaphor. International Journal of Psychoanalysis, 79(5): 923-936.

Boskin, J. (1987) The complicity of humour: the life and death of Sambo. In: J. Morrell (ed.): The Philosophy of Laughter and Humour. New York: State University of New York Press.

Boulton, M. and Smith, P. (1992) The social nature of play fighting and play chasing: mechanisms and strategies underlying co-operation and compromise. In: J. Barlow et al. (eds.): The Adapted Mind Oxford: Oxford University Press.

Bradney, P. (1957) The joking relationship in industry. Human Relations, 10: 179-187.

Brandon, D. (1996) Mind dancing: humor and psychotherapy. Changes, 14(IV): 259-267.

Brazelton, B. (1992) Touchpoints. London: Viking.

Brazelton, B. and Cramer, B. (1991) The Earliest Relationship. London: Karnac.

Brenman, M. (1952) On teasing and being teased and the problem of moral masochism. Psychoanalytic Study of the Child, 7: 264-285.

Britton, R. (1989) The missing link: parental sexuality in the Oedipus complex. In R. Britton, M. Feldman and E. O'Shaughnessy (eds.) The Oedipus Complex Today: clinical implications. London: Karnac Books.

Britton, R. (1998) Belief and Imagination. London: Routledge.

Brodzinsky, D. and Rubien, J. (1976) humor production as a function of sex of subject, creativity and cartoon content. Journal of Consulting and Clinical Psychology, 44: 597-600.

Bryant, J. Brown, D., Parks, S., and Zillman, D (1983) Children's imitation of a ridiculed model. Human Communication Research, 10: 243-255.

Buckman, E. (1994) humor as a communication facilitator in couples therapy. In: E. Buckman (ed.) The Handbook of Humour: clinical applications in psychotherapy. Melbourne, FL: Krieger.

Buckwalter, K. (1994) What is the impact of humor as a coping strategy by nurses working in psychogeriatric settings? Journal of Psychosocial Nursing in Mental Health Services, 29(7): 42-43.

Byrne, D. (1958) Drive level response to humor and the cartoon sequence effect. Psychological Reports, 4: 439-442.

Caper, R. (1999) A Mind of One's Own. London: Routledge.

Carotenuto, A. (1986) Kant's Dove: The History of Transference in Psychoanalysis. Wilmette, IL: Chiron Publications.

Carroll, J. and Schmidt, J. (1992) Correlation between humorous coping style and health. Psychological Reports, 70, 402.

Carson, T. and Adams, H. (1980) Activity valence as a function of mood change. Journal of Abnormal Psychology, 89: 368-377.

Carver, C. et al. (1993) How coping mediates the effect of optimism on distress: A study of women with early stage breast cancer. Journal of Personality and Social Psychology, 65: 375-390.

Castonguay, L. et al. (1996) Predicting the effect of cognitive therapy for depression: A study of unique and common factors. Journal of Consulting Clinical Psychology, 64: 497-504.

Cavell, M. (1998) In response to Owen Renik's 'The analyst's subjectivity and the analyst's objectivity' International Journal of Psychoanalysis, 79(b): 1195-1202.

Chaplin, C. (1960) 'Sayings of the week', The Observer (London), 17, June.

Chapman, A. (1983) humor and laughter in social interaction and some implications for humor research. In: P. McGhee and J. Goldstein (eds.) Handbook of humor Research. New York: Springer-Verlag.

Charles, L. (1945) The clown's function. Journal of American Folklore, 58: 25-34.

Chasseguet-Smirgel, J. (1988) The triumph of humour. In: H.P. Bloom, Y. Kramer and A.D. Richards (eds) Fantasy, Myth and Reality: essays in honour of Jacob A. Arlow. Madison, CT: International University Press.

Chiaro, D. (1992) The Language of Jokes. London: Routledge.

Christie, G. (1994) Some psychoanalytic aspects of humour. International Journal of Psychoanalysis, 75: 479-489.

Clay, R. (1997) Research has harnessed the power of humour. American Psychological Association Monitor, September 1997, pp 1-3. URL www.apa.org/monitor/september97/humour.html.

Cogan, R., Cogan, D., Walts, W., and McCue, M. (1987) Effects of laughter and relaxation on discomfort thresholds. Journal of Behavioural Medicine, 10: 139-144.

Cohen, T. (1978) On Metaphor. In: S. Sacks (ed) Metaphor and the Cultivation of Intimacy: Chicago: University of Chicago Press.

Coltart, N. (1993) Slouching towards Bethlehem. London: Free Association Books.

Condon, W. Sander, L. (1974) Synchrony demonstrated between movements of neonate and adult speech. Child Development, 45: 456-462.

Coser, R. (1960) Laughter among colleagues. Psychiatry, 34: 81-95.

Couch, A. (1979) Therapeutic functions of the real relationship in psychoanalysis. Unpublished paper. Revised version of a paper on 'The role of the real relationship in analysis' given at a scientific meeting in the Boston Psychoanalytic Society, 10 January.

Cousins, N. (1979) Anatomy of an Illness. New York: Norton.

Cousins, N. (1985) The therapeutic value of laughter. Integrated Psychiatry, 3: 112-114.

Dana, K. (1994) humor as a diagnostic tool in child and adolescent groups In: E. Buckman (ed.) The Handbook of Humour: clinical applications in psychotherapy. Melbourne, FL: Krieger.

Danzer, A. Dale, J. Klions, H. (1990) Effects of exposure to humorous stimuli on induced depression. Psychological Reports, 66: 1027-1036.

Darwin, C. (1872) The Expression of the Emotions in Man and Animals. London: John Murray.

Davis, H. and Fallowfield, L. (1991) Counselling and Communication in Healthcare. Chichester: Wiley.

Dean, R. (1997) humor and laughter in palliative care. Journal of Palliative Care, 13(1): 34-39.

Deayton, A. (1999) A History of Alternative Cabaret. BBC UK Documentary.

Dillon, K. and Totten, M. (1989) Psychological factors, immunocompetence, and health of breast feeding mothers and their infants. Journal of General Psychology, 150: 155-162.

Dixon, N. (1980) Humour: A cognitive alternative to stress? In: I. Sarason and C. Spielberger (eds) Stress and Anxiety, Vol.7. Washington: Hemisphere.

Dooley, L. (1934) A note on humour. Psychoanalytic Review, 21: 49-58.

Doolittle, H. (1956) Tribute to Freud. New York: Pantheon Book.

Douglas, M. (1966) Purity and Danger. London: Routledge.

Douglas, M. (1975) Implicit Meanings. London: Routledge and Kegan Paul.

Dovidio, J. (1984) Helping behavior and altruism: an empirical and conceptual overview. In: L. Berkowitz (ed.) Advances in Experimental Social Psychology, 17. New York: Academic Press.

Driessen, H. (1997) Humour, laughter and the field: reflections from anthropology. In: J. Bremmer and H. Roodenburg (eds) A Cultural History of Humour. Cambridge: Polity Press.

Dugas, J. (1902) Psychologie du Rire. Paris: Hachette.

du-Pre, A. (1998) humor and the Healing Arts: a multimethod analysis of humor use in health care. London: Laurence Erlbaum.

Eco, U. (1983) The Name of the Rose. London: Pan Books.

Ellis, A. (1977) Fun as psychotherapy. Rational Living, 12: 2-6.

Ellis, S. (1978) Right on: humour, the wonder drug. Nursing Times, November 1792-1793.

Emerson, J. (1969) Negotiating the serious import of humour. Sociometry, 32: 169-181.

Erdman, L. (1993) Laughter therapy for patients with cancer. Journal of Psychosocial Oncology, 11(4): 55-67.

Erskine, A. and Judd, D. (1994) The Imaginative Body. London: Whurr.

Fairbairn, W. (1958) On the nature and aims of psychoanalysis. International Journal of Psychoanalysis, 39: 374-385.

Feingold, A. and Mazella, R. (1991) Psychometric intelligence and verbal humor ability. Personality and Individual Differences, 12: 427-435.

Feldman, M. (1989) The Oedipus Complex: manifestations in the inner world and the therapeutic situation. In: R. Britton, M. Feldman and E. O'Shaughnessy (eds): The Oedipus Complex Today. London: Karnac Books.

Fenichel, O. (1946) The Psychoanalytic Theory of Neurosis. London: Routledge.

Ferenczi, S. (1911) The psychoanalysis of wit and the comical. In: Further Contributions to the Theory and Technique of Psychoanalysis. London: Hogarth Press.

Ferenczi, S. (1928) The elasticity of psychoanalytic technique In: Final Contributions to the Problems and Methods of Psychoanalysis. London: Karnac Books.

Fine, G. (1976) Obscene joking across cultures. Journal of Communication, 26: 134-140.

Fine, G. (1979) A History of Psychoanalysis. New York: Colombia University Press.

Fine, G (1983) Sociological approaches to the study of humour. In: P. McGhee and J. Goldstein (eds.) Handbook of Humour Research. New York: Springer-Verlag.

Fine, G. (1984) Humorous interaction and a social construction of meaning: making sense in a jocular vein. Studies in Symbolic Interaction, 5: 83-101.

Fisher, S. and Fisher, R. (1981) Pretend the World is Funny and Forever: A psychological analysis of comedians, clowns and actors. Hillsdale, NJ: Erlbaum.

Fogel, A., Dixon, K. Hsu, H., Messinger, D., Nelson-Gones, C. Nwokah, E. (1997) Communication of smiling and laughter in mother/infant play: research on emotion from a dynamic systems perspective. New Directions for Child Development, 77: 5-24.

Fonagy, P. and Target, M. (1996) Playing with reality, 1. International Journal of Psychoanalysis 77(3): 217-233.

Fonagy, P. Steele, H., Moran, G., Steele, M. and Higgett, A. (1991) The capacity for understanding mental states: the reflective self in parent and child and its significance for security of attachment. Infant Mental Health Journal, 13: 200-217.

Frank, A. and Gunderson, J. (1990) The role of the therapeutic alliance in the treatment of schizophrenia. Archives of General Psychiatry, 47: 228-233.

Frankl, V. (1959) Man's Search for Meaning. Boston, MA: Beacon Press.

Frankl, V. (1965) The Doctor and the Soul: from psychotherapy to logotherapy. New York: Knopf.

Freeman, T. (1998) But Facts Exist: an enquiry into psychoanalytic theorising. London: Karnac Books.

Freud, A. (1954) The widening scope of indications for psychoanalysis: discussion. Journal of the American Psychoanalytic Association, 2: 607-620.

Freud, S. (1905a) Jokes and their relation to the unconscious (SE8). London: Hogarth Press.

Freud, S. (1905b) Three Essays on the Theory of Sexuality. London: Penguin.

Freud, S. (1909) Five lectures on psychoanalysis (SE11). London: Hogarth Press.

Freud, S. (1911-1915) Papers on technique (SE12: 83-173). London: Hogarth Press.

Freud, S. (1912) The dynamics of transference (SE12: 99-108). London: Hogarth Press.

Freud, S. (1913) On beginning treatment (SE12). London: Hogarth Press.

Freud, S. (1917) Mourning and melancholia, 11 London: Penguin.

Freud, S. (1920) Beyond the pleasure principle, 11. London: Penguin.

Freud, S. (1924) The loss of reality in neurosis and psychosis, 10. London: Penguin.

Freud, S. (1925) Negation (SE19: 235-239). London: Hogarth Press.

Freud, S. (1927) humor (SE21: 161-166). London: Hogarth Press.

Fridlund, A. (1998) Television interview. 'Beyond a Joke', Horizon, BBC, 5 November.

Friedman, L. (1988) The Anatomy of Psychotherapy. Hillslade, NJ: Analytic Press.

Friedman, R. (1994) Using humor to resolve intellectual resistances. In: H. Strean (ed.), The Use of humor in Psychotherapy. Northvale: Jason Aronson.

Fry, W. (1994) The biology of humour. International Journal of humor Research, 7(2): 111-126.

Fry, W. and Allen, M. (1975) Make 'em Laugh. Palo Alto, CA: Science and Behaviour Books.

Fry, W. and Savin, W. (1988) Mirthful laughter and blood pressure. humor 1: 49-52.

Gaberson, K. (1991) The effect of humorous distraction on pre-operative anxiety. ARON Journal, 54: 1258-1263.

Gedo, J. (1979) Beyond Interpretation. New York: International University Press.

Gelkopf, M. and Kreitler, S. (1996) Is humor only fun, an alternative cure, or magic: the cognitive therapeutic potential of humour. Journal of Cognitive Psychotherapy, 10(4): 235-254.

Gelkopf, M. and Sigal, S. (1995) It is not enough to have them laugh: hostility, anger and humor coping in schizophrenic patients. Humour, 8: 273-284.

Gelkopf, M., Kreitler, S. and Sigal, S. (1993) Laughter in a psychiatric ward: somatic, emotional, social and clinical influences on schizophrenic patients. Journal of Nervous and Mental Disease, 181(5): 283-289.

Gill, M. (1979) The analysis of transference. Journal of American Psychoanalytic Association, 27:261-288.

Gilman, S. (1988) Disease and Representation: images and illness from madness to AIDS. New York: Cornell University Press.

Gitelson, M. (1952) The emotional position of the therapist in the psychoanalytic situation. International Journal of Psychoanalysis, 33: 1-10.

Goffman, E. (1967) Interaction Ritual. Chicago: Aldine.

Golan, G., Rosenhan, E. and Jaffe, Y. (1988) humor in psychotherapy. British Journal of Psychotherapy, 4: 393-400.

Goldstein, J. (1976) Theoretical notes on humour. Journal of Communication, 26: 104-112.

Goleman, D. (1996) Emotional Intelligence. London: Bloomsbury.

Gomez, L. (1997) An Introduction to Object Relations. London: Free Association Books.

Goodall, J. (1968) The behaviour of free-living chimpanzees in the Gombe Stream Reserve. Animal Behaviour Monographs, 1: 165-311.

Goodchilds, J. (1959) Effects of being witty on position in the social structure of a small group. Sociometry, 22: 261-272.

Goodchilds, J. (1972) On being witty: causes, correlates and consequences. In: J.H. Goldstein and P. McGhee (eds) The Psychology of Humor, Theoretical Perspectives and Empirical Issues. New York: Academic Press.

Grace, A. (1991) Comedians. Charlottesville, VA: Professional Photography Division Eastman Kodak Company and Thomassen-Grant.

Greenberg, J. (1996) Psychoanalytic words and psychoanalytic acts. Contemporary Psychoanalysis, 32: 195-203.

Greenson, R. (1967) The Technique and Practice of Psychoanalysis. London: Hogarth Press and Institute of Psychoanalysis.

Greenson, R. and Wexler, M. (1969) The non-transference relationship in the psychoanalytic situation. International Journal of Psychoanalysis, 50: 27-39.

Gregory, J. (1924) The Nature of Laughter. New York: Harcourt Brace.

Grinder, R. (1940) Reminisces of a personal contact with Freud. American Journal of Orthopsychiatry 10: 850-854.

Grotjahn, M. (1957) Beyond Laughter New York: McGraw Hill.

Grotjahn, M. (1971) Laughter in group psychotherapy. International Journal of Group Psychotherapy, 12: 234-238.

Gruner, C. (1976) Wit and humor in mass communication. In: A. Chapman and H. Foot (eds.) humor and Laughter: theory, research and applications. London: John Wiley.

Hager, A. (1998) Lear's fool. In: V. Janik (ed.) Fools and Jesters in Literature, Art and History Westport, CT: Greenwood Press.

Haig, R. (1986) Therapeutic uses of humour. American Journal of Psychotherapy, 40: 543-553.

Haig, R. (1988) The Anatomy of Laughter: biopsychosocial and therapeutic perspectives. Springfield, IL: Charles C. Thomas.

Hamilton, V. (1996) The Analyst's Preconscious. Hillsdale, NJ: Analytic Press.

Hampes, W. (1994) Relation between intimacy and the multidimensional sense of humor scale. Psychological Reports 74: 1360-1362.

Harelson, W. and Stroud, P. (1967) Observations of humor in chronic schizophrenics. Mental Hygiene, 51: 458-461.

Harlow, J. (1999) Lottery sends in clowns to cheer up NHS. Sunday Times (London), 28 February: 7.

Hayworth, D. (1928) The social origin of the function of laughter. Psychological Review, 35: 367-384.

Hazlitt, W. (1885) Lectures on the English Comic Writers. London: George Bell.

Heimann, P. (1950) On countertransference. International Journal of Psychoanalysis, 31: 81-84.

Heimann, P. (1960) Countertransference II. British Journal of Medical Psychology, 33: 9-15.

Herth, K. (1990) Contributions of humor as perceived by the terminally ill. American Journal of Hospital Care, 7(1): 36-40.

Hesse, H. (1965) Steppenwolf. London: Penguin.

Heuscher, J. (1993) Kierkegaard's humor and its implications for indirect humorous communication in psychotherapy. In F. William and W. Salamek (eds.), Advances in humor and Psychotherapy. Sarasota, FL: Professional Resource Press.

Hinds, P., Martin, J. and Vogel, R. (1987) Nursing strategies to influence adolescent hopefulness during oncologic illness. Journal of the Association of Paediatric Oncological Nursing, 4: 14-22.

Hoffman, I. (1987) The Value of uncertainty in psychoanalytic practice. Contemporary Psychoanalysis, 19: 389-422.

Holden, R. (1993) Laughter: The Best Medicine. London: Thorsons.

Hopkins, J. (1996) From baby games to let's pretend. Journal of the British Association of Psychotherapists, 31(1) Part 2: 20-27.

Horvath, A. and Luborsky, L. (1993) The role of the therapeutic alliance in psychotherapy. Journal of Consulting and Clinical Psychology, 61(4): 561-573.

Hudak, D., Dale, J. Hudak, M. and Degood, D. (1991) Effects of humorous stimuli and sense of humour on discomfort. Psychological Reports, 69: 779-786.

Isola, A. and Kurki, A. (1997) humor as experienced by patients and nurses in aged nursing in Finland. International Journal of Nursing Practice 3(1): 29-33.

Jacobson, H. (1997) Seriously Funny. London: Viking.

Jacobson, H. (1999) Jokes that save us from ourselves. Evening Standard (London) 17 March, 13.

Janik, V. (1998) Fools and Jesters in Literature, Art and History. Westport, CT: Greenwood Press.

Janus, S. (1975) The great comedians: personality and other factors. American Journal of Psychoanalysis, 35: 169-174.

Jenkins, R. (1988) Acrobats of the Soul: comedy and virtuosity in contemporary American theatre. New York: Theatre Communications Group.

Jenkins, R. (1998a) Taishu Engeki: subverting the patterns of Japanese culture. In: V. Janik (ed.) Fools and Jesters in Literature, Art and History. Westport, CT: Greenwood Press.

Jenkins, R. (1998b) Penasar of Bali: sacred clowns. In: V. Janik (ed.) Fools and Jesters in Literature, Art and History. Westport, CT: Greenwood Press.

Johnson, A. (1990) A study of humor and the right hemisphere. Perceptual and Motor Skills, 90: 995-1002.

Johnson, H. (1990) humor as an innovative method for teaching sensitive topics. Educational Gerontology 16(6): 547-559.

Jones, E. (1929) Psychoanalysis. New York: Cape and Smith.

Jones, E. (1957) The Life and Work of Sigmund Freud, Vol. 3. London: Hogarth Press.

Jones, J. (1916) The theory of symbolism. In: Papers on Psychoanalysis. London: Baillière, Tindall and Cox.

Jones, J. (1974) Quoted in: Jones, J. and Liverpool, H. (1976) Calypso humor in Trinidad, in A. Chapman and H. Foot (eds) humor and Laughter, Theory and Research and Applications. London: John Wiley.

Joseph, B. (1985) Transference: the total situation. International Journal of Psychoanalysis, 66: 447-454.

Kagan, J. (1971) Change and Continuity in Infancy. New York: John Wiley.

Kahn, W. (1989) Toward a sense of organisational humour: implications for organisation diagnosis and change. Journal of Applied Behavioural Science, 25: 45-63.

Kane, T., Siels, J. and Tedeschi, J. (1977) humor as a tool of social interaction In: A. Chapman and H. Foot (eds) It's a Funny Thing, Humour! Oxford: Pergamon Press.

Kant, I. (1892) Critique of judgement. In J. Morreall (ed.) The Philosophy of Laughter and Humor. New York: State University of New York Press.

Kaplan, H. and Boyd, I. (1965) The social functions of humor on an open psychiatric ward. Psychiatric Quarterly, 39: 502-515.

Kavanagh, D. and Bower, G. (1985) Mood and self efficacy: impact of joy and sadness on perceived capabilities. Cognitive Therapy and Research, 9: 507-525.

Keenan, B. (1992) An Evil Cradling. London :Hutchinson.

Kelley, M., Jarvie, G., Middlebrook, J. McNeer, M. and Drabman, R. (1984) Decreasing burned childrens' pain behaviour. Journal of Applied Behavioural Analysis, 17,: 147-158.

Keltner, D. and Bonanno, G. (1997) A study of laughter and dissociation: distinct correlates of laughter and smiling during bereavement. Journal of Personal and Social Psychology, 73(4): 687-702.

Kernberg, O. (1982) The theory of psychoanalytic psychotherapy. In: S. Slipp (ed.): Curative Factors in Dynamic Psychotherapy. New York: McGraw Hill.

Kierkegaard, S. (1841) The Concept of Irony. Bloomington: Indiana University Press.

Killinger, B. (1977) The place of humour in adult psychotherapy. In: A. Chapman and H. Foot (eds) It's a Funny Thing, Humour! Oxford: Pergamon Press.

King, P. (1977) Affective responses of the therapist to the patient's communication. International Journal of Psychoanalysis, 61(4): 561-573.

Klapp, O. (1972) Heroes, Villains and Fools: the changing American character. Englewood Cliffs, NJ: Prentice Hall.

Klauber, J. (1986) Difficulties in the Analytic Encounter. London: Free Association Books and Maresfield Library.

Klein, M. (1930) The importance of symbol formation in the development of ego. In: Love, Guilt and Reparation London: Virago.

Klein, M. (1935) A contribution to the psychogenesis of manic depressive states. In: Love, Guilt and Reparation. London: Virago.

Klein, M. (1961) Narrative of a Child Analysis. London: Hogarth Press.

Klerman, G. Weissman, M. Rounsaville, B. and Chevron, E. (1984) Interpersonal Psychotherapy of Depression. New York: Jason Aronson.

Kline, P. (1977) The psychoanalytic theory of humor and laughter. In: A. Chapman and H. Foot (eds) It's a Funny Thing, Humour! Oxford: Pergamon Press.

Koestler, A. (1964) The Act of Creation. London: Arkana, Penguin Books.

Kohler, W., (1925) The Mentality of Apes. New York: Harcourt Brace.

Kohut, H. (1966) Forms and transformations of narcissism. Journal of the American Psychoanalytic Association, 14: 243-272.

Kohut, H. (1971) The Analysis of The Self. Madison: International Universities Press.

Kohut, H. (1984) How does analysis cure? In: A. Golding (ed.) Chicago: University of Chicago Press.

Kreitler, S., Dreschler, I. and Kreitler, H. (1988) How to kill jokes cognitively: The meaning and structure of jokes. Semiotica, 68: 297-319.

Kris, E. (1938) Ego development and the comic. International Journal of Psychoanalysis, 19: 77-90.

Kris, E. (1952) Psychoanalytic Explorations in Art. New York: International University Press.

Krupnick, J. et al. (1996) The role of the therapeutic alliance in psychotherapy and pharmacotherapy outcome: findings in the NIMH Collaborative Research Programme. Journal of Consulting Clinical Psychology, 64: 532-539.

Kubie, L. (1971) The destructive potential of humor in psychotherapy. American Journal of Psychiatry, 127: 861-866.

Kuhlman, T. (1988) Gallows humor for a scaffold setting: managing aggressive patients on a maximum-security forensic unit. Hospital and Community Psychiatry, 39(10):1085-10.

Kuhlman, T. (1993) humor in stressful milieus. In: W. Fry and W. Salmeh (eds.) Advances in humor and Psychotherapy. Sarasota, FL: Professional Resource Press.

Kuiper, N. and Martin, R. (1993) humor and self concept. International Journal of Humour, 6: 251-270.

Lachmann, F. and Beebe, B. (1996) Three principles of salience in the patient-analyst interaction. Psychoanalytic Psychology, 13: 1-22.

Lachmann, F. and Lichtenberg, J. (1992) Model scenes: implications for psychoanalytic treatment. Journal of the American Psychoanalytic Association, 40: 117-137.

Lambert, M. (1989) The individual therapist's contribution to psychotherapy process and outcome. Clinical Psychology Review, 9:469-485.

Lambert, M., Shapiro, D. and Bergin, A. (1986) The effectiveness of psychotherapy. In: S. Garfield and A. Bergin (eds) Handbook of Psychotherapy and Behaviour Change. New York: Wiley.

Lambert, R. and Lambert, N. (1995) The effects of humor on secretory immunoglobulin A levels in school age children. Paediatric Nursing, 21(1), 16-19.

Langs, R. (1976) The Bipersonal Field. New York: Jason Aronson.

Lee, S. (1997) Tell us a joke, then. Time Out, 29 January, 18-20.

Leech, C. (1968) Twelfth Night and Shakespearean Comedy. Toronto: University of Toronto Press.

Le Goff, J. (1997) Laughter in the middle ages. In: J. Bremmer and H. Roodenburg (eds) A Cultural History of Humour. Cambridge Polity Press.

Lemma, A. (1993) The design and evaluation of a training package for staff working with people with learning disabilities. Unpublished dissertation, The British Psychological Society.

Lemma, A. (1999) Containing the Containers: the effects of training and support on burnout in psychiatric nurses. University of Surrey (in preparation).

Levine, J. (1961) Regression in primitive clowning. Psychoanalytic Quarterly, 30: 72-83.

Levine, J. and Redlich, F. (1955) Failure to understand humour. Psychoanalytic Quarterly, 24: 560-572.

Levy-Strauss, C. (1949) The Elementary Structures of Kinship. London: Social Science Paperbacks.

Lewis, P. (1987) Laughter and humour – does it have a place in group analysis? Group Analysis, 20: 367-78.

Lipton, S. (1977) The advantages of Freud's technique as shown in his psychoanalysis of the Rat Man. International Journal of Psychoanalysis, 58: 255-273.

Little, M. (1951) Counter-transference and the patient's responses to it. International Journal of Psychoanalysis, 32: 32-40.

Locke, K. (1996) A funny thing happened: The management of consumer emotions in service encounters. Organisation Science, 7(1): 40-59.

Loewenstein, R. (1958) Remarks on some variations in psychoanalytic technique. International Journal of Psychoanalysis, 39: 202-210.

Lorenz, K. (1994) Man Meets Dog. New York: Kodansha America.

Lorenz, K.(1966) On Aggression. New York: Harcourt, Brace and World.

Malcolm, J. (1981) Psychoanalysis: The impossible profession. New York: Knopf.

Martin, R. (1989) humor and the mastery of living: Using humor to cope with the daily stresses of growing up. In: P. McGhee (ed.) humor and Children's Development: a guide to practical applications. New York: Haworth Press.

Martin, R. and Dobbin, J. (1988) Sense of humour, hassle, and immunoglobulin A: evidence of the stress moderating effect of humour. International Journal of Psychiatry and Medicine 18(2): 93-105.

Martin, R. and Lefcourt, H. (1983) Sense of humour as a moderator of the relation between stressors and mood. Journal of Personality and Social Psychology, 45: 1313-1324.

Martineau, W. (1972) A model of the social functions of humor In: J. Goldstein and P. McGhee (eds): The Psychology of Humour. New York: Academic Press.

Marx, G. (1959) Groucho and Me. New York: Random House.

Marziali, E. (1984) Three viewpoints of the therapeutic alliance. Journal of Nervous and Mental Disease, 172(7): 417-423.

Masson, J. (1998) Dogs Never Lie About Love. London: Vintage.

Mast, G. (1973) The Comic Mind. New York: Bobbs-Merrill.

May, R. (1953) Man's Search for Himself. New York: Random House.

Mayer, J. and Bremer, D. (1985) Assessing mood with affect sensitive tasks. Journal of Personality Assessment, 49: 95-99.

McDougall, L. (1920) The Group Mind. New York: Puttenham.

McGhee, P. (1974) Development of children's ability to create the joking relationship. Child Development, 45: 552-556.

McGhee, P. (1979) Humour: Its Origins and Development. San Francisco: W.H. Freeman.

McClelland, D., Cherrif, A. (1997) The immunoenhancing effects of humour on secretory IgA and resistance to respiratory infections. Psychology and Health, 12(3): 329-344.

Meadows, S. (1993) Children's Cognition. London: Routledge.

Mehta, G. (1998) Snakes and Ladders. London: Virago Press.

Meltzer, D. (1978) The clinical significance of the work of Bion. In: The Kleinian Developments Part 3. Strathtay, Perthshire: Clunie Press.

Menninger, K. (1958) Theory of psychoanalytic technique. New York: Basic Books.

Meredith, G. (1956) An essay on comedy. In: W. Sypher (ed.) Comedy: London: Johns Hopkins University Press.

Milner, M. (1985) The role of illusion in symbol formation In: M. Klein, P. Heimann, R. Money-Kyrle (eds) New Directions in Psychoanalysis. London: Maresfield.

Milton, J. (1997) Why assess? Psychoanalytical assessment in the NHS. Psychoanalytic Psychotherapy, 11(1): 47-58.

Minden, P. (1994) Humour: a corrective emotional experience. In: E. Buchman (ed.): The Handbook of Humour: Clinical Applications in Psychotherapy. Melbourne, FL: Krieger.

Mindess, H. (1971) The sense in humour. Saturday Review, 21 August, 10.

Mitchell, S. (1993) Hope and dread in psychoanalysis. New York: Basic Books

Mollon, P. (1993) The Fragile Self. London: Whurr.

Monro, D. (1951) Argument of Laughter. Melbourne: Melbourne University Press.

Moran, C. and Massam, M. (1997) An evaluation of humor in emergency work. Australasian Journal of Disaster and Training Studies, 3: 1-9.

Morreall, J. (ed) (1987) The Philosophy of Laughter and Humor. New York: State University of New York Press.

Morreall, J. (1991) humor and work. Humour, 4(3): 359-373.

Mulkay, M. (1988) On Humour, its Nature and its Place in Modern Society. Cambridge: Polity Press.

Nerhardt, G. (1970) humour and inclination to laugh: emotional reactions to stimuli of different divergence from a range of expectancy. Scandinavian Journal of Psychiatry, 2: 185-195.

Nezu, A., Nezu, C. and Blisset, S. (1988) Sense of humour as a moderator of the relationship between stressful events and psychological distress: a prospective analysis. Journal of Personality and Social Psychology, 54: 520-525.

Nilsen, A., Donelson, K., Nilsen, D. and Donelson, M. (1987) humour for developing thinking skills. Humour, 44: 63-75.

O'Connell, W. (1976) Freudian humour: the eupsychia of everyday life In: A.J. Chapman and H. Foot (eds): humor and Laughter: Theory, research and applications. London: John Wiley.

O'Shaughnessy E. (1964) The absent object. Journal of Child Psychotherapy, 1: 160-165.

Oberdorf, C. (1932) Kidding – a form of humour. International Journal of Psychoanalysis 13: 479-480.

Obrolik, A. (1941) Gallows humour. American Sociological Review, 47: 709-713.

Offen, J. and Burrough, L. (1987) The benign aspects of the strong superego: theoretical and technical considerations. Current Issues in Psychoanalytic Practice, 4: 35-45.

Ogden, T. (1985) On potential space. International Journal of Psychoanalysis, 66: 129-141.

Oppenheim, D. Simmons, C. and Hartmann, O. (1997) Clowning on children's wards. Lancet, 350: 1838-1840.

Orwell, G. (1961) The art of Donald MacGill. In: Collected Essays. London: Heinemann.

Overholser, J. (1992) Sense of humor when coping with life stress. American Journal of Sociology, 47: 799-804.

Palmer, J. (1987) The Logic of the Absurd. London: BFI Publishing.

Palmer, J. (1994) Taking humour Seriously. London: Routledge.

Panksepp, J. (1998) Television interview. 'Beyond the Joke', Horizon, BBC, 5 November.

Paolino, T. (1982) A therapeutic relationship in psychoanalysis. Contemporary Psychoanalysis, 18: 218-234.

Parkin[KL6], (1997) humor Theorists of 20th Century. New York: Edwin Mellen Press.

Pasquali, G. (1986) Some notes on humour in psychoanalysis. International Review of Psychoanalysis, 14: 231-236.

Pellegrini, D., Masten, A., Garmazy, N., Ferrarese, J. (1987) Correlates of social and academic competence in middle childhood. Journal of Child Psychology and Psychiatry, 28: 699-714.

Pellegrini, T. (1998) Television interview. 'Beyond the Joke', Horizon, BBC, 5 November.

Penjon, A. (1893) Le rire et la liberté. La Revue Philosophique, 42: 80-97

Perelberg, R. (1999) (ed.) Psychoanalytic Understanding of Violence and Suicide. London: Routledge.

Phillips, A. (1993) On Kissing, Being Tickled and Being Bored. London: Faber.

Phillips, A. (1998) The Beast in the Nursery. London: Faber and Faber.

Piaget, J. (1951) Play, Dreams and Imitation of Childhood. New York: Norton (original French edition, 1945).

Pierce, R. (1994) Use and abuse of laughter in psychotherapy. In: H. Strean (ed.) The Use of humor in Psychotherapy. Northvale: Jason Aronson.

Pine, F. (1981) In the beginning: contributions to a psychoanalytic developmental psychology. International Review of Psychoanalysis, 8: 15-33.

Plato (1925) Philebus (ed. Harold Fowler). London: Heinemann.

Poland, W. (1994) The gift of laughter: on the development of a sense of humor in clinical analysis. In H. Strean (ed.), The Use of humor in Psychotherapy'. Northvale: Jason Aronson.

Pollio, H. and Edgerly, J. (1976) Comedians and comic style. In: A. Chapman and H. Foot (eds.) humor and Laughter: Theory, research and applications. London: John Wiley.

Poon, L., Martin, P., Clayton, G., Messuer, S., Noble, C. and Johnson M. (1992) The influence of cognitive resources on adaption in old age. International Journal of Ageing and Human Development, 24: 31-46.

Porterfield, A. (1987) Does sense of humor moderate the impact of life stress on psychological and physical well being? Journal of Research in Personality, 21: 306-317.

Prerost, F. (1987) Health locus of control, humour and reduction in aggression. Psychological Reports, 61: 887-896.

Prerost, F. (1989) Theory and practice: intervening during crises of life transitions: promoting a sense of humour as a stress moderator. Counselling Psychology Quarterly, 2(4): 475-480.

Proops, G. (1997) Pull the other one. Elle magazine, November: 160.

Provine, R. (1992) Contagious laughter: laughter is a sufficient stimulus for laughs and smiles. Bulletin of the Psychonomics Society, 30: 1-4.

Provine, R. (1998) Television interview. 'Beyond the Joke', Horizon, BBC, 5 November.

Provine, R. and Fischer, K. (1989) Laughing, smiling and talking: relation to sleeping and social context in humans. Ethology 83: 295-305.

Pugh, G. (1977) The Biological Basis of Human Values. New York: Basic Books.

Radcliffe-Brown, J. (1952) On joking relationships. In: Structure and Function in Primitive Society. London: Cohen and West.

Ramachandran, V. (1998) The neurology and evolution of humour, laughter and smiling: the false alarm theory. Medical Hypotheses, 51(4): 351-354.

Rappaport, D. (1998) Destruction and gratitude: some thoughts on 'The use of an object'. Contemporary Psychoanalysis, 34(3): 369-378.

Ravella, N. (1988) The serious business of humor in therapy. Journal of Strategic and Systemic Therapies 7(2): 35-40.

Reddiford, G. (1980) Imagination, rationality and teaching. Journal of Philosophy of Education, 14(2): 205-213.

Reddy, V. (1991) Playing with other's expectations: teasing and mucking about in the first year. In: A. Whiten (ed.): Natural Theories of Mind. Oxford: Blackwell.

Redlich, F., Levine, J. and Sohler, T. (1950) A mirth response test: preliminary report on a psychodiagnostic technique utilising dynamics of humour. American Journal of Ortho-Psychiatry, 21: 717.

Reich, A. (1949) The structure of the grotesque – comic sublimation. Bulletin of the Menninger Clinic, 13: 212-216.

Reich, W. (1949) Character Analysis. New York: Noonday Press.

Reik, T. (1936) Surprise and the Psychoanalyst London: Kegan Paul.

Reik, T. (1954) Freud and Jewish wit. Psychoanalysis, 5: 13-28.

Renik, D. (1993) Analytic interaction: conceptualising technique in light of the analyst's irreducible subjectivity. Psychological Quarterly 62: 553-571.

Renik, D. (1998) The analyst's objectivity and the analyst's subjectivity. International Journal of Psychoanalysis, 79(3): 487-497.

Richman, J. (1996) Points of correspondence between humour and psychotherapy. Psychotherapy, 33(4): 560-566.

Rim, Y. (1988) Sense of humor and coping styles. Personality and Individual Differences, 9: 559-564.

Roberts, F. and Johnson, D. (1958) Some factors related to the perception of funniness in humour stimuli. Journal of Social Psychology, 46: 57-63.

Roberts, G. (1993) The devil and comedy. In: K. Cameron (ed.) humour and History. Oxford: Intellect.

Robinson, V. (1991) humour and Health Professions. Thoroughfare, NJ: Slack.

Roncoli, M. (1971) Bantering: a therapeutic strategy with obsessional patients. Perspectives in Psychiatric Care, 12(4): 171-175.

Rose, G. (1969) 'King Lear' and the use of humor in treatment. Journal of the American Psychoanalytic Association, 17: 927-940.

Rosenberg, L. (1991) A qualitative investigation of the use of humour by emergency personnel as a strategy for coping with stress. Journal of Emergency Nursing, 17(4): 197-203.

Rosenheim, E., Tucucinu, F. and Dimitrovsky, L. (1989) Schizophrenics' appreciation of humour as therapeutic interventions. Humour, 2: 141-152.

Rosten, L. (1961) The Return of Hyman Kaplan. New York: Harper.

Rosten, L. (1994) Carnival of Wit. New York: Plume Books.

Roth, A. and Fonagy, P. (1996) What Works for Whom. London: Guildford Press.

Rothbart, M. (1976) Incongruity, problem solving and laughter. In: A. Chapman and H. Foot (eds.) humour and Laughter: theory, research and applications. London: John Wiley.

Roustang, F. (1987) How do you make a paranoid laugh? Modern Language Notes, 102: 707-718.

Russell, E. (1991) The excited child. Australian Volume of Psychotherapy, 10(2): 166-179.

Sacerdoti, G. (1992) Irony through Psychoanalysis. London: Karnac Books.

Safran, J., Crocker, P., McMain, S., and Murray, P. (1990) The therapeutic alliance rupture as a therapy event for empirical investigation. Psychotherapy, 27: 154-165.

Safranek, R. and Schrill, T. (1982) Coping with stress: does humour help? Psychological Reports, 51: 222.

Salameh, W. (1983) humor in psychotherapy: past outlooks, present status and future frontiers In: P. McGhee and J. Goldstein (Eds.) Handbook of humor Research. New York: Springer-Verlag.

Saltzman, C., Luetgart, M., Roth, C., Creaser, J. and Howard, L. (1976) Formation of a therapeutic relationship. Journal of Consulting and Clinical Psychology, 44(4): 546-555.

Sameroff, A. (1983) Developmental systems: contexts and evolution. In: W. Massey (ed): Massey's Handbook of Child Psychology, 1. New York: Wiley.

Sandler, J. and Sandler, A. (1997) A psychoanalytic theory of repression and the unconscious. In J. Sandler and P. Fonagy (eds), Recovered Memories of Abuse. London, Karnac Books.

Sandler, J., Holden, A., Dare, C. (1973) The Patient and the Analyst. London: Karnac Books.

Sands, S. (1984) The use of humour in psychotherapy. Psychoanalytic Review, 71(3): 441-460.

Saper, B. (1987) humour in psychotherapy: Is it good or bad for the client? Professional Psychology: Research and Practice, 18(4): 360-367.

Satow, R. (1991) Three perspectives on humour and laughing: classical object relations and self psychology. Group, 5(4): 242-245.

Schafer, R. (1960) The loving and beloved superego. Psychoanalytic Study of the Child, 15: 163-188.

Schlesinger, K. (1979) Jewish humour as Jewish identity. International Review of Psychoanalysis, 6: 317-330.

Schopenhauer, A. (1981) Die Velt als Wille und Vorstellung. Leipzig: Brockhaus.

Schultz, T. (1976) A cognitive developmental analysis of humour. In: A. Chapman and H. Foot (eds.) humour and Laughter, Theory and Research on Applications. London: John Wiley.

Searles, H. (1979) Counter Transference and Related Subjects. Madison: International University Press.

Segal, H. (1957) Notes on symbol formation. International Journal of Psychoanalysis, 38: 391-397.

Shatzky, J. (1988) Schlemiels and Schlimazels. In: V. Janik (ed.) Fools and Jesters in Literature, Art and History. Westport, CT: Greenwood Press.

Shaw, F. (1998) Interviewed by J. Rees, 'She's an Inspiration', Independent on Sunday, 14 June: 16.

Simon, J. (1990) humour and its relationship to perceived health, life satisfaction, and morale in older adults. Issues in Mental Health Nursing, 11: 17-31.

Simons, C., McCluskey-Fawcett, T., and Papini, D. (1986) Theoretical and functional perspectives on the development of humor during infancy, childhood and adolescence. In: L. Nahemow, A. McLuskey-Fawcett and P. McGhee (eds): humor and Ageing. Orlando, FL: Academic Press.

Sinason, V. (1996) 'But psychotherapists don't laugh, do they?' Psychoanalytic Psychotherapy in South Africa, Summer, 19-31.

Singer, D. (1968) Aggression, arousal, hostile humour and catharsis. Journal of Personality and Social Psychology, 8: 1-14.

Skynner, R. and Cleese, (1993) Life and How to Survive It. London: Methuen.

Sloboda, J. (1998) The Musical Mind: The Cognitive Psychology of Music. Milton Keynes: Open University Press.

Smith, D. (1991) Hidden Conversations: An Introduction to Communicative Psychoanalysis. London: Routledge.

Smith-du Pre, A. (1992) humor in the hospital: an ethnographic study of the communicational aspects of humor shared by patients and caregivers. Unpublished masters thesis, University of South Western Louisiana.

Solomon, J. (1996) humour and ageing well: a laughing matter or a matter of laughing? American Behavioural Scientist, 39(3): 249-271.

Solzhenitsyn, A. (1973) The Gulag Archipelago. New York: Harper and Row.

Spruiell, V. (1985) The joke in 'The Moses of Michaelangelo': imagination and creativity. Psychoanalytic Study of the Child, 40: 473-492.

Spurling, S. (1951) On the psychodynamics of teasing. Paper read at the annual meeting of the American Psychoanalytic Association, May 1951.

Sroufe, V. and Waters, E. (1972) The ontogenesis of smiling and laughter: a perspective on the organisation and development in infancy. Psychological Review, 83: 173-189.

Stanton, M. (1990) Ferenczi: reconsidering active intervention. London: FAB.

Steiner, J. (1993) Psychic Retreats. London: Routledge.

Stephenson, R. (1950) Conflict and control function of humor. American Journal of Sociology, 56: 569-574.

Sterba, R. (1982) Reminiscences of a Viennese Psychoanalyst. Detroit: Wayne State University Press.

Stern, D. (1977) The First Relationship. Cambridge, MA: Harvard University Press.

Stern, D. (1985) The interpersonal world of the infant. New York: Basic Books.

Stern, D., Sander, L., Nahum, J. et al. (1998) Non-interpretative mechanisms in psychoanalytic therapy: the 'something more' than interpretation. International Journal of Psychoanalysis, 79(5): 903-922.

Stolorow, R. and Attwood, G. (1992) Contexts of Being. Hillsdale: Analytic Press.

Stone, L. (1961) The Psychoanalytic Situation. New York: International University Press.

Stone, L. (1997) Laughing in the Dark: a decade of subversive comedy. Hopewell, NJ: Ecco Press.

Storr, A. (1988) Solitude. London: Flamingo.

Strachey, J. (1934) The nature of the therapeutic action in psychoanalysis. International Journal of Psychoanalysis, 15: 127-159.

Strean, H. (1993) Jokes: Their Purpose and Meaning: Northvale: Jason Aronson.

Strean, H. (1994) (Ed.) The Use of humor in Psychotherapy. Northvale: Jason Aronson.

Symington, N. (1993) Narcissism: A New Theory. London: Karnac Books.

Sypher, J. (ed.) (1956) Comedy. London: Johns Hopkins University Press.

Szasz, T. (1963) The concept of transference. International Journal of Psychoanalysis, 44: 432-443.

Tarachow, S. (1963) An Introduction to Psychotherapy. New York: International University Press.

Tennant, K. (1990) Laugh it off – the effect of humour on the well being of the older adult. Journal of Gerontological Nursing, 16(12): 11-17.

Thackeray, W. (1995) The Four Georges and the English Humorists. London: Sutton Publishing.

Thompson, S. and Spacapa, S. (1991) Perceptions of control in vulnerable populations. Journal of Social Issues 47(4) 1-21.

Thorson, J., Powell, F., Sarmany-Schuller, I., Hampes, W.P. (1997) Psychological health and sense of humour. Journal of Clinical Psychology, 53(6): 605-619.

Trice, A. and Price-Greenhouse, J. (1986) Joking under the drill: a validity study of the coping humour scale. Journal of Social Behaviour and Personality, 1: 255-265.

Tronick, E. (1989) Emotions and emotional communication in infants. American Psychologist, 44(2): 112-119.

Turner, R. (1980) Self-monitoring and humour production. Journal of Personality, 48: 163-172.

Vaillant, G. (1971) Theoretical hierarchy of adaptive ego – mechanisms. Archives of General Psychiatry, 24: 107-117.

Van Hooff, J. (1972) A comparative approach to the phylogeny of laughter and smiling In: R. Hinde (ed.): Non-verbal Communication. Cambridge: Cambridge University Press.

Veitch, R. and Griffitt, W. (1976) Good news-bad news: affective and interpersonal effects. Journal of Applied Social Psychology, 6: 69-75.

Vergeer, G., Macrae, A. (1993) Therapeutic use of humour in occupational therapy. American Journal of Occupational Therapy, 47(8): 678-683.

Viederman, M. (1991) The real person of the therapist and his role in the process of psychoanalytic cure. International Journal of Psychoanalysis, 39: 451-489.

Vinton, K. (1989) humour in the workplace: it's more than telling jokes. Small Group Behaviour 20: 151-166.

Vorhaus, J. (1994) The Comic Toolbox. Beverley Hills, CA: Silman-James Press.

Walsh, J. (1928) Laughter and Health. New York: Appleton.

Warner, S. (1991) Humour: a coping response for student nurses. Archives of Psychiatric Nursing, 5: 10-16.

Watson, M. and Emerson, S. (1988) Facilitating learning with humour. Journal of Nursing Education, 27(2): 89-90.

Weisfeld, G. (1993) The adaptive value of humour and laughter. Ethology and Sociobiology 14(2): 141-169.

Welsford, E. (1935) The Fool: His Social and Literary History. London: Faber and Faber.

White, C. (1998) The anthropology of fools. In: V. Janik (ed.) Fools and Jesters in Literature, Art and History Westport, CT: Greenwood Press.

Wilde, L. (1973) The Great Comedians. Syracuse, N.J.: Citadel Press.

Williams, P. (1999) Internet Discussion; Non-interpretative mechanisms in psycho-analytic psychotherapy by Stern et al. International Journal of Psychoanalysis , 80(1): 197-211.

Winnicott, D. (1947) Hate in the counter-transference. In: Collected papers: London: Tavistock Publications.

Winnicott, D. (1954) Metaphysical and clinical aspects of regression within the psy-choanalytic setting. In: Through Paediatrics to Psychoanalysis. London: Karnac Books.

Winnicott, D. (1965) The Maturational Processes and the Facilitating Environment. London: Karnac Books.

Winnicott, D. (1971) Playing and Reality, London: Routledge.

Wolf, Z. (1988) Nurses' work: the sacred and the profane. Philadelphia: University of Pennsylvania Press.

Wolfenstein, M. (1951) A phase in the development of children's sense of humour. Psychoanalytic Study of the Child, 6: 336-350.

Wolff, H., Smith, C. and Murray, H. (1974) The psychology of humour, 1, a study of responses to race disparagement jokes. Journal of Abnormal and Social Psychology 28: 341-365.

Wormer, K. and Boes, M. (1997) humour in the emergency room: a social work per-spective. Health and Social Work, 22(2): 87-92.

Yerkes, R. (1943) Chimpanzees: A Laboratory Colony. New Haven, CT: Yale University Press.

Zelazo, P. (1972) Smiling and vocalising: a cognitive emphasis. Meryl Palmer Quarterly, 18: 349-365.

Zelazo, P. and Komer, M. (1971) Infants smiling to known social stimuli and the recognition hypothesis. Child Development 42: 1327-1339.

Zetzel, E. (1956) Current concepts of transference. International Journal of Psychoanalysis 37: 369-376.

Zetzel, E. (1970a) Therapeutic alliance in the psychoanalysis of hysteria. In: The Capacity for Emotional Growth. London: Hogarth Press (originally published 1958)

Zillman, D. and Bryant, J. (1974) Retaliatory equity as a factor in humour appreci-ation. Journal of Experimental Social Psychology, 10: 480-488.

Zillman, D. and Cantor, J. (1976) A disposition's theory of humour and mirth. In: A. Chapman and H. Foot (eds) humour and Laughter, Theory and Research and Applications London: John Wiley and Sons.

Ziv, A. (1976) The effects of humour on creativity. Journal of Educational Psychology, 3: 318-322.

Ziv, A. (1981) The self-concept of adolescent humorists. Journal of Adolescence, 4: 187-197.

Ziv, A. (1983) The influence of humour as atmosphere on divergent thinking. Contemporary Educational Psychology, 8: 413-421.

Ziv, A. (1984) Personality and Sense of Humor. New York: Springer.

Ziv, A. and Gadish, O. (1989) humour and marital satisfaction. Journal of Social Psychology, 129: 759-768.

Zwerling, I. (1955) The favourite joke in diagnostic and therapeutic interviewing. Psychoanalytic Quarterly, 24: 104-114.

Index